Pick of Punch

"Bless my soul! That's the most overactive thyroid gland I've ever removed."

Pick of Pu

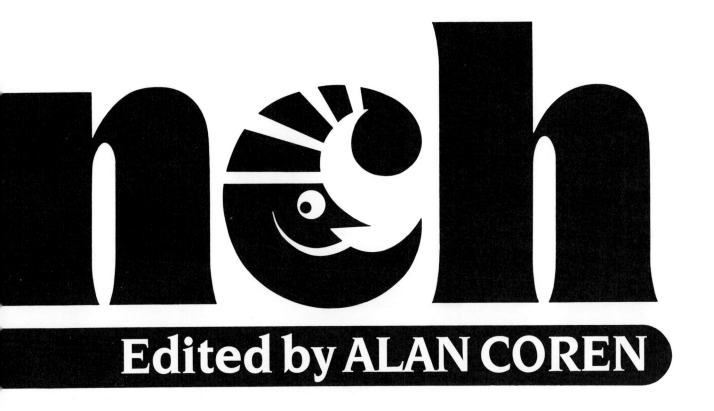

punch

Edited by ALAN COREN

HUTCHINSON
London   Melbourne   Sydney   Auckland   Johannesburg

© Punch Publications 1985

All rights reserved

First published in Great Britain in 1985
by Hutchinson & Co (Publishers) Ltd

An imprint of Century Hutchinson Ltd

Brookmount House, 62-65 Chandos Place, London WC2N 4NW

ISBN 0 09 1619408

Printed in Great Britain by
Redwood Burn Ltd., Trowbridge, Wiltshire
and bound by WBC Bookbinders Ltd, Maesteg, Mid-Glamorgan

"Well, Piglet, that's the last we'll see of his ruddy computer."

BUMP
BUMP
BUMP

CONTENTS

"Did you know the Waterhouses were leaving today, Douglas?"

INTRODUCTION

There's a library here at Punch, packed to the gunwales with the comic arcana of a hundred-and-whateveritis years, and most days the place teems with po-faced academics from the round earth's imagined corners, asking all manner of daft questions, such as *Why you put John Donne quotation in first line of introduction 1985 Pig of Bunch, in my country this cause much puzzlement?* and so forth.

These good folk are all here to do theses on English humour, having wormed the necessary ackers out of gullible paymasters as different as the Albanian Jape Institute and North Dakota Wimmin Against Mink. All over the planet, it seems, thousands of worthy and well-endowed foundations are eager to cough up folding money in order to get to the bottom of why British people of sound mind sometimes fall to the carpet and roll around helplessly. Quite why either they or their earnest emissaries should want to do this has never been entirely clear to me or to my library staff, who took the job because of what they believed to be the unrivalled opportunities it offered for staring out of the window and knocking off early.

Questioned, the seekers after codswallop will invariably reply that a country's sense of humour is an invaluable key to its national character. I look at them for a bit.

They in their turn gaze at the bound volumes which contain the 300,000 pages of comedy that I and my predecessors have bolted together since 1841, and come over a bit faint. Is there, they enquire, any, how you say, short cut, we have twelve-month deadline for Ph.D., have you perhaps one small book which shows British sense of humour, therefore national character, we must also read Dickens, Thackeray, P. G. Woodlouse, we have only one pair of hands, what you got?

It is for them, and them alone, therefore, that Pick of Punch is designed. It is the distillation of a year's comic graft. It is packed with things like anti-nuclear underwear, suicide notes from cats, HM the Q's day off, coke-filled snooker stars, Gorbachev's sex life, reincarnation as a sideboard, the death of Hollywood, gay boatpeople, Etonian cannibals, how to buy an empire and how to grow a husband from cuttings, Nazi sandwiches, the Lady Di gondolier scandal, all that stuff.

Quite what it tells us about the British character, I haven't the foggiest idea. But then, it wasn't meant for us at all. It was meant for them. I hope it's some help.

AC

AMAGING GRACE

"I've been looking all over for you."

"Kong, kong, kong, kong!"

"Any questions?"

"No encores – I know only two numbers."

Alan COREN

"The last-minute cancellation of the Canadian visit does of course leave a large gap in the diary which probably cannot be filled at this late date. The Queen will be at something of a loose end."

Palace spokesman

One is One and All Alone

MONDAY

Got up, finally,

Sat at escritoire. Filled in all o's on front page of one's *Telegraph*. Put paperclips in long line. Pushed paperclips into little pile. Straightened paperclip and cleaned old bits of soap out of engagement ring. Bent paperclip back to original shape. Put paperclip back in little pile and tried to identify it with eyes shut.

Noticed tiny flap of wallpaper curled back from skirting just behind escritoire. Took one's Bostik out of escritoire drawer, put little smear on wall, little smear on wallpaper, pressed down wallpaper.

Picked old dried crusty bits off one's Bostik nozzle.

Read Bostik label. It is good for glass, wood, ceramics, light metal, leather, and plastic, whatever that is. If one gets it in one's eyes, one should wash it out immediately.

Saw fly go past.

Saw fly come back.

Watched wallpaper curl off wall again.

Turned on *Play School*. Noticed flat head on presenter. Summoned Lady Carinthia Noles-Fitzgibbon, who confirmed head not normally flat. She enquired if she should summon Master of the Queen's Ferguson. One told her no, one was perfectly capable of fiddling with one's apparatus oneself.

One was in fact quite grateful.

Took lift to West Loft. Keeper of the Queen's Smaller Gifts (West Loft Division) most helpful. One had, according to his inventory, been given a zircon-encrusted ratchet screwdriver by King Idris of Libya, following 1954 reciprocal trade agreement on depilatory soup. During Keeper's search for this item, put on alligator's head presented by Friends of Mbingele National Park on the occasion of one's Silver Wedding. A snug fit, but some tarnish on the molars.

Keeper rather taken aback upon return to find one in alligator's head and Mary Queen of Scots' execution frock, but recovered admirably. Having to suppress his distress at poor Professor Blunt's departure has matured him considerably; one may soon allow him to fondle the odd corgi.

Returned to one's apartment. *Play School* now finished, so put on one's husband's video recording of yesterday's *Postman Pat*. It is now Mrs Goggins the Postmistress who has a flat head.

Applied screwdriver to hole in back of one's apparatus. Blue flash. Zircons all blown off. One's husband burst in, ranting: apparently, one's husband's Hornby Dublo layout had fused itself to nursery floor.

One's husband now at worse loose end than

ever, stormed off in foul mood to put up shelf in garage. Has been talking about putting up shelf in garage since Suez.

Lunch. First lunch alone since October, 1949.

Moulded mashed potatoes into Grampians, poured gravy in to simulate Loch Rannoch, cut pea in half to make two ferries. Had ferry race by blowing down one's straw. Left-hand pea won.

Knighted it with fork.

After lunch, one's husband stormed in again, carrying gold claw-hammer (Ghana, 1962), diamanté pliers (Melbourne, 1968), set of inlaid mother-of-pearl ring-spanners (Tongan gift on occasion of PoW's first tooth), and shouting *Where one's bloody zircon-encrusted screwdriver?*

Stormed out again with rather nice Louis XV rosewood side-table, muttering *Soon chop up this tarty Frog rubbish, make bloody good plank, this, rip a couple of brackets off that poncey Tompian clock upstairs, shelf up in two shakes of a CPO's whatsit.*

Fusebox Poursuivant arrived to repair apparatus. Commanded to remain and play I-Spy. One won.

Bed at 8.15, with ocelot-bound *Fifty Things To Do On A Wet Day* (New Zealand, 1978). Made flute out of old sceptre. Played *God Save One*.

TUESDAY

Woke early, made hat from *Telegraph*.

Drew up list of all one's acquaintances with spectacles. Compared it with list of all one's acquaintances with flat feet.

Watched one's husband rush in clutching bloodstained thumb, shouting *Where bloody Dettol, where bloody Elastoplast?* Watched him rush out again.

Sudden brilliant thought. Decided to make one's own breakfast. Cheered to find nursery kitchen empty. Recognised frying-pan. Put egg in frying-pan. Oddly, egg did not go yellow and white, egg just rolled around in frying-pan, went hot, then exploded.

Had bath.

Rang TIM, Weather, Cricket Scores, Puffin Storyline. Listened to Mrs Goggins story. Rang Starline: good day for throwing out old clothes, will meet interesting short man with financial proposition, a loved one will have exciting news in evening.

Threw out old clothes and waited for interesting short man. Did not come, so got old clothes back. Put them into symmetrical heaps.

In evening, loved one stomped in with exciting news: Louis XV garage shelf had fallen on Rolls, dented bonnet, knocked off wing-mirror.

Bed at 9, with interesting book. There are 3,786 Patels in it.

WEDNESDAY

Got up, put *Telegraph* in bucket of water. Added flour, as recommended by *Fifty Things To Do On A Wet Day*, made papier-maché head of Mrs Goggins.

Removed old glove from pile waiting for interesting short man, put it on, poked forefinger into Mrs Goggins, did puppet-show for corgi.

Corgi passed out.

Rang 246 8000 again, but no further news of interesting short man or his financial proposition. Nothing about one's dog falling over, either. However, it is a good day to go shopping. One leapt at this! Why had one not thought of it sooner?

One has never been shopping.

It being a fine day, one decided to slip out quietly in sensible shoes and headscarf, and walk up Constitution Hill to Knightsbridge. Most interesting. Sixty-two street lamps.

Several Japanese persons stared at one strangely. At Hyde Park Corner, a taxi-cab driver slowed, pushed down his window, and shouted "I bet you wish you had her money!"

Quite incomprehensible.

One recognised Harrods at once, from their Christmas card. One went inside. Most impressive. One selected a jar of Beluga caviare, a rather splendid musical beefeater cigarette-box with a calculator in its hat, a pair of moleskin slippers, a Webley air-pistol, and a number of other items one might never have thought of to help one while away the remainder of one's spare fortnight, and one was quite looking forward to strolling back to the Palace, putting one's mole-shod feet up, treating oneself to a spoonful or two of the old Royal Fish roe while potting starlings through the window and totting up the toll on one's loyal Yeoman calculator to the stirring accompaniment of *Land Of Hope And Glory*, when one suddenly felt one's elbow grasped with an uncustomarily disrespectful firmness.

"Excuse me, madam, but I wonder if you would mind accompanying me to the Assistant Manager's office?"

One was aware of a grey-suited person.

"Normally," one replied, "one allows it to be known that one is prepared to entertain a formal introduction. One then initiates the topic of conversation oneself. It is normally about saddles. However, one is prepared to overlook the protocol occasionally. One assumes the senior staff wishes to be presented?"

FRIDAY

Got up, slopped out.

One might, of course, have made a fuss. One might, for example, have pointed out to one's Assistant Manager – the entire place is, after all, By Appointment – that not only does one never carry money, but that money actually carries one, and would therefore serve as a convenient identification.

One chose, however, to retain one's headscarf, one's glasses, and one's silence; since something had suddenly dawned on one.

Thus, yesterday in Bow Street, being without visible means of support, one was not even given the option to seven days. One now has a rather engaging view of Holloway Road, albeit only from the upper bunk, a most engaging companion with a fund of excellent stories, and a mouse, and one is already through to the South Block ping-pong semi-finals.

Tonight, there is bingo, rug-making, cribbage, aerobics, bookbinding, squash, pottery, chiropody, raffia work, community singing, petit-point, judo, darts, and do-it-oneself. One can hardly wait to see what tomorrow may bring!

One is, in short, amused.

"Heavens, we don't stone people for adultery any more – she's a West Ham supporter."

HALDANE

"He's a parrot's parrot."

"He's decent enough, but, intellectually, we're worlds apart."

"Don't you think that we should at least try to talk him out of it?"

"I warn thee, wife, it's me or the ouija board!"

ANNUAL RESULTS:
CHAIRMAN'S STATEMENT

Chairman: Basil Boothroyd

A Satisfactory Year

Despite a highly competitive market place and downward trends in purchasing power, your company has continued trading throughout 1984. Both directors have voted to conceal their surprise at this, and to express cautious optimism for at least the foreseeable future.

Principal Activities

Your Literary Division again achieved a viable plateau of emolument, substantial investment being made in United Stationery, British Telecommunications, Southern Typewriter Servicing and British Imperial Tobacco. In excess of 18,000 miles of travel was undertaken by your Commuter Division, all between Haywards Heath and London Bridge. Losses were limited to one umbrella.

As in past years, your Food Production Division has sustained a high level of proficiency at a split level of cooker, notwithstanding upward progressions in raw material costs and the holding down of the Division's deployable resources to limits agreed in 1979. Foodstuff deliveries have consistently been honoured as per contract, instances having occurred where table-ready products have even been delivered prior to consumer-outlet requirements.

On your Managing Directress's recommendation these have been either left on the table for later discussion or referred back to cold storage pending conclusion of *Match of the Day*.

Repairs and Maintenance

Pursuing your Board's policy of controlled outgoings under this head, necessary refurbishments have been kept to the minimum, other than in the matter of Extraordinary Items.

Extraordinary Items

Brickwork dislodged from the Head Office chimney unfortunately destroyed a birdbath and concrete owl in the underlying staff recreation complex. Withdrawals from your numbered Post Office account enabled the structural renovations to be put in hand as a matter of urgency, and builders were at work within a month. Expenditure on a further owl and bath was thought unjustified at prevailing prices. Your auditors have accordingly written them down to a revised book value as window-box hardcore. It is anticipated that the sites will afford expansion potential for wider dispersal of leisure furniture and an expected free gift of barbecue components from a Mail Order subsidiary.

At a hurriedly convened meeting in the Na-

tional Car Park, Worthing, in mid-August, your directors sought to allocate responsibility for the explosion of six $1\frac{1}{2}$-litre tonic bottles in the rear of your company car, with consequent depreciation in your upholstery, earlier grocery purchases and no-claim bonus. Though no conclusion was reached, it was minuted that windows should be left minimally unclosed in the event of a further hot summer, provided that continued deterioration in draught-proofing had not by then rendered such provision superfluous. A proposal to limit your company's tonic-related gin consumption was rejected as impracticable. It was however agreed that conservation of lemon-segments for recycling should be practised even more rigorously, up to the socially acceptable limit of not having been noticeably sucked.

Ancillary Staff Remuneration

On the motion of Mrs B. Killick (co-opted) your Graded Employment Joint Consultative Committee unanimously voted an increment of 15 per cent to £4.75 per hour, taking effect Thursdays 9.30 a.m. to 12 noon if fine. Your company will supply cleaning requisites as before, including tea, ready listening, sprays, polishes and your Chairman's old underwear.

Welfare

Safe and congenial working conditions have as usual received prime consideration by your Board. A smell of fish on the company's upper floors was eventually traced to a melting electrical point and at once remedied by the removal of the plug. Following your Chairman's backward fall on to a metal waste-disposal receptacle, still gripping the front of a drawer, worm in his desk has been treated and no recurrence is anticipated. His period of voluntary convalescence was fortunately not concurrent with that of your Managing Directress. The collapse of a glass shelf and hippopotamus soap-holder into the executive bath prior to her entry should have been notified by the resident Maintenance Unit, who was severely reprimanded. Only minor cuts were sustained by the Directress concerned, and she has now been able to resume her seat on the Board. A proposal to replace the hippopotamus was put, but overruled by the casting vote of your Chairman on the grounds of expense and bad dreams.

Sales

Sales have been vigilantly attended. Notable acquisitions on advantageous terms have been your company's set of matching luggage (Grand Birthday Event) and a padded casual aged-look pig-skin split storm-trekker executive blouson with desk-reinforced elbows (Fire Damage, Everything Must Go). Further comparably beneficial additions to your company's fixed assets are in prospect as 1985 approaches (Slashing January Opportunities).

Entertainment and Hospitality

Though aware of competitors' extensive disbursements on block bookings for business associates at Goodwood, *The Mousetrap*, the Raymond Revuebar and the Lord's Test, your company has decided on modest investment only in these areas.

In July a party of thirteen close affiliates visited Whipsnade under escort by your Managing Directress, a similar exercise being projected over the Christmas period *(Mother Goose)*. No new business seems likely to accrue from these operations. It is your Chairman's view that more directly profitable use may be made of available reserves, presently standing at a £25 travellers cheque and the sterling equivalent of 3,062 Spanish pesetas. Meanwhile the painting of the company's front door has again had to be postponed, with no replacements as yet for the disappeared bootscraper, dustbin and south-east shutter from the main Head Office frontage opposite the Wellington Arms.

Encouraging Outlook

In conclusion, and in pursuance of company policy of full and clear information for shareholders, your Chairman gives his unhesitating assurance that with due attention to a stabilised cash-flow deficit, spot market marginals, strategic discount sector options, and short-term down-builds in extended finance debt funding within operating capability parameters, your company can confidently look forward to another remarkable year. ℮

"For a while we weren't sure we were going to make it. Wallace has done his back again."

"What a trouper!"

"No, you may __not__ be tried by twelve good dogs and true."

DICK VOSBURGH

THE QUACK AND THE DEAD

CLARENCE NASH, husband of Margie, father of Kay and Peggy and grandfather of eight, died on February 20th at the age of eighty.

The media reported this fact all over the globe and it was even the subject of a Radio 2 *Thought for the Day*. But it wouldn't have been world news if Nash hadn't been the voice of Donald Duck. A pity Clarence Nash didn't receive commensurate attention when he was still among the living.

Look up his name in Ephraim Katz's 1,266-page *Film Encyclopedia* and you won't find it. Ah, but if you look under Donald Duck, you still won't find it. You will simply see:

DONALD DUCK. Popular cartoon character introduced by Walt Disney in 1936 in the short *Orphans' Benefit*. Like all Disney characters, the little duck, usually clad in sailors' blue and white, has distinctive human characteristics. Unlike the calm Mickey Mouse, he is an excitable little fellow, hot headed and always eager to challenge adversaries.

As a rival cartoon company put it, that's all, folks. Well, that isn't enough.

NASH, CLARENCE. Voice specialist. Musician. Born 1904 in Watonga, Oklahoma. In his youth, studied the mandolin and learned to imitate the farm animals around him. At thirteen, acquired a baby billy-goat and learned to imitate him too.

Spent the 1920s as an entertainer, playing the mandolin and doing his barnyard impressions for rural audiences from Missouri to Louisiana. Arrived in Los Angeles during the Depression with his bride Margie and a resolve to forget show business. Landed a job driving a pony-drawn milk cart for the Adohr Dairy, billed as "Whistling Clarence the Adohr Bird Man".

One legendary day in the early '30s, after two years of Percy Edwardsing around LA, he parked his milk cart outside the Disney Studios, crossed his fingers and requested an audition. Request granted. Was halfway through his repertoire when Disney shouted to his yes-men, "That's it – our talking Duck!" Nash was astonished. Especially as he'd been doing his baby billy-goat. The important thing was that the voice inspired the creation of a unique cartoon character.

Despite what Katz stated, Donald Duck made his debut in *The Wise Little Hen, (The Orphans' Benefit* was his second film) and the nautical duck with the long pointed bill – it was later bobbed – soon caught the public's imagination. Donald's bad temper was Disney's idea; Nash had always regarded the goat/duck voice as lovable and had never thought of blowing his top in it. Every time he did, audiences demonstrated with hard cash that they preferred the irascible Donald to the rascible Mickey. It's not known how Mickey felt about the competition, but Grace Moore made it more than plain. Asked to follow Donald on a radio programme, the soprano shouted: "I'm not doing any show with any damn duck!"

Although Margie warned Clarence when he first signed with Disney that the job probably wouldn't be permanent, the trick voice he perfected at thirteen was still supporting them both at umpteen. 1983 saw the release of *Mickey's Christmas Carol,* an odd swan song for the Duck; it miscast him resoundingly as

Scrooge's happy-go-lucky nephew.

Happy-go-lucky indeed! The duck the world laughed at for over fifty years was more like his uncle Scrooge, angrily shaking his feathered fist and squawking unintelligibly. The Sunday after Nash's death, BBC2's *News Review* commemorated his passing by showing him speaking in Donald's voice. The programme provides sub-titles for deaf viewers and for the first time in my life I knew what the duck was saying. But how did the BBC know?

When I met Jim Backus, I noticed he had the same weird chortle as his alter ego, Mr Magoo. He nodded, saying, "The first time the guys who dreamed up the character heard this laugh of mine, they yelled 'That we've got to use!'" He then spoke about being cast as Brassbound in a West Coast stage production of *Captain Brassbound's Conversion*. At the first reading, he saw the stage direction "Brassbound laughs" and automatically laughed his own laugh. Greer Garson, who was playing Lady Cicely Waynflete, did a Grace Moore and shouted, "I'm not acting in Shaw with *Magoo!*"

To do Popeye's voice – as Jack Mercer did for over forty years – you had to force yourself to believe the old vaudevillian's credo (as outlined in *The Sunshine Boys*) that words with "K" are funny. Otherwise you couldn't say lines like, "Olive, this roask beef is like a beautiful symphkony," without getting embarrasked. His Olive was the talented Mae Questel – so talented that for a time during World War II, she did Popeye's voice as well. Then there was Verna Felton, who played elephants in *Dumbo* and *Jungle Book,* and was married to Lee Millar, who barked for Pluto.

The best-known voice in animation is unquestionably Mel Blanc, whose versatility verges on sci-fi. He's Bugs Bunny, Sylvester, Tweetie Pie, Yosemite Sam, Foghorn Leghorn, Pepe Le Pew, Porky Pig, Speedy Gonzales, Daffy Duck, Barney Rubble in *The Flintstones,* and in some commercials, Elmer Fudd. Blanc's Daffy Duck lisp (and who could be daffier than a drake who thinks he's a duck?) was based on the lisp of Leon Schlesinger, who produced the Warner Bros cartoons from 1936-42. The first time Schlesinger heard Daffy, his reaction was, "Thay, where'd you get a thwell voithe like that?" Impure speech is Blanc's meat; Porky stammers, Elmer can't pronounce his R's, L's or W's, and the S's of Sylvester's "Sufferin' succotash!" keep getting in Tweetie's eye.

Blanc's master-voice is Bugs Bunny – the Groucho of Cartoonland, forever brandishing a carrot instead of a cigar. The dialogue in Bugs's cartoons is pretty Marxian too:

"Batten down the hatches!"

"I've battened 'em down already, Cap'n!"

"Well batten 'em down again – I'll teach those hatches!" Unlike Clarence Nash, who was long denied a credit on the screen, Blanc has for years been identified by the words: "voice characterizations Mel Blanc". He says he got the credit in lieu of a pay rise. (The Bros Warner were very hard of spending.) Tha-tha-that's nearly all, folks, but first: Succotash is an American cooked dish made of beans, corn and, if you wish, red and green peppers.

Just thought you'd like to know.

On A Society Rumour
The duchess is with child. O blest fertility.
Confounding all who doubt the duke's virility.
Last night a footman claimed responsibility.

On A Surrogate Mother
Alone, the dark Samantha met her doom –
A rented mother in a rented room.

The Vision-Mixer
The vision-mixer died and went to Hell.
Or was it Heav'n? Alas, he could not tell.

The Passing of the Third-Floor Back
A flash, a bang. . . . No death was ever neater.
The Third-Floor Back has by-passed his
last meter.

The Death Of Mrs Bloggs
Death handed Mrs Bloggs the frozen mitt.
"Well, this is it," she said, "well, this is it."

The British Disease
All trades, from manual to supervisory,
Denounce the latest offers as derisory.
But ah, the pubs are happy as the thrall
Of vicious serfdom smothers one and all.

To A Well-Known Journalist
You have integrity. We do not doubt it.
But, God Almighty, don't go on about it.

The Tomboy Tamed At Last
The wild Lucinda, that enchanting hoyden,
Was sobered by a honeymoon at Croydon.

The Folly of Women
As battered barks make for a hostile shore.
So every battered wife goes back for more.

The Dying Copywriter To His Love
Farewell, that mane of sun-spun gold!
Tomorrow I'll be stiff 'n' cold,
And other hands shall then caress
Your longer-lasting loveliness.
But may I hope that, ere I die,
One tear may moisturise your eye?
And let my tomb proclaim with pride
The love that cleansed deep down inside.

Satan On The Line
And now, our latest phone-in to the Devil.
Good morning, Lucifer – Good morning, Neville —
What is the greatest triumph you can show
Over the last two thousand years or so? —
Without a doubt, I'd say it's Video.

In Search of Sanctuary
Where, in this world, can Julia's lovers be?
Ask of the swallows, sporting fancy-free.
Ask of the wind. . . but, much more usefully,
Ask on the oil-rigs in the northern sea.

On A Tax Inspector
This public servant, whom we clothe and nourish,
Scourges the just and lets the unjust flourish.

A Conversation In Fleet Street
Good morning, editor – Good morning, sneak –
I've brought you this – Well, well, another leak –
I'll need cash down – But this stuff's pretty weak –
Good morning, editor – Good morning, sneak.

On A Grandmother
What? Twice a gran at thirty-one?
Then someone must have jumped the gun.

On A Lady Friend
My Love in her attire doth show her wit,
With "MIND MY MILK BAR" stretched from
tit to tit.

So That's All Right, Then
Maisie said, "I'm preggers, Ma.
Shall I stay, or say ta-ta?"
Ma said, "Better ask your Pa."
Pa said, "Che sera sera."

More Victorian Values
The good girls sat round bored. The not-so-good
Filled Hostels for the Fallen Sisterhood.

Objection
With belly-dancing one is quickly sated.
The belly should be stuffed and not gyrated.

Travel Note
In India's temples there are naughty thingamies.
What is the naughtiest of all? The lingam is.

The Spoilers
The bloody Tyrant leaves the landscape wrecked,
As also does the bloody Architect.

The Fortunate Ones
Lord, what luck! In Maracaibo,
Fukushima and Odessa
Folk have never heard of Vita,
Or Virginia, or Vanessa.

The Servant Problem
The Jeeves from Spain is jailed again,
    Luigi's at the *vino,*
And in her lair the Swede au pair
    Has trapped the Filipino.

The Sticking Point
In seven days God fashioned stars and seas,
Volcanoes, wart-hogs, men and women, fleas.
"There's only one thing I will not create,"
Said God. "That's monosodium glutamate."

Headlines
Nothing makes the spirit sag
More than "VICAR'S PLEA FOR DRAG."
Nothing lifts the spirits like
"POLY LECTURERS ON STRIKE."

Lift Up Your Hearts
Say not the struggle naught availeth!
Whom one judge frees, another jaileth.

E S Turner

HANDELSMAN

ACADEMICIAN IMPOSSIBLE!

or, *The Light that Failed to Fail*

In the autumn of his life, neo-classicist Pratt Fall needed increasingly powerful spectacles.

THE FACT WAS THAT FALL WAS OUT OF STEP WITH THE ART WORLD.

FREAKY FABLES

MORAL: Over-draw not, lest ye be overdrawn.

KEITH WATERHOUSE

Military Two-Step

Dear Yorkshire Arts,

I should like to apply for the post of Dance Officer as advertised in *The Guardian*. Though no longer in full-time employment, I was (until taking voluntary redundancy) Chief Waltz Co-ordinator for this area, and still keep my hand in as Adjutant of a Territorial Formation Dancing Battalion, and cha-cha visitor to our local Borstal. My c.v. will prove I have the necessary experience:

Education: Minnie del Monte's School of Dance. Field Marshal Haig Memorial Tap-dancing Scholar at Miss Tremayn's Academy for Dance Officer Cadets. Victor Sylvester Lines, Sandhurst. After army training in various aspects of the Dance, continued to learn in the Ballroom of Life.

Qualifications: School certificates in flamenco, choreography and applied folk dancing. Considerable field experience in Gay Gordons, Lancers etc. Passed officers' instruction courses in (1) unarmed dance hall combat, (2) stripping down and naming of parts of the rumba, (3) night Morris dancing. Twice leader of Army Pas de Deux team, Royal Tournament (won against Royal Marines twosome on both occasions). In civilian life, extensive knowledge of olde tyme dancing at community leisure centre and town hall levels.

Work experience: After waltzing out of Sandhurst in 1949, and failing to be accepted by the Highland Fling Regiment owing to a slight tango wound sustained while on manoeuvres at the Hammersmith Palais, I obtained a commission with the Royal Army Corps de Ballet where, among other duties, I was i/c Western District Leotard Maintenance Depot, later assuming responsibility for both block toe and soft toe ballet-shoe dumps.

1950-53: Transferring to the King's Own Light Fantastic Regiment, I was given command of a quickstep platoon and posted immediately to Korea. Saw action at the Starlight Room and the Fragrance and Jasmin Dance Halls, Seoul. Mentioned twice in despatches – (1) for leading a palais glide under fire, and (2) for my platoon's part in overcoming a foxtrot emplacement and capturing fifteen enemy taxi dancers. Present at South Korea v. North Korea Come Dancing finals.

1953-57: Home posting to British Army Dance Headquarters, H. M. Ballroom, Aldershot, with rank of captain. Allotted task of co-ordinating all regimental dinner-dances. Detached on tour of Mecca Ballrooms to study at first-hand the big band sound and report back on its applicability to Naafi hops. Detached to Catterick Novelty Dance Range as member of team investigating infiltration of jitterbugging by a foreign power (under Section Three of the Official Secrets Act, dealing with classified dance steps, I am unable to expand on this important mission).

1957-59: Upon the King's Own Light Fantastic merging with the Lancashire Clog Regiment and the Surrey Soft Shoe Shuffle Brigade to become the Royal Sequence Dancing Corps under army reorganisation, was posted to West Germany for a two-year tour of the North Atlantic Hokey Cokey Alliance (NAHCA) with the substantive rank of major. Gained valuable first-hand experience of the schottische and took part in Exercise Madame Jessie – executing the Pas de Basque in arctic conditions (Jeré with demi-ronde up Alp. Assemblé to ball of right ski. Slight plié and coupé in snowdrift.) Subsequently conducted survival course requiring combined allied Moonlight Saunter forces to carry out armed promenade turns in sub-zero temperatures.

1959-62: Returned to British Army Dance Headquarters as Rationalisation Officer, with responsibility for co-ordinating and harmonising steps of the Royal Empress Tango which were differing from garrison to garrison and in some cases from mess to mess, with officers stepping L.F. forward and leftwards in the first diagonal chassé while non-commissioned officers would be stepping L.F. forward and rightwards. During this period attended Madame Jessie's Officer Training College for re-training in Doris Waltz, Lilac Waltz, and Magenta Modern Waltz under fire.

1963: Conducted court of inquiry into isolated outbreaks of rock'n'roll at certain army depots, the rejected findings of which led to the celebrated Colchester Assembly Rooms Mutiny, where an officer and eighty-five other ranks were charged with forming an unlawful conga in protest at new Queen's Regulations, imposed against my advice, forbidding unauthorised steps. Had my superiors accepted my recommendation that rock'n'roll training courses be instituted, and a modified, strict tempo version of rock'n'roll under proper supervision be allowed in army dance halls, that uprising would never have taken place. (Nor, I venture to add, did the "top brass" learn from their mistakes – hence the Camellia Tango Guards breakdancing riots of recent memory.) Resigned commission in disgust.

1964-68: On returning to "civvy street", accepted position of Dance Adviser to the Confederation of British Industry, my main role being to tour factories and shipyards and iron out the demarcation disputes over "who does what" in the Waverley Two Step etc which at that time were seriously bedevilling our export drive. With the active support of the TUC Slow Waltz Committee, I drafted the guidelines leaflet, "Left Foot Forward, Reverse, Inwards Progressive Turn" which did much to harmonise canteen dances throughout industry. Here my experience as Rationalisation Officer with British Army Dance Headquarters stood me in good stead: where – say – boilermakers and woodworkers were deadlocked, with both sides stubbornly refusing to be the lady, delicate negotiations proceeding literally step by step were necessary and a high degree of expertise required. The still popular Brothers' Two Step, where the partners perform their glissades arm in arm with neither leading, owes its conception to my conciliatory role in the lightning dance strikes of the Sixties.

1968-74: My task with the CBI completed, and having no desire to sit about waiting to step into dead men's dancing pumps in the role of Chief Dance Executive, I turned to pastures new and a rewarding career in local government. Commencing as Scottish Reel Consultant to Cairnborough City Council, I quickly rose "through the ranks", so to speak, in a succession of advisory posts up and down the country, ultimately becoming Director of Bevindon District Council Polka, Royal Empress Tango and Azalea Foxtrot Department. During this period I formulated the Council's Nuclear Dance strategy, evolving an Evacuation Waltz for use in underground ballrooms in the event of a nuclear attack.

1974-82: Was successful among 250 applicants in securing the position of Chief Waltz Co-ordinator for S. Loamshire. Immediately instituted a policy of licensing discos with regular inspections of same to ensure that disco dancing was at all times being performed to the standards of the International Dance Teachers' Association. Had responsibility for funding and overseeing a wide spectrum of council-sponsored dance activities ranging from a Gay Gay Gordons Workshop to a single-parent Gainsborough Glide group. In my period there, S. Loamshire became the first county authority ever to win the Yvonne Spatchwick Latin Dancing Bronze Medal. On the principle of "quitting while one is ahead" I then took early retirement. However, the pull of the ballroom is as strong as ever, and, if appointed, I look forward to leading Yorkshire Arts in the dance I shall invent to celebrate – T' Tykes' Tango.

"Mr Marplew, you have two minutes on the works of John Buchan starting. . .

. . .Now, what are the thirty-nine steps?"

". . .Um, the thirty-nine steps is an. . .

. . .Aargh . . .!!!"

DREDGE

Michael BYWATER
Cat off a Hot Tin Roof

THEY say everything passes in front of your eyes as you go down, but it's the twenty-seventh floor now and all I can see is old Mrs Dobryanowitz sat in her recliner tickling that dumb old tabby. She's got *The 700 Club* on and a can of pretzels in her fat paw, and she's watching the guy in the bright blue suit talking about miracles, and she takes a pretzel, then she gives one to the dumb old tabby, and that's all I see because I'm on my way down, and it'll take more than a lousy miracle to stop me now. Which suits me fine.

It would be nice to say it had been an interesting life, but it wouldn't be true, and I figure that now is not the time to start lying. Things have always been sorta short on fascination, not that I'm complaining; that's the way it is for us, half the time you're asleep, the rest of the time things kinda swim in and out of your line of fire, like coming round from the stuff they gave me when the guy in the white coat finished off for good the only part of my life which really had any direction to it.

The Contexts caused that thing to happen. It was the second thing they ever did to me, the first being they picked me up and took me back to their apartment. I'm passing the Mcguires', apartment now and they're stuck into each other as usual, except I note that she's got a Moulinex electric carver in her hand this time. Okay, it's unplugged at the moment but theirs is a smart apartment and well-supplied with power points, so it's fair to assume that things are taking a turn for the worse for the McGuires, and also for me. To be frank about it, I am rapidly becoming a victim of gravity and before I discover the final truth about our ability to land on our feet in any situation, I would like to answer for myself the difficult question about why the hell I let the Contexts pick me up and take me home.

I could tell them for a pair of schleps the minute I set eyes on them. There was something about Arnie Context that said "real estate", from his brand new topsiders to his malt-thickened hairstyle, taking in the Rogers Peet leisure suit on the way, and Topey fitted right in with that in her designer drawstring sweat-pants and that $150 hair colour job that screamed of metal salts and hypochlorite, but which you could be sure she shrugged off as the sunshine beating down on their Fire Island retreat. I put them down as the kind who would have had some nice Afghan called Julius with an out-of-work ballet dancer to come in and feed the poor bastard and walk him round South Central Park while Arnie and Topey Context were out shifting real estate.

But it turned out they were starved for animal love, this being a serious decision which they had reached while strolling in Washington Park rubbernecking dive sickies, which I could tell the minute I saw them. I was heading east along Bleeker Street before taking a left up McDougal, because I always like to hit the Square in that corner to take in the action

before I made my choice, given that making my choice had some purpose in those days, and I could hear Topey kvetching Arnie about some lousy Lhasa Apso she wanted even before the topsiders (his) and the Nike Hi-Siders (hers) came into eye-level.

I'm out of 19th and passing the window of 1821 now, which has always been something of a mystery to me but is now solved with the sight of a strawberry blonde hooker in a Giorgio Armani *mouchoir* relieving a fattish, sweating businessman of $100, and so it's not the time to recall the slush that the Contexts came out with as they picked me up. Normally I'd have had their eyes out the moment they bent down, but I was feeling somewhat sluggish on account of Marc and Karl, two beefy fags I used to hang around with on Christopher Street, had given me a chunk of fine Gold in my Purina chow that afternoon and it had slowed my reflexes.

At first I was glad of the narcolept for permitting me to get into a situation which I figured would repay handsome dividends. Sure, East 67th Street was kind of a long way from Washington Square, but things were getting a little hot for me and although staking out a whole new territory was sort of a pain, I felt confident I could handle it. I had a good build and I always looked well turned out and I figured a challenge was what I needed.

So I let the Contexts take me back to their apartment in the very building of which I am now passing the 14th floor and making the

"At least the French can't complain we're not true Europeans any longer."

incidental but illuminating discovery that the Reverend Julio Anodyne inhabits a distinctly un-clerical apartment, the whole studio room being a kind of shrine to Elvis Presley, including a life-size model of the guy which Julio is kneeling before, and for the first couple of days everything was fine.

It was on day three that I came back after settling a small dispute over the waste plot behind Douggie's Bar. I was pretty exhausted and not very pleased to be greeted with Topey yelling, that cat *stinks*, and Arnie agreeing and Topey saying, well have him *done*, Arnie, have him *done*, and Arnie saying, I couldn't, they're all small and furry and think of the pain, and Topey saying, what are you, Arnie, some kind of *pervert*, Christ you make me *sick*, you can never make a lousy *decision*, I can't even bear to *look* at you, you're so *fat* and *bloated*, you swell up in the heat like some goddamned damp, spotty, poisoned *dog*, no *wonder* we don't make love any more, I think you maybe do this subconciously to punish me.

So Arnie is some kind of feeb, a wimp, because instead of ripping this unpleasant person to shreds he just says, okay, hon, I'll get him fixed tomorrow, if we'd got a Lhasa Apso there'd have been no problem.

I feel obliged to draw a veil over what happened after that, except to say that I am now passing apartment 1218, moving slightly eastwards in the evening breeze, and neither the sight of Mrs Abse taking her breasts off in the bathroom nor the prospect of the sidewalk moving towards me at a leisurely pace fill me with particular horror relative to the agonies of that day.

Arnie and I returned to the apartment that evening to find Topey in tears. I was feeling rather weak but I managed a pitiful combination hobble-and-drag across the deep-pile wall-to-wall, so Topey redoubles her sobbing and starts yelling at the wimp Arnie, and the Contexts swing into marital overdrive while I lapse into the trance which has characterised much of my life, before and since, but which was especially exemplified by the events of that day. (Were I a philosopher I might also say that New York was exemplified also thereby: one's manhood is removed while one sleeps and there is no right of appeal.)

I awoke, or came round, to find Topey gone and Arnie drunk on Chivas Regal, which many might regard as a pretension but when taken in the context of Context's other pretensions took on the appearance of extreme restraint.

Topey came back two days later, in the company of a bearded youth in russet clothing. A Prince of Peace, she called him, who preached gentleness and wholism and cut off my Purina chow because it was unnatural. I wasn't too happy about the diet of mung beans and soya curd, and nor was Arnie. The creep took to wandering aimlessly between his jacuzzi and his short-wave, his video and his synthesizer, turning things on and off, making odd noises with the blender during the night and generally consuming Con Ed power to no purpose. As a tactic it was fruitless, because Topey still followed him around the apartment dressed in her sable-trimmed Serendipity *peignoir*, now dyed russet, yelling at him that he was heartless, a wimp, how could he mutilate a poor innocent animal, and so on.

It's hard to say why now, as I pass apartment 712 wherein Mr Zuntz and Mrs Kugelmass (of 931) are making love while wearing Ronald Reagan masks, but I felt some sympathy with the wimp Context as things went from bad to worse, and when I followed him to an immoral club called The Zoo one Saturday I knew how he felt; a man could get a steak at The Zoo, and a woman, and a drink, and he didn't have his wife sitting around the apartment with a bearded Prince of Peace and the Prince of Peace's girlfriend, a six-two, 160 pound mulatto with fists like hams and an appetite for novelty like we are supposed to have for cream.

So when the wimp Context comes home this afternoon to find his wife in the sack with the Mulatto while the Prince of Peace intones phrases from St Julian of Norwich through a microphone while standing on the remains of Context's video, I am ready to be sympathetic, because Context has a client with him to whom he wishes to sell some real estate and this scene perhaps makes Context feel a little uneasy about the impression he is making on the client.

And I remain sympathetic (I still feel sympathetic even now, as I pass 308 and observe not without a final pang of pleasure the sight of Mr Pinkus thrashing his Schnauzer) when the client screams "Claude!" and the Prince of Peace chokes into his megaphone and the Mulatto leaps off Mrs Context and lays out the client and the Prince of Peace bends over the client and begins kissing his eyelids and Mrs Context takes the revolver out of the Kleenex dispenser and begins firing widely and wildly and Arnie Context starts yelling, it's that goddamn lousy cat, we were happy, rich and upwardly-mobile until that stinking cat came along, and then the cops bust in and one of them takes a look at me and kicks me right in the source of my greatest regret, and I give a kind of yell and leap onto the window-sill.

Which is when it strikes me. And I look out. And it seems a long way down. So I look back into the room, then out again, and it doesn't seem so far any more, and the air is warm, and I review my life, which has been reasonably interesting but on the whole lacking in any real substance, consisting largely of wandering around following various instincts which demand much and give little in return, and making strange and pointless noises in my throat for no reason except that they stop people from kicking me, though not always, and I think, what the hell.

So I step out and it's quite pleasant and now I'm passing apartment 101 in which Mr Splanck the experimental artist is sitting by his telephone with a look of naked hopelessness on his grey sagging face, and very shortly now I am going to discover if there is a God, for us, and if He is a panther or a jaguar or a cheetah or even, as some people say, a tree. ℮

"Gerald, do you remember how I used to say your head was shaped like an onion?"

"Know what I miss, Lennie? I miss the boos."

DICKINSON'S SAFARI

"Even they've left the breakfast!"

"Ask them how many beads for a full service and a new half-shaft."

"My God, you're right – it isn't a mirage."

"I hope your husband realises that giraffe rides are not included in the overall price of the holiday?"

"She says you only get the free road map with purchases of over ten gallons."

Janet St. Clair

Fair Warning

> **"Music and Mardi Gras are as indigenous to New Orleans as moisture."**

Call me sentimental, then. But I concluded virtually forthwith that I'd preferred New Orleans *before* this "last great extravaganza" (to purloin from Loozy-ana's Governor Edwards what could conceivably be construed as a description itself perhaps encroaching upon the extravagant) "that will be available for people of this century." Oh, the Louisiana Exposition is undeniably every penny's worth an 80-acre, $350-million World's Fair. But a certain irony attaches to this sprawling, spurious, hydroponic, hothouse-pink and turquoise-plastic, hybrid New Orleans being planted, force-fed and harvested in the very heart of the lush and fecund Real Thing.

Because the new New Orleans has been the world's best world's fair for at least the last couple of centuries. Surrounded severally by vast, bittersweet, oyster-laden Lake Ponchartrain, the murky, meandering Mississippi River, and trackless channels of catfish swamp and bayou, it has remained through time a literal island unto itself; a city like no other.

Yet its character defies classification: it is Caribbean, cajun, Caucasian, creole, backwoods redneck and African Black; reggae to rag time, bluegrass to blues; Baptist, Catholic, Muslim and Voodoo. Somehow this *bouquet garni* of cultures and customs simmers successfully in the effluvial soup of its encircling Southern waters, and imparts to the tropical steam of New Orleans a heady zest distinctively its own.

The Fair – and its concessionaires – sought to clone this aqueous cultural phenomenon, then charge fifteen clams a crack to see it. The theme, "The World of Rivers. . . Fresh Water as a Source of Life", was as compatible to this master-plan as carp to a bayou. Gargantuan green 'gators, pink pelicans, carmine crawdads and turqoise turtles line the famed fountain-and-waterfall waterfront "Wonder Wall" and oversee the vendors hawking shrimp jumbalaya, filé gumbo, fried catfish po-boys and oyster muffuletta. Nor did Expo merchants for a moment forget that music and Mardi Gras are as indigenous to New Orleans as moisture: sticky children clutching pecan pralines and wiggly rubber reptiles adhere to sweat-shiny adults wearing glittery carnival tee-shirts and Bourbon Street visors. Fair-fabricated Dixie in even more highly concentrated doses is for sale in such Southern salmagundis as the Jazz Creole Buffet Fireworks Mississippi Riverboat Cruise.

But do I erroneously imply that Expo '84 offers nothing but Louisiana purchases? That would be unjust: the exhibits are fabulous. I can't imagine even the most curmudgeonly of Scrooges leaving the Chinese or Canadian pavilions, for example, still begrudging the price of an entry ticket. Many participating nations display samples of their finest art and artifacts, and several even feature native artisans in action.

And the incredible plethora of live entertainment – much of it transplanted nearly intact from the seamy streets and smoky clubs of the Real New Orleans – leaves one utterly aboggle with sound and spectacle. Around each periwinkle stall and fountain is yet another group of musicians: jazz, gospel, rhythm and blues, zydeco, country, soul and folk. Interspersed therein are jugglers, dancers, puppeteers and plays. Very Big Names and First Class Acts await ticket-holding amphitheatre patrons, where, between country rock layers of Oak Ridge Boys, Merle Haggard and Linda Ronstadt, such gems as the Tokyo Ballet and English National Opera can often be excavated.

Even so, one given to wistful reminiscence of old New Orleans can tolerate only so many 30-foot nearly-nude concrete Nereids and steamboat calliope renditions of *Are You From Dixie?* before hankering to paddle upriver a stretch. And so, pushing my way through reeking, sweltering throngs, past mammoth plaster mermaids, and out garishly festooned purple gates, I escaped into the indolently thick atmosphere of the steamy Real Thing. Shuffling as determinedly as one can through

"It takes him ages to put up a set of bloody shelves."

BANX

that sensuously sultry fog masquerading as air, I passed the new, glass, high-rise hotels on Canal Street, then plodded torpidly down dirty, dilapidated Decatur to the funky decadence of the old French Quarter.

Just as the first rumblings of thunder announced a forthcoming summer's storm, I slumped into my chair in the covered courtyard of that venerable old New Orleans institution, the Café du Monde, and waited languidly for my beignets and chicory-laced *café au lait*. The sudden torrential tropical rains that sent sightseers squealing and splashing pell-mell across Jackson Square lent that perfect backdrop, I observed aesthetically, against which I might most picturesquely swaddle myself in gloomy nostalgia for those good ol' days in old New Orleans.

Conveniently overlooking the tiny truth that this was actually only my third visit, I leaned back in attentive emulation of native lassitude and surveyed the World's Fair tourists with a tolerantly amused indifference. A gust of river wind sprayed my entire shirtfront with damp powdered sugar; I remained placidly *pococurante*. The Fair, I at length pronounced, as if I knew whereof I was pronouncing, is all well and good. But it can never capture the dignity, the style, the exuberance of New Orleans.

The Dignity of the meticulously preserved old Southern mansions of St Charles Avenue; of the huge black ladies in their gaudy caftans, sitting in stately silence like African Queens, fishing the tepid lakes of City Park. The Style of the intricately-wrought iron balustrades and jungle-covered courtyards; of the cemeteries, where miniature cities of ornately-carved tombs traditionally keep their habitants high and dry; and of the shabby streetcars, still in their Tennessee Williams paint. The Exuberance of Marie Laveau feathers-and-pigs'-knuckles Voodoo; of huge wire baskets of crawling, clawing crabs and crawdads being lowered into vast bubbling vats of spicy water; of the Jazz Festival, Mardi Gras, the Quarter. . .

I heaved a wonderfully histrionic heavy sigh, then ambled with woebegone resignation back toward the Fair for more ice-cream, cajun-dogs and fresh water pamphlets.

Night fell. The pavilions locked up; the ticket-takers and all those sticky kids and weary parents went home.

And then, before my very eyes, the most amazing metamorphosis occurred: the New Orleans World's Fair turned into the Real Thing. The gates swung open, and the boundaries dissecting Fiction fom Genuine began to fade. Bands played on, and everybody began laughing and dancing in the steets with friends who had only moments before been perfect strangers. Under the late-night lights, the towering concrete mermaids and 'gators, the garish gold cherubim, and the flags, streamers and banners of the hydroponic hothouse hybrid all took on the magical cast of one gigantic Mardi Gras float; of one fantastic polychromatic island situated in the antic midst of yet another.

It was an E-ticket ride. It was a real Jazz Creole Buffet Fireworks Mississippi Riverboat Cruise. Now, mind, it was only my third visit, but it sure felt like New Orleans to me. ℮

"Sorry about that – he's allergic to cats."

"It seemed a shame to waste it."

ERICH VON STROHEIM
as "MAD MICK" MALLOY

HEDY LAMARR
as DAWN PATROL

ALEXANDER NEVSKY
as HIMSELF

MARLENE DIETRICH
as NANOOK

PAUL ROBESON
as COUNT ZEPPELIN

THEY WERE TOO YOUNG TO LOVE – AND TOO OLD TO DIE!

Busby Berkeley's

SINK THE POTEMKIN!

THE EPIC THAT BRINGS THE TRUE HORROR & FUTILITY OF WAR MOVIES TO THE SCREEN!

PRODUCED & DIRECTED BY BUSBY BERKELEY. WITH A CAST OF THOUSANDS APPEARING IN ALPHABETICAL ORDER

BARRY FITZGERALD
as THE RED BARON

ELISHA COOK JR
as HINDENBURG JR

BASIL RATHBONE
as ABU DE SOUFFLE

C. AUBREY SMITH
as RED RIVER

JEAN GABIN
as ADMIRAL TIOMKIN

The Western Front, 1916. A bullet-riddled Sopwith Camel (Richard Attenborough) crash-lands in dense fog at Von Richtofen's airfield (1). The pilot, war-weary Major "Mad Mick" Malloy, is entertained by the shell-shocked Red Baron himself (2). Schtoned on Schnapps, they agree to destroy the battleship *Potemkin*, whose commander, Admiral Dmitri Tiomkin, has been selling maggoty whisky and lousy theme music to both sides (3).

Loading a couple of Richtofen's Fokkers (Curt Jurgens & Conrad Veidt) with bombs, they set out for Odessa but are forced down by a mysterious single-engined woman, the lovely Dawn Patrol, who thinks they're gorgeous (4). She forces them down again, and persuades them to leave the war and join her in a musical extravaganza starring her as the Kaiser (5).

Nothing much happens for ages after that, except that "Mad Mick" and Richtofen fall in love with Dawn and one of them falls into a shell-hole and drowns (6).

From then on the plot weakens, everyone being shot by snipers while trying to catch a war-weary butterfly (John Mills) (7). The war, which is hell, goes on.

JACKSON

"Our spells have never been the same since we got the bleedin' wok."

"Cuckoo."

"It's about time you realised, Elmsworthy, that I've made more calculated guesses than you've had hot dinners."

Debriefing

YOUR CUTS TONIGHT:
SPECIAL RADIO TIMES SHOCK HORROR ISSUE

Sunday

ROYAL VARIETY PERFOR-MANCE: Due to budgetary considerations, the need to recoup £7 million by Jan 1st etc, this will feature just the One Ronnie plus a lot of close-ups of HM the Queen Mother since she is non-Equity and therefore doesn't qualify for appearance fees. In a further attempt to raise funds, the BBC is proud to announce a special new concession whereby those viewers willing to put £25 in the post, preferably in used fivers with non-traceable serial numbers, will be allowed to switch off their sets before the appearance of Bonnie Langford.

For £50 they will be allowed to switch off before Max Bygraves, and for £350 they will be allowed not to watch at all.

DID YOU SEE? Meanwhile on BBC2 Ludovic Kennedy will be introducing a special Royal Variety edition; as it has not been possible to hire critics, this week's edition will feature highlights from the Queen Mother's appearance at the 1983 Royal Variety Performance: these will be followed by black-and-white extracts from the 1947 Royal Variety Performance now out of copyright.

Monday

PANORAMA: Fred and the late Dick Emery with an especially hard-hitting investigation into why precisely thirty top BBC executives, together with wives and in certain cases people who are still other people's wives, have been living for the last month in a hotel in Singapore attending conferences on the future of Indonesian broadcasting at licence-payers' expense. This programme is subject to abrupt last-minute cancellation if the flights from Singapore are coming in on time during the late afternoon.

FRANK DELANEY: It will be noticed that the BBC is now eager to employ large numbers of jovial Irish monologists. This cuts down on the need to employ studio guests, and allows one camera to be locked off in mid-close-up while all others in the studio go home before overtime rates apply.

Those already at home will of course then have to go out to the pub in order to avoid the programme, but this need not be at the BBC's expense.

Tuesday

LAME DUCKS: Hilarious new sitcom in which our two likely lads (Billy Cotton Jr and Alasdair Milne) take the bus to Downing Street in the hope of winning another half-million pounds in the great Daily Mirror Licence Competition. Ronnie Barker guest-stars as Mrs Thatcher with Anton Diffring as Robert Maxwell. Next week: Will The Libyans Send Us A Cheque?

WE MISS MISS WORLD: Irate viewers hoping for the restoration of beauty contests are invited to gather on the pavement outside White City tube station where they will be addressed by Michael Grade, who is himself hoping to open a boutique in Malta any day now.

Wednesday

THE OTHER HALF: Isaac and John Pitman with another tragic investigation into what it is like being married to a BBC executive on £100,000 a year plus free videotapes of Esther Rantzen in labour.

THE TRIBAL EYE: David Attenborough interviews Fay and Huw Weldon, last survivors of a remarkable civilisation in which it was possible to make programmes that people actually wanted to watch for less than thirty thousand pounds a second not including repeats of *Dallas.*

Thursday

BREAKFAST TIME: This will in future be Continental only, no orange juice or fried eggs; coffee will be extra.

I'VE GOT A SECRET: Seven governors of the BBC, many of them still alive, have to guess precisely when in January 1985 the first commercial will be broadcast on Radio 2; they then have to guess by what month in 1986 the BBC will have been totally disbanded and sold to British Telecom shareholders or Virgin Airlines.

Friday

OXBRIDGE BLUES: Frederic Raphael's chilling account of five thousand arts graduates leaving Oxford every morning in the hopes of a job with Humphrey Burton, many of whom are now having to write Channel Four programme notes instead.

CALL MY BLUFF: The postmaster-general is challenged to explain why a licence fee of £5000 per annum might affect the outcome of the next election.

By Appointment Only

Brit Tel Com/./././. Share Line

Your Questions Answered

Just what exactly is this power behind the button?

Usually about 9 volts at room temperature for the person of average height and build. In some backward areas, British Telecom/././././. may still be the power behind the dial. If you are in any doubt you should consult a qualified electrician before applying for shares.

Just what exactly is this British Telecom anyhow?

In most instances, British Telecom/././././. is the power behind the button. Today's state-of-the-art button technology means that it will soon be commonplace for every household to have more than two thousand telephones implanted on a button no bigger than your fingernail or an average-sized coat button. These buttons will be able to perform a multiplicity of buttoning tasks up to a thousand times faster than switching on a light bulb.

Just how much is all this going to cost?

Every little helps. For example, £10 buys a Postman Pat novelty button telephone, for £100 you could have your name engraved on a telegraph pole of your choice, or £1,000 is enough to supply the average 3-bedroomed house with a 256K button telephone able to word-process, revolutionise washday, banish cold starting problems, record BBC-1 whilst you are away, etc etc. Within a very few years it should be possible to control a 9lb boil wash from outer space via your button telephone.

I've heard a lot of exciting talk about cordless telephones. Just what exactly is a cordless telephone anyhow?

Cordless telephones are tomorrow's technology here today. Already British Telecom/././././. has more than 10,000 cordless telephones in phone boxes across

the length and breadth of Britain and many inner city areas also have telephones with no handset, no buttons, no dial and no coin-boxes either. In case of difficulty, your messages should be sent first class post and are guaranteed to arrive within ten working days.

Can anyone apply to buy British Telecom/././././.?

Provided you have a bank account and can read a prospectus at 6ft (if necessary with the aid of spectacles), you should in most cases be able to apply to buy all or part of British Telecom/././././. There are a number of exceptions to this general rule, for example, concerning Soviet subjects or those persons who between the nights of 20 November 1984 and 28 November 1984 expect to be confined to prison. If you are in any doubt as to your eligibility to purchase British Telecom/././././. you should have a word in the first instance with your local priest or a registered general practitioner.

Will my TV reception be affected by the sale of British Telecom/./././.?

Probably not. Areas of low pressure can sometimes affect older persons or some pets but the sale of British Telecom/././. is not expected to cause congestion.

Just what happens if I am on holiday abroad?

In most cases, you will still be able to buy all or part of British Telecom/./././. provided you can satisfy the local authorities that you are aged between 5 and 85 and are the holder of a valid Post Office licence. Some special flights

have been arranged from major EEC participating countries and all applications made to British Consulates or overseas PABX supervisors will be handled in the strictest confidence. In certain areas of the Far East, you should dial or enter 0272 0272 0272 0272 for further information.

How can I be certain that my money will get through to where it is desperately needed?

British Telecom/./././. has an international network of BritTelComShareApp sorting centres second to none. BritiTelComShareApp centres are

manned round the clock on a 24-hour basis. If you should experience any difficulty understanding the 24-hour clock you should dial or enter the BritTelComClockSpeak service on (027272727 if you are outside the 10-mile fisheries limit) 272 272 272 272 272 and ask the operator for FreeBritTelComSpeak.

Just how will this affect my pension rights?

Under Article 272 272 272 of the EuroTelCom Convention, no salesman will call. Your Telecom/./././. shares are yours to examine in the comfort and privacy of your own home. If you are not entirely satisfied and delighted with your purchase of all or part of British Telecom/./././., simply return your TelComShareApp vouchers in the NO envelope to Dept 272 272 272 272 272, Goonhilly Downs, BT1 272X.

LARRY
AS SEEN ON TV

DEAR UNCLE MAC

A wonderful new readers' advice service

glory and the dream? The great tourer of state rattles at last into its final ditch, the chauffeur homeward plods his weary way, the headlamps are going out all over Europe.

I hope this has been of some help.

Yours sincerely,
Stockton

Dear Uncle Mac,

I am the ex-manager of Queen's Park Rangers, and I do not know which way to turn. Can you advise me?

Yours,
Alan Mullery MBE

My dear M'be,

As the chap whose nostrils picked up the first gamey inkling of the wind of change, I am deeply touched that one of the Empire's dusky sons should have turned once more to the mother country when the straits became dire.

I am informed that Queen's Park Rangers is a footer team. Ah, how the words roll back the arches of the years – I see them now, as if it were yesterday, Jessie Matthews, Charles Lawton, the unforgettable Henry James! It is not now as it hath been of yore, M'be, the great boot of state sinks into the mud, the sun sets on the umpire, our balls drop into the encroaching rough.

Provided you are not the unspeakable ruffian who sold Mr Gilson his frightful car, I trust this advice is what you were seeking.

Yours sincerely,
Stockton

Dear Uncle Mac,

Can you settle a bet? My best friend Sharon says Buff Orpington is the capital of Majorca, but I think it is Cliff Richards' real name.

Which of us is right?

Yours faithfully,
Tracey Twistleton-Wickham-Fiennes

My dear Tracey,

Surely, there need be no cause for discord and acrimony between you? Surely, you must be able to find a way to resolve your common differences in common aims? Is what divides you so much more important that what binds you together with hoops of steel?

When I was a young man, before that terrible war which ravaged our tragic continent and bore its finest sons away on its dreadful tide, men of goodwill would have sat down together and agreed upon a middle way: that, for example, Cliff Majorca was the capital of Buff Richards.

Is that not a wiser course than to allow the great Sharon of state to turn slowly on her once-proud side and sink forever beneath the wave of despair?

Yours sincerely,
Stockton

Dear Uncle Mac,

I recently come by a Nippobishi Loganberry 1.6 GLX out of *Exchange & Mart,* and I quote, nice runner, £2,750, only when I took my good lady and her friend Avril up the tupper last Tuesday, the gearstick come off in my hand and there was yours truly stood in the road like a prat, never mind miles from bleeding anywhere and was there an AA man, was there buggery.

What I want to know is, can I do the vendor for making good same? He is a blackie, if that comes into it.

Yours truly,
B. E. Gilson

My dear Mr Gilson,

When I was a boy, this great island of ours was criss-crossed with leafy winding lanes down which the young folk would whizz in their two-seater Bogworts and Wolfbanes and Cowslips between hedgerows ablaze with Frazer Nash and Armstrong Siddeley. I myself had a little Old Man's Beard, I recall, with a big dickie.

Eheu fugaces, Mr Gilson! Whither has fled the

PHILIP HOOD

AT THE Olympics in California last month, after another minor social gaffe by the almost anonymous Neil Macfarlane, Britain's Minister of Sport, the heavy betting insisted he would be replaced in Mrs Thatcher's September shuffle by Colin Moynihan, the sparky young Tory MP for Lewisham East, who was actually taking part in the Games as coxswain to the British rowing eight.

It seemed a good wheeze. At only 28, the diminutive Moynihan, it was supposed, could speak roughly the same sporty language as Daley Thompson and Tessa Sanderson – and indeed, back home, would even be able to bend a sympathetic ear to mumbling Charlie Magri's latest post-fight excuse in the dressing-room, for had not he, Moynihan, also been an Oxford boxing blue in the flyweight division?

Came the Olympic race: Moynihan's crew not only did worse than expected, it did very badly indeed. That did not matter, of course – the great thing is to take part, and all that stuff – but then was reported a fact that caused Ladbroke's Westminster odds to be wiped clean off the blackboard. Moynihan, dejected at his crew's defeat, publicly burst into tears. *Dammit! The fellow's a blubber!* No Tory could be Wetter.

A Minister of Sport is, in fact, only an Under-Secretary of State at the Department of Environment. The job was "invented" by Harold Wilson as one of his white-hot gimmicks in the 1960s, but was immediately established as fairly indispensible by the enthusiasm and politicking of Denis Howell, who is still considered by all sport as its Hon Min, although he has not held the post for over six years.

Before even the hapless Macfarlane, successive Conservatives had never got to grips with the job. At a sportswriters' gathering I remember Eldon Griffiths absentmindedly reading a speech prepared for a group of policemen – "This nation is deeply proud of the integrity of such a fine body of men as you, etc. etc. . ." It started to go down smarmingly well with us before we sniggeringly twigged the truth. Griffiths was followed by Hector Monroe, a similar daydreamer, languid and lofty; at one Sportsman of the Year do in a seedy West London ballroom, where beer was the order of the day, I bought him a glass of port: he stared at it, sniffed it, gave it back, sighed, got up, and vaguely wandered away, never to be seen again. . .

Sport, let's be honest, doesn't really matter. Over the years we have had general elections won or lost by the Poor Laws, the Corn Laws, never the Denis Laws: the ticket has been the Servicemen's Vote, the Housewives' Vote, You've Never Had It So Good, You've Never Had It, or the *Gotcha!* Falklands Factor. . . Never, remotely, a Sportsmen's Vote? If such a thing came to pass in the next year or so, then the Labour Party would win by a landslide.

Neil Kinnock's genuine and articulate devotion to Welsh rugby union is a pleasure. It was a ruddy shame, man, as well as a giggle for his opponents, that he was obliged to sit out last season's internationals at Cardiff Arms Park on account of some pathetically misguided Welsh clubs agreeing to scrum down with the pariahs of South Africa. I hope he has sorted that one out for the forthcoming season: his strength is as the good guy, bellowing on the

terraces with you and me; not the distant, suited statesman up in the committee box as some of his advisers see him, I fancy.

Well before Nye Bevan, young Kinnock's boyhood heroes had been long determined – Gilbert Parkhouse, Glamorgan's cultured creamer at cricket; John Charles, soccer's regal giant, and Cliff Morgan, Cardiff's pinball fly-half with the hopscotch footwork.

With Roy Hattersley, as readers of these pages know, first loves were Yorkshire cricket and Sheffield soccer: and you never forget the first times. A couple of years ago I was chatting, amiably and after-breakfast blearily, to Labour's deputy leader in the foyer of the Queen's Hotel in Leeds on the Test Match Saturday morning. He was edgy, looking over my shoulder to the door. Suddenly, he blushed into the shining morning face of youth, the eyes cleared, and he was up with his satchel and off – for Sir Len Hutton was giving him a lift to the ground. No politician even can ever have looked so justifiably pleased with himself. If he did nothing else in his life, he had still made it in the bigtime – for, once, Hutton drove Hattersley to Headingley.

Labour's record has always been pretty good at this sort of thing. Clement Attlee could, by all accounts, quote verbatim whole chunks of *Wisden*, certainly the scorecards of the Harrow v Eton match at Lord's. Hugh Gaitskell was less of a team man, but he followed closely the results of Wimbledon and the Open golf: at Winchester one of his biggest disappointments was to fail to win the senior steeplechase, for which he was hot favourite. But no reports say he blubbed.

Harold Wilson, too, tells you he was a nifty

"No wonder the poor devil went crazy."

sprinter in his youth. I've never dared ask him if he found the clogs a hindrance. On Yorkshire cricket teams you could never fault him, and without even organising a pause for a puff of St Bruno he can still rattle off the Huddersfield Town side of 1937 – "Hesford, Craig, Mountford, Willingham . . . . ." When Tony Crosland was Foreign Secretary, he would beg leave for a brief adjournment of high level talks in faraway places, and he and his entourage would go into a huddle around the shortwave radio. Orders from Carlton House, presumed the foreigners. Not a bit of it. Tony was checking the Test score on the BBC World Service.

Once Crosland begged off an urgent Heathrow meeting with whistle-stop Kissinger at the very height of the Rhodesia crisis. The US envoy later found that Crosland's "absolutely vital and crucial constituency engagements in Grimsby" in fact represented a 90-minute top-of-the-table promotion clash between Town and Gillingham. Another time, some months later, Crosland took Kissinger to watch Chelsea at Stamford Bridge: Kissinger became hooked on the game there and then, and a few years on became the first president of the US Soccer League.

Michael Foot's first question of a teatime Saturday was always "How did Argyle get on?" and, to be sure, one of the sights of last season during Plymouth's grand and unlikely run in the FA Cup was of the venerable patriarch and former prophet arriving at the ground with his nephew, Paul, and being persuaded against his will to have a seat in the directors' box instead of behind the goal on the terraces. If not, sir, I'm afraid we'll 'ave t' confiscate that stick, sir, sorry sir.

The Tories have never been able to match this sort of thing. Moynihan should have known he was on to a loser in more ways than one. They had Chris Chataway, of course, but whatever happened to him? And Jeffrey Archer, another very former MP, once sprinted

for Britain at the White City in 1966, twelve years after Cecil Parkinson had shown his paces at the same place in the annual match between the combined universities of England and USA. See what I mean?

Even the Tories' grouse-moor image has taken a beating since the year dear old Willie Whitelaw enraged all Scotland when, for fun, he persuaded his bodyguard to shoot a bird with his police pistol. And that from a former Captain of the R & A. Mrs Thatcher herself has not helped. Her sense of humour is as sidesplitting as Ken Dodd's compared to her awareness of sport. We all know how she was asked, after the 1978 Cup Final, to choose the man of the match. "Whymark in the No 10 shirt," she announced in an attempt at a joke. The nation was convulsed – her acolytes had forgotten to tell the lady that Whymark, amid headlines an acre thick, had cried off injured on the morning of the match.

Then there was that picture of her a year or two back when she entertained the England soccer team at Downing Street. She is holding a football high in the air but looks frowningly nonplussed even though Keegan, Brooking and Co are nearly falling out of the photograph in mirth. One of the midfield men had just said to her – "Hey, missus, I bet that's what you'd like to be doing with every striker's balls!"

Ted Heath, of course, had his *Morning Cloud*, which proved a good Central Office winner for a while. Then it sank, and so did he. Sir Alec Douglas Home was a goodish cricketer who once played for Middlesex in the days when knights were bowled and professionals knew their place. The late Ian Peebles, lovely man and one of the best *real* cricketers to come out of Scotland, once told me of the day he asked Sir Alec to play for his village team at Uddingston.

The local lads couldn't get over it for years – during the course of the game, the noble visitor wore, at different times, more than half a

dozen various and gaudy coloured caps.

Peebles would also enchant you with the account of the time he talked sport with Winston Churchill. The old boy could, apparently, hold forth for hours on the pleasures of polo or pig sticking – "But when he learned I was a cricketer he dismissed his own career at the game as having ended with a broken finger when he was ten. He could not remember the rules or the names of the implements at all, but the delivery was tremendous, enhanced by those squishy sibilants. Prompted occasionally by myself, he warmed to his tale – 'The ball came pascht,' he said, 'and hit the little things behind – what are they called? – ah, yesh, the schtumpsh!'"

Harold Macmillan liked sport. In his speech at the 1979 Boat Race dinner at the Savoy, he yearned: "In my day one could go into sports without having first to go into a long test to discover whether you are a man or a woman. Those were the times when games were games and sport was sport. As a young man I took a great interest in cricket, knew all the batting averages and all the great players of the day, Hobbs and Hayward, terrible degenerate days when you could still play a match between the Gentlemen and Players . . . . Reactionary, regressive, awful, I suppose. Still, a happy world . . . . " And he would bet sixpences with Nanny on the outcome of the Boat Race.

How would Saatchi & Saatchi have laundered that? Indeed, how would they have polished Disraeli's image? In a letter to his mother from Malta in 1830 he related he was unwell after being struck by a ball in the officers' rackets court. "The ball had then lain at my feet. Finally I picked it up and handed it to a rifleman standing nearby, and requested him to forward its passage into the court, as, do you know mother, I have never thrown a ball in my life."

Could it be that sport, one day, might even win or lose an election? Harold Wilson still reckons that England's World Cup soccer defeat on the very eve of the 1970 poll contributed to the nation's V-sign. No doubt that America's lorryload of gold medals at their village sports last month will boost Reagan's vote this winter – just as Joggin' Jimmy Carter lost the Presidency the day he fainted during that half-marathon.

Talking of which . . . . at the finishing line of the spectacularly successful London Marathon earlier this summer, I stood next to Labour's GLC leader, Ken Livingstone, who had upstaged Mrs Thatcher again and was preeningly accepting bouquets and cheers as we awaited the leaders on Westminster Bridge. News was seeping back from the course. An innocent American journalist with a short-wave radio sidled up and told us that at the halfway stage the leading British woman runner was an unlikely, freckle-thighed, middle-aged, matronly, blue-vested North London housewife *with red hair and a furrowed, earnest, determined look . . . .*

It turned out, of course, to be the amazing Joyce Smith, the Hertfordshire mother of two.

But, for one glorious moment, Red Ken had blanched and seemed almost on the point of tears.

Mossleworth Reporter

MOSSLEWORTH BORING SHOCK

MOSSLEWORTH IS THE MOST effing boring bloody dump in the effing world, according to 100% of young readers. Asked whether, you know, like, Mossleworth was the most effing boring bloody dump in the effing world, 100% of young readers said, "Right, this is it, right?"

Typical of young readers' comments was Julie Barmie, 15, of Tunnel Road. "Mossleworth is the most effing boring bloody dump in the effing world," said Julie, 15.

Others said:
*Nowt to do
*Boring
*Boring
*Nowt to do
*Boring
*Boring
*Boring
*Nowt to do

Full Story: page 3

GLAMOROUS SHARON KARKER, 13, pictured "ready for work" outside the Badminton Courts, Eckersdyke Street (See Entertainments).

WAYNE COMES OUT- AND IT'S A BIG ONE

LIKE LAST FRIDAY WAS A B-I-I-I-G night for Wayne Ackersthwaite, 17, of Eucris Avenue, right? Like Wayne was all kind of psyched up for a thing with glamorous Kikki Bong, 15, when like suddenly he come out, yeah? This is it, right?

And it was a big one, real big. And red, with an effing great yellow head. And right on the end of his, like, nose. I mean, the lads really give him a going over, a real old dose of the verbals, right? Eh?

As for Kikki, well, she told him where to get off, right? Well you would, woun't you? Specially where her Dad, Ng Deng Bong, he's got this takeaway up by the Flying Horse, "E dun't like want spotty thingy all over the thingy, I mean," says glamorous Kikki. "Right? I mean, this is it, right?"

Hard cheese, Wayne, 17. Har har har.

MOSSLEWORTH YOUTH GETS JOB

IT'S A HAPPY NEW YEAR for Baz Dork, 16, of Skelmersdale Bank. Baz, 16, has got a job as a pallet loader with J&B Chandra (Pallet Loading) Holdings, the well known Mossleworth pallet loading company. "It was like a bit of luck like," says Baz, 16. "And it means a Happy New Year for me, right?"

Baz's stroke of luck came when one of the existing pallet loaders was sacked for fighting. His new girlfriend, Tracey Lunk, who lives up them new flats behind the Bingo, says, "This is it, right?"

OTHER MOSSLEWORTH YOUTH LOSES JOB

IT'S AN UNHAPPY NEW YEAR for young Derek ("Doz" to his mates) Appen, 16. Doz, of that block of thingies, what's its name, Glen-bleeding-holme or summat like that, says he was sacked for fighting.

"I was sacked for fighting," says Doz, 16. "My girlfriend, Tracey Lunk, who lives up them new flats behind the Bingo, was putting it about with some other bloke an I reckon it was him, right, but I couldn't see to be sure." Doz's ex, Tracey Lunk, who lives up them new flats behind the Bingo, says, "This is it, right?"

FISH FOUND IN CANAL

A FISH WAS FOUND in the Mossleworth Canal earlier this week. It was a roach or gudgeon or summat, reckons Kevin Widdowson, 13, who made the discovery. "I don see what's so effing special about some effing fish," says Kevin, 13.

"Oh-oh, here comes Old Indian Summer."

"I've been thinking, Grace, these precious days I'd rather not spend with you."

"Could you both try and think of something that doesn't bring tears to your eyes?"

FFOLKES SINGS SEPTEMBER SONG

"Don't you just feel Keats all over the place?"

"I'm sorry, the sap doesn't rise again for another six months."

"Don't even ask. 'Autumn Leaves'."

Hunter DAVIES

Father's Day

Square Deal

"I got in front of her and enunciated my English more clearly this time. Some of these Italians can be a bit slow."

FLORA doesn't like it when we have words. It's usually pretty silly, about who's stupid fault it was that we have ended up doing this stupid thing, and it usually ends up pretty silly as well, arguing about who it was who started the argument or, even worser, who brought it up again. All the normal family stuff.

This time, please gather round, I can see a few seats left at the front there, don't be shy, this time we were just too shattered to shout for very long, and it did end ever so happily.

It happened last week in Tuscany. We had gone for five days, me and my wife and Flora, because we both wanted to do some research for various books we are currently working on. Me and the missus, that is. I don't think Flora

has started her first book. She's only eleven, but she'd better hurry up. Sometimes I feel so tired.

We had spent the morning in Siena, watching the preparations for the Palio, this historic horse race they have round the central square. We had failed to buy tickets, which was probably just as well, as 200,000 spectators were expected and it was already standing room only in the surrounding streets and alleyways. So we decided to visit San Gimignano, one of the most beautiful places in the whole of Italy, so every guide told us.

We had had Jimmy Jimmy on our list for several days. We had been calling it that partly because I had still not quite come to grips with the Italian language, or the lire, but also as a

joke. Flora has this phrase she says when she catches people out, such as elderly Wrinklies, when they have lied or exaggerated or just made a genuine mistake. "Jimmy Jimmy," she says, rubbing her chin. Don't ask me the derivation. Far too hot for that.

We set off for Jimmy Jimmy about mid-day, leaving the hordes, estimating that we would be there in under an hour, just in time for lunch. My wife was navigating and she did very well, getting us safely off the bit of autostrada from Siena, and we were soon following the signs to San Jimmy. We saw it first in the distance, an amazing walled town, just as the books described it, on a hill in the distance, with towers and battlements, the sort of skyline that travellers must have seen all over Italy, back in the fourteenth century.

We climbed up and up a narrow, twisting road and eventually made it through the town wall and into the old quarter and by a terrific bit of luck we managed to park near the centre. Well, it wasn't really luck. The place was deserted. Every Italian, not just every tourist, was obviously in Siena for the day.

We had parked near a street called Via 20 Settembre. Flora asked why it was called that but I told her to ask Jake, next time we meet him. He's the expert on Italian history. I looked it up on the San Jimmy map and there it was, but couldn't find the next street we came to. Typical. All week we had been struggling with the *Michelin* guide. They never seem to put on their town maps the actual street you happen to be standing in. But I worked out the general direction and eventually we reached the Duomo. Cathedral to you, dum-dum. Next to it, just as the map said, was the Museum of Sacred Art. It looked quite cool inside. After lunch I might give it three seconds of my valuable time.

We really felt we were in medieval times. The old town was so marvellous and atmospheric, cut off from all modern life, with no nasty modern buildings and hardly any cars. Walking round the ancient streets, we realised we were the only tourists in the whole town. Clever old us, choosing the Palio day.

We stood in the central square, wondering where the restaurants might be. My wife looked up the *American Express* Florence and Tuscany guide, a book I can heartily recommend, and she happened to see them refer to the main square in San Gimignano as being *triangular*. We happened to be standing in a main square which was *rectangular*.

Now take this easy, Hunt. Even I know the difference, though it's centuries since I did geometry. Stupid guidebooks. As the author of several, I know how untrustworthy we can all

"Me too. I can get all this at home."

be at times. But the Duomo was in the right place on the map, so was the little museum, and the Via 20 Settembre. Perhaps this wasn't the main square after all.

The square was deserted. It was siesta time. All the locals still at home must be inside asleep, or watching television. I caught a glimpse of an old woman, flitting from one dark alleyway to another, and I raced after her and in my fluent English I asked where the Piazza del Cisterna was. This is what they call their main square in San Jimmy.

She tried to escape, but I got in front of her and repeated my question, enunciating my English a bit more clearly this time. Some of these Italians can be a bit slow. She shook her head, so I got out the guidebook and showed her the name I was looking for on the map.

Now this is always a mistake. My wife started muttering, don't be stupid, how cretinous, she won't understand a map, locals never do. This is true. My father-in-law Arthur knows Cumberland backwards, every secret road and route, but show him a map and he's lost. He has his own map in his head, one which Mercator could never reproduce.

Suddenly, the old woman burst out laughing and launched into fluent Italian, forgetting for a moment I was a visiting foreign idiot in my Marks and Spencer shorts and ancient Green Flash. She pointed over the town walls into the far distance. It slowly struck us what had happened. We were not in San Jimmy. We were in some place called Colle di Val D'Elsa, an equally ancient medieval walled town on a hill, with a Duomo, a museum, a 20th September street.

It was your stupid fault, you were supposed to be navigating. Oh no it wasn't, you parked the car and you said that's the Duomo and that's the main square, you halfwit, you have buggered up the whole day now.

Shush, said Flora, it doesn't matter, let's just have an ice cream and forget lunch.

I'm not staying here, said my wife. And I'm not leaving now, so I said. It's another eight kilometres to the right place, and I'm shattered and starving and anyway I've got a good parking place. But there's no place to eat, and *you* can't go without eating, you pig, I know you.

To the right of the Duomo I noticed a sort of hardboard hut, a make-shift shop set up in a passageway, and on the pavement in front a handwritten scrawl which said, "Oasis for Tourists". I went across and it was just a shack selling trinkets, awful glass ornaments, the sort you win on fairgrounds. It seemed to be run by a local peasant-looking family. There was a mum in black and two daughters beside the souvenirs and a dad with brawny arms who was sitting in the shade at a table eating what looked like a half a cow.

He waved his half cow at me, like Desperate Dan, and kissed his fingers and went yum yum yum, or whatever is the Tuscan for yum yum. Something else to ask Jake.

Do you do food, I asked, and one of the girls, aged about sixteen, produced a menu on a scrap of paper. She was doing English at school and was quite good, if hesitant, though she wasn't helped by her Dad who continued to shout in Italian at her and at me, shaking his cow, and encouraging me to sit down and tuck in.

My wife was still in the square, doing her Greta Garbo act, I want to be alone and have nothing to do with this tomfoolery. Flora was looking miserable, wishing we would stop arguing. I went over and told them I had discovered this trific little place, look just over there.

I persuaded them to at least look, but my wife quickly stopped. I am not eating *there*. You two can go. I'll wait. Oh God, I said, this is supposed to be a family holiday, all friends together, a cultural experience which little Flora will never forget, now *you're* being silly. So come on. Sometimes I can be so dominant.

We were there for almost three hours, the only customers they had, and we had the most enjoyable meal of the whole holiday. My wife's salami was incredible, while me and Flora had excellent spaghetti bolognaise. The bread was great, and you know how rotten Italian bread usually is. The father made us join him in sharing his own chianti, when our bottle had finished, then he sent his daughters off to get us fresh apricots and peaches. He forced brandy upon me and his wife went to their own home to make me real coffee.

For an hour I discussed Graham Souness's chances next season and what a pity that they hadn't got Rush or best of all, Dalgleish. I asked about Rossi and he made a face and put his thumbs down. You forget that one country's national hero is not necessarily a local hero, not if he happens to play for a team you don't support. I told him about the time I went with Tottenham Hotspur when they played AC Milan in Milan. It turned out to be his team.

When the bill came, for this incredible meal, it came to 8,400 lire. I have it in front of me. Even I could work out that it was ridiculously cheap. We had guzzled and drunk for almost three hours, yet the bill was just over £3. Prices in Italy are about the same as here, so it should have been about £15 to £20. I queried it, but the father waved and shouted some football slogan, then he sent a daughter to get some huge peaches for us, twenty in all, and presented them to us in a plastic bag. I made the whole family line up and I took their photograph. Must send them one, if it ever comes out.

Later that day, I met the Director of the British Institute in Florence, and I told him what had happened. He said that Colle was one of his favourite places in Tuscany, so we had had a lucky mistake, but the price of the meal, he just couldn't understand it. The father must just have charged me for the bottle of wine, and for some reason let me off everything else.

Why? My wife thinks it was because of a misunderstanding between my pigeon English and his Italian and that he thought I actually *played* for Spurs. Don't you remember, he asked for your autograph after he had given you the bill? Perhaps.

I like to think it was because we are part of that wonderful worldwide brotherhood of Fathers. That's the explanation I prefer. ❧

FRED AGNOSTIC

BEWARE OF THE DOG

The Rabbi was a hoot and so was the Priest. The Jehovah's Witnesses weren't a bundle of laughs but...

the Buddhists had some very good gags and the Methodist had me rolling in the aisles...

but when you come right down to it...they all tasted the same!

Rev B.C.

WHAT WILL YOU GET WHEN YOU DIVIDE ONE BY THREE?

I GIVE UP!

THE FATHER, SON AND HOLY GHOST!

BEATS ME!

BLONDIE & RUNCIE

MADAM, YOU'VE BEEN IN THAT BOOTH FOR AN HOUR!

Telephone

I CAN'T GET THROUGH TO ANYBODY!

Telephone

WHY DON'T YOU JOIN US ANGLICANS?

WE HAVE A DIRECT LINE!

BROTHER BRISTOW

REMEMBER ME, ATKINS? THE REPENTANT SINNER, BRISTOW!

THE LORD SHALL PRESERVE THY GOING OUT, AND THY COMING IN, FROM THIS TIME FORTH, AND EVEN FOR EVERMORE....

SOB SOB

IN MY FATHER'S HOUSE ARE MANY MANSIONS ...TWICE AS MANY AS THE CHESTER-PERRY BUILDING!

UNCTION UNCTION

FATHER FEIFFER

IF YE HAD NOT PLOWED WITH MY HEIFER, YE HAD NOT FOUND MY RIDDLE... AND WHY LEAD YE, YE HIGH HILLS?...

DEAD FLIES CAUSE THE OINTMENT OF THE APOTHECARY TO SEND FORTH A STINKING ODOUR...

AND ALL THE RIVERS RUN INTO THE SEA; YET THE SEA IS NOT FULL... BE INSTANT IN SEASON, OUT OF SEASON...

THE DEVIL MAY HAVE ALL THE BEST TUNES BUT WE HAVE ALL THE BEST QUOTES!

RELIGIOUS NUTS

I AM A VERY FRIENDLY MOONIE··· I ALWAYS TRY TO HAVE A KIND WORD FOR EVERYONE

HI, CHARLIE BROWN..WHERE ARE YOU GOING?

TO ETERNAL DAMNATION!

OH...

HAVE A **NICE** ETERNAL DAMNATION THEN!

ANDY CAPLAN

I SUPPOSE YOU'RE GOING TO SAY 'THE WAGES OF SIN IS DEATH', RABBI?

ON THE CONTRARY, ANDY, I DON'T THINK YOU WILL HAVE TO WAIT THAT LONG FOR YOUR PAY PACKET!

BISHOP of ID

YOU KEEP ASKING FOR MORE MONEY

WE HAVE TO··· THE CHURCH HAS EXPENSES YOU KNOW!

I SUPPOSE THE COST OF LIVING DOES KEEP RISING

NOT TO MENTION THE COST OF EVERLASTING LIFE!

TINTIN in South America

What's a Contraceptive, Your Holiness?

My child, why concern yourself with such trivialities?

One can travel the world and lead a full happy life without ever needing one!

Take me, for example!

?

GARFIELD the Church Cat

GREAT SERMON THIS MORNING, VICAR··· NEVER HEARD SO MANY BELLY LAUGHS!

MORE FUN THAN THE OLD DAYS··· BUT THERE **ARE** DISADVANTAGES···

WHEN THE ROLL IS CALLED UP YONDER, I WANT TO BE ABLE TO HEAR MY NAME!

Dear Nurse Garsmold:

As a kitchen extractor hood consultant, I meet all sorts, plus a different stratum altogether at my bonsai tree circle (Tuesdays). Furthermore, collecting peculiar headlines, e.g. MAN HAD TURTLE UNDER CARDIGAN, has taught me, over the past twenty years, that life does not hold many surprises for the person who keeps his wits about him.

However, I have been followed to our holiday chalet at Jaywick Sands by a darkie with a medallion and a strange walk who we parked next to in a lay-by on the A 603 to allow our youngest, Tina, to bring up a whelk. You will gather from this that I am a family man, and nothing like this darkie has ever happened to me before, except a man with a labrador when I was a scout, and I called the conductor and that was the end of it.

The thing is, though, that he has an interest in midget trees, unlike my wife Yvonne, who cannot stand anything Jap. I know this, because he followed me when I went down The Three Jolly Gulls on our first night and started a conversation, and I did not want to appear prejudiced, after all he might want a kitchen extractor hood one day, you never know in my line. But after I got launched into my favourite topic, the Nikimoto Pine, only four inches tall but delivers a full crop of titchy little cones every October, he suddenly put his hand over mine and said I had lovely eyes, they sort of lit up when I got enthusiastic.

I do not know which way to turn. Obviously, I would rather he was a woman, I would leave Yvonne like a shot, but you cannot wait all your life for a girl with an interest in little oriental flora to come along, I am 42 next birthday. What should I do?

<u>Arthur Tenby</u>

Dear Nurse Garsmold,

They have this game in Horremolinos-del-Mar, where a holidaymaker is buried by his wife and the wine-waiter from their hotel, and then the wife and the wine-waiter go off and leave him, and the winning holidaymaker is the one who stays in his hole longest, and he gets a fabulous bottle of Widdlo de Caballo sparkling wine.

I have won this contest five years running. The photo shows me winning this year's one, where I stayed in the hole nine days, with no ill effects except the sun dried up the two ballpoints in my top pocket. The wine waiter's friend come out regular and fed me paella, so a good time was had by all! What I want to know is, is this a record?

<u>R. F. Wiggins</u>

Dear Nurse Garsmold,

I enclose a picture of me, taken in Bognor in 1923.
As you will see, the lady on my right bears a striking
resemblance to the lady on my left, except for being a
head taller. The one on my left is my wife, who I married
on the Tuesday of that week, since you did not hang about
when you were a member of the Lost Generation etc., you
must have read about it, there's been books, films, all
sorts of stuff.

It was not till I got home to Waynefleet that I realised
I had married the wrong one. My wife wore high heels at the
Registry Office, and I never twigged she was short until
we got home. I thought I had married the tall one, Wanda
I think her name was. My question is: could I change
wives at this late date? I think I saw Wanda getting on a
bus at New Cross last Friday, she was still tall, if 81, and
I wouldn't mind making a fresh start. I know there have
been changes in the divorce laws recently, and I thought
you would be in a position to advise me.

Edmund Karb

Nurse Garsmold:

Being a typist with some light clerical
ies but definitely no tea-making etcetera,
t is what juniors are for, I told them, I
d myself on holiday here in fabulous
nigreen, and I have a problem, well query,
ally.

I am not forward, due to a strict Morden
pbringing, Sunday School, father clipping ear,
and so forth, but I am on the pill, also all
kitted up, and being 32 reckon we only pass this
way but once and who am I saving it for, as it
were.

Anyway, I have met a nice man on this beach
we have, well, I say beach, it is more of a sort
of large board really, with that plastic grass
they have at greengrocers, when they have plums
on it and so forth; he is called Pedro and he puts
the parasol out of a morning, in its concrete thing
due to where the wind comes from Gibralter, I think
he said, it is not easy to tell with (a) the wind,
(b) him speaking Spanish, mainly, and (c) a growth
on his lip, a bit like a cobnut, only with hairs
on it.

Anyway, he says I can have the good deckchair
he normally saves for special guests, if I go to
his hut for a siesta. It is not much of a hut, it
has a tin chimney and a dog tied to the doorknob,
but Pedro says he has got beer in it and a Li-Lo.
What I want to know is, is this "the real thing",
or should I wait for Mr Right, as I still have
nine days left and have not peeled yet?

Selena Perrins

Dear Nurse Garsmold:

Here I am, just arrived on a Greek island,
not sure which, I think it ends in -os, it has
Red Barrel and Big Macs and a Berni Inn, so you
can probably identify it off a map.

The thing is, I paid £267 in Macclesfield
for a singles holiday to meet the man of my
dreams as per brochure, but when I got here to
see who they had teamed me up with, he was not
finished. On the brochure where they had this
picture of the men of your dreams, they was all
bronzed and muscular with little bums and dark
curly hair. Mine is called Cyril and he is still
white all over except for his little thin face
which is bright red and skinned, he looks like a
boiled prawn, and he is virtually bald with no
muscles at all, all his bulk is in this sort of
oval backside he's got, which he keeps in a pair
of baggy black woollen trunks with the label
showing. He has also got a Arthur Scargill hat
with CHARTERED SURVEYORS DO IT ON THE LEVEL round
the peak.

Have I got a claim against Funsingles (Macclesfield) Ltd? I have complained to the courier on
Thingos, and he has promised that Cyril will be
finished very soon, he will go brown and get his
muscles up etc. as per brochure, but personally I
have my doubts, I have seen stick insects with
better biceps. If I kick up enough stink, would
they move me to a more developed specimen? Please
advise soonest, I am sick of sleeping in the bath.

Miriam Spofe

Alan BRIEN

Johnson and Johnson

"Old Dread-Death and Dread-Devil Johnson, that teacher of moping and melancholy. . . If the writings of this time-serving, mean, dastardly old pensioner had got a firm hold of the people at large, the people would have been bereft of their very souls. These writings, aided by the charm of their pompous sound, were fast making their way, till light, reason, and the French Revolution came to drive them into oblivion: or, at least, to confine them to the shelves of repentant, old rakes, and those old stock-jobbers with young wives standing in need of something to keep down the unruly ebullitions which are apt to take place while their 'dearies' have gone hobbing to 'Change."

In the bi-centenary year of Johnson's death, when his home-town of Lichfield is in a continuous spate of commemoration and a wonderful exhibition of Johnsoniana collected from all over the world has just opened at London's 105 Piccadilly, this summing up of his influence, from William Cobbett's *Journal* for November 1822, appears particularly unpersuasive. Much more probable now seems Boswell's cocky crow of 1793 – "I have Johnsonised the land, and I trust they will not only TALK, but THINK, Johnson."

Still, amid this grand chorus of magnified praise, as the anarchic Right shoulder Johnson high, proclaiming him as the rationalist who never ceased to be a believer, the radical who remained a Tory, Karl Marx in negative, the incarnation and apotheosis of dialectical idealism – Richard Ingrams editing a new collection of Mrs Thrale's anecdotes, Malcolm Muggeridge about to be revealed as the 1984 President of the Johnson Society – I find it salutary to browse among some of the dissenting opinions.

Cobbett's onslaught I had forgotten until I came across it in Peter Levi's introduction to the Penguin bi-centenary edition of Boswell and Johnson's separate accounts of their tour of the Western Isles. Checking it against the text in another source, I was irritated to find that Levi, despite his obeisance to its author ("This side of idolatry, Cobbett is my hero") manages to misquote the extract, importantly if not crucially. And though he doubts whether Cobbett's Johnson ever really existed, and praises Johnson's observations of Scotland as far more informative and useful than Cobbett's of 60 years later, he admits – "It remains true that he who dines with Johnson should use a long spoon."

"As the anarchic Right shoulder Johnson high, it is salutary to browse among some of the dissenting opinions."

In fact, if you turn to Cobbett's account, *Tour in Scotland*, coincidentally just re-issued in paperback by the Aberdeen University Press, you find some of his jokes and jests have a very contemporary ring (Lord Grimond, in his foreword, compares them to *Private Eye*) such as:

Dr Dread-Devil said that there were *no trees* in Scotland. I wonder how they managed to take him round without letting him see trees. I suppose that lick-spittle Boswell, or Mrs Piozzi, tied a bandage over his eyes, when he went over the country I have been over. I shall sweep away all this bundle of lies.

Johnson's reputation has suffered the usual see-saw rise and fall over the two centuries, though it has never fitted the popular image of him, passed along from generation to generation by those who have never read him. Even today, according to Dr Graham Nicholls, curator of the birthplace, most visitors have heard of him as "the artist starving in the garret, getting his recognition only after he is dead". They are surprised – "perhaps a little disappointed" – to discover that at least from his mid-fifties, for the last third of his life, he was quite well-off, with a pension that relieved him

of the need to work for his living, and one of the leading celebrities of his day.

The great service that Boswell did was to equip him with a second fame, as a man, as a figure stepped out from behind his pages, as an almost fictional character, who was, as Macaulay said, "more intimately known to posterity than other men are known to their contemporaries". Whenever his essays, or poems, or drama were no longer used even by scholars, there was always the Great Cham (Smollett's phrase) of the pubs and the clubs to be remembered. Coleridge, for example, was confident that Johnson had been "really more powerful in discoursing *viva voce* in conversation that with his pen in hand. It seems as if the excitement of company called something into his reasonings which in his writings I cannot see. His antitheses are almost always verbal only: and sentence after sentence in the *Rambler* may be pointed out to which you cannot attach any definite meaning whatever."

This is from Coleridge's own *Table Talk*, a record of witty, brilliant, sometimes silly or just odd remarks that are now far more attractive and interesting to us than his run of prose works. Incidentally, the birthplace museum in Lichfield has on display copies of the *Rambler*, and I must say I had always assumed this was a weekly magazine, like *The Spectator*, say, to-day, with leaders, readers' letters, departments for reviews of books and plays. It is rather a shock to find that what Johnson sold, and the public bought, was simply one essay, printed in large type, the first paragraph of which began on the front page under the title and ran on to the last.

The peculiar progress that Macaulay noted of development from a classic in your own lifetime to a companion to posterity has not pleased some commentators in either guise. Shaw went so far as to assert that the second ruined the first, in a typical, unfavourable comparison with himself – "I have not wasted my life trifling with literary fools in taverns as Johnson did when he should have been shaking England with the thunder of his spirit." Leavis thought the cult of the clubman obscured his real virtue ("a serious interest in things of the mind"). And I cannot resist citing Lytton Strachey's tribute, somewhat over-familiar, like everything to do with Bloomsbury, but still striking:

> Johnson's aesthetic judgements are almost invariably subtle, or solid, or bold; they have always some good quality to recommend them – except one: they are never right.

Dr Nicholls says that in 1784 the people of Lichfield showed no exceptional respect for the local boy made good in the big city. His father, local businessman and politician, had been popular in his day – Johnson records with pride he was due to take his ceremonial Ride as Sheriff of the city the day after Samuel was born. But his social status could not have been very high: travelling round the countryside with his stock of books, putting them up for sale in the marketplace, he was only a cut above any other commercial traveller. Anyway, great difficulty was experienced raising even the money needed for "the modest monument in the Cathedral".

For the next 100 years, "Lichfield slept as did its appreciation of Johnson." A few tourists came in the early nineteenth century to talk to Johnson's black manservant, Frank Barber, who had inherited most of his property and settled there, where his descendants, no longer bearing any trace of dark skin, still live. "Boswell's Johnson", like an outsize refugee from a Dickens novel, was the one the Victorians cherished. Nobody could accuse Lichfield, until the 20th century, with a population of only 10,000, of exploiting him. You couldn't even visit the birthplace most of the time as it went through being a grocer's shop, a lodging house, a newspaper office (*The Lichfield Mercury*), a draper's and haberdasher's, "Dr Johnson's Coffee House", and finally a dental surgeon's office and surgery. ("Artificial Teeth Painlessly Fitted by Atmospheric Suction at one-third the usual charges. No extraction necessary: perfect and permanent: life-like appearance.")

In 1900, the owner, a Mr G. H. Johnson, died and directed in his will that the property, for which he had paid £900 in 1887, should be offered to the Corporation of Lichfield for only £250. The offer was accepted and Colonel Councillor Gilbert, who produced the money,

"As long as there's nothing wrong with me, I'll be getting back to Jupiter."

was made an Honorary Freeman in recognition of his generosity. No one seems to have made any public acknowledgement of the enterprise of Mr Johnson.

Dr Nicholls contrasts the difference between Lichfield's reaction to the first centenary of Johnson's death in 1884 – nothing; and that of the bi-centenary of his birth in 1909 – a banquet with a former Prime Minister, Lord Rosebery, as guest of honour. What had happened, he believes, is that during those 25 years there had been a revolution in Johnsonian scholarship – "People were beginning to see that they were both great writers as well as colourful personalities."

Even today, in Lichfield, though you cannot catch a citizen who does not know that Sam Johnson was born here, many still tend to wonder whether it is really worth all the trouble – "Surely he was only a minor figure?" And Dr Nicholls is obliged to pump up a few statistics. Johnson is among the three, or perhaps four, most written-about writers in English literary history. He is the most widely-quoted prose writer in English *in the world*. "I tell them that those who know him only as a personality have all the pleasures and insights of his writing to come."

Nevertheless, a fantasy portrait of Dr Johnson still forms itself out of the ectoplasm of the popular mind and inserts itself between reality and myth.

"Late 20th-century man seems desperate to equate a Johnsonian love of life with a love of sex. There are always those who retail the legend that somewhere in the city is 'the room where Johnson took his women'," says Dr Nicholls. "The story has proved difficult to

deflate even when the total lack of evidence is pointed out."

Lichfield itself has not always had the best of presses over the years. Perhaps the most dismissive summing-up coming from Henry James – "The place is stale without being antique," he writes after a visit in 1872, going on to remark that this may explain "the Doctor's subsequent almost ferocious fondness for London".

It's true that Johnson left a gap of around 20 years when he never made the journey from London back to Lichfield. But once his mother was safely dead, as it would appear, he began to make annual pilgrimages, often with Boswell, and was embarrassingly fulsome in his tributes to the place – "the most sober, decent people in England, the genteelest in proportion to their wealth" – even that old stager – "they speak the purest English."

Dr Nicholls makes a good case for Lichfield being an exceptional nursery of literary talent. When you consider its size, to produce, as well as Johnson, David Garrick, Joseph Addison, Elias Ashmole, Richard Garnett and Erasmus Darwin, is not a bad haul.

Not many of us nowadays read this Darwin, grandfather of Charles, or care that he anticipated some of his grandson's discoveries in the field of evolution. But if nothing else, Erasmus can lay claim to the status of a prophet. We all know Tennyson's forecast of "aerial navies grappling in the central blue". But what about this, penned a century before?

> Soon shall thy arm, Unconquer'd Steam, far
> Drag the slow barge, or drive the rapid car;
> Or on wide waving wings expanded bear
> Thy flying chariot through the fields of air. ℮

Ciao Principe Carlo
Benvenuto Principessa D

One's quick squint at Italy and so on

MONDAY

TRH are in Rome, a terribly old place, where apparently Romans once lived. Hang on, it's Florence. TRH arrive Florence to sign Visitors' Book and greet a number of Florentines. TRH visit a bridge and a cemetery. Separate engagement for Her Royal Highness to receive gift of a porcelain wolf. TRH attend reception at *Ristorante Pasta Gloria* to inspect flood damage to fresco.

TUESDAY

Still Florence, noted for its old part. TRH received by a Prefect, amidst waving. Embark HMY *Britannia* off Leghorn for journey along the sea. TRH change shoes. HMY *Britannia* berths at a coastal place. TRH board Tiger Moth of The Queen's Flight en route to Villa Ambrosia, a bat sanctuary and spa for afflictions of the spleen. TRH visit a charming bastion and later attend a mime of *Pinocchio*.

WEDNESDAY

Grottoes.

THURSDAY

Visit to plastic raincoats factory on the Po. TRH are shown Piedmont, Lombardy and the Alps before luncheon in the old quarter of Omo with monks and a Chamber of Deputies. TRH see a large Tintoretto and the old steps at the Palazzo Gran Turismo. His Royal Highness attends a performance of *Turandot* given by the Sub-Aqua Club of the British Consulate in Polenta. Embark in Royal Barge.

FRIDAY

Disembark from Royal barge to inspect quay. Morning at the Hospice for the Hard of Hearing, Salmonella. Packed luncheon at nearby volcano. Her Royal Highness is barouched to an archaeological area. His Royal Highness swims to Venice.

SATURDAY

Visit to a canal, followed by a short tour of another canal by boat. TRH arrive Doge's Boatyard to learn of importance of boats to Venetians. TRH attend St Mark's Square for coffee and to be presented with a souvenir whistling gondola yo-yo by local noblemen. One more church, then home.

Rimini · Cappucc
Jimini · Pi
Salame
Tombola · Zanu
Oratorio
Marconi
Maserati
Im
Valpolice
Allegro con Fuoco · Pront
Volvo
Polpi-in-Purgatorio · Cornetto
Scusi
Grissini

One or two Italians One has met

Commendatore Umberto Martini Rosso:
A politician and Prime Minister Mondays and Thursdays. Laughs and sings frequently, often without obvious cause.

Giuseppe Craxi:
Another politician, Prefect of Something-or-Other, but taller.

Ettore Praxi:
Rather small politician, but nicely spoken

Licenzio Taxi:
Bullet-proof chauffeur and Wharfinger-in-Waiting to The Quirinale.

Professore Edmundo Rosso:
Man of letters, Accademia di Belle Arti, Scienze, Studi Classici, Economico-Agraria, Etnografia e Tagliatelle. Firm handshake.

Dottore Salvatore Campanile:
Socialist Minister of Hydraulics and useful shot.

Osvoldo Palazzo Ducale:
Custodian of Pinacoteca Comunale di San Pellegrino. Shouts.

Suo Holissimo Karol Wojtyla:
Ex-patriate cleric with, curiously, an Ealing accent. Wishes a very happy summer to us all in 22 languages.

Enzo Campari:
Court Correspondent, *Corriere dello Fascismo*. No relation.

Carabiniero Soave Magnum:
One's Private Detective.

Lena Zabaglione:
Entertainer of sorts. Odd she's never heard of The Goons.

One's handy phrase-book

Some really pretty straightforward words and what they seem to mean to the Italian people when one says them out loud:

a [pronounced ''ah''] means at. Example: a mare – at sea
e [as in e(gg)] means and. Example: A e B – A and B
i [pretend it is ''e''] means the, when there are lots.
Example: i rossetti – the lipsticks
o [as in (h)o(t)] – means or. Example: bagno o doccia – bath or shower

One or two much harder things to say, best left to one's lady-in-waiting or equerry:

Sono molto lieto di fare la sua conoscenza – Hello
Molto bene, grazie – One is feeling jolly well, actually
Vorrei shampo e messa in piega – One wants a shampoo and set
Unpo' di piu qui – Spot more off round here, one thinks

io

Mt. Edna

Vigilante

Colada

"Hear ye! Hear ye! Hear ye! Hamleys will remain open in the evenings till 8.00 during the holiday season!"

"Realistic goals bring realistic gains."

Adjusted

"Good evening, mam. May I work your party for a 50/50 split of the take?"

"I want to wish each and every one of you a Merry Christmas: Merry Christmas, Mr and Mrs Albert Netzel; Merry Christmas, Waldo T. Hollenbeck; Merry Christmas, Dedee Roylander; Merry Christmas, Reverend Dettmar; Merry Christmas, Otis Ragoonath, Jr.; Merry Christmas, Bess and Stevie Obermeyer; Merry Christmas, Officer Mellenger; Merry Christmas, the Copperdahl twins . . . "

" . . . And now, dear friends, Merry Christmas and a Happy New Year to all of you from all the Luddingtons. P.S. Attached is a list of all our achievements, awards, promotions, cups, ribbons, medals, encomiums, prizes and citations for the year."

" . . . And a Polly parrot in a pear tree!"

Simon
HOGGART

ON THE HOUSE

> "I was staying in the hotel next to the Grand, and watched the explosion cause the TV set to perform a brief, stately dance."

A BOMB does not only rip away the front of a building, leaving it exposed like an open dolls' house, but it does the same for people's private lives. What brilliant pyjamas some of our Cabinet members wear; what a contrast to their predictable sub-fusc working clothes! What a joy it must be for them to throw aside their dark blue suits, striped shirts and discreetly patterned ties, then climb into silk more vivid and colourful than Kubla Khan can have worn.

Some people, by contrast, must feel intolerably vulnerable in their nightwear, and they spent quite some time dressing properly after the explosion, with cuff-links and neatly tied shoelaces. I was staying in the Metropole, the hotel next to the Grand, and watched the quake cause the TV set in my room to perform a brief, stately dance, as if in some whimsical Czech cartoon film.

When I got downstairs to the sea front a few minutes later, I found to my surprise that I had put on a tie, knotted carefully in the correct place. I suppose that when you are agitated, it takes less effort to perform the familiar daily rituals, than it does to decide what would be the most practical course of action.

I wondered too why people felt, sporadically, so light-hearted after the explosion. Part of it must have been relief, of course; it hadn't happened to them, just as hearing the crack of a rifle tells you that the bullet has not hit you, since it would arrive before its sound. Principally it was because we didn't know that anyone was dead.

It seemed obvious that they must be, since the hotel had been crowded and a large part of it was now dust and rubble. But for hours nobody brought news of any serious injuries, and long before Norman Tebbit was rescued the first people were coming back from the hospital, some bruised, some with arms in slings, all being slapped on the back and helped to brandies. In a curious way we began to believe in a miracle which had not happened.

The most striking figure there was Greg Knight, the MP for Derby North, who has an enormous mound of curly hair which winds round at peculiar angles, like a collapsed candy floss. He had been downstairs in the Grand at the time of the blast, and his hair was thick with the dust, so he looked like Little White Sambo.

As the BBC began its morning bulletins, I saw another victim, Agriculture Minister Michael Jopling, hunched over a radio in the lobby of the Metropole. I moved near to listen and heard the voice say: "Cereal prices have held steady. . ." Mr Jopling must have been the only person in Brighton that morning tuned to *Farming Today*.

Of course the IRA misread people's reactions to the bombing, though I doubt if it had much to do with the self-congratulatory assurances that this was because we were all British. Partly this is because a bombing is a shared experience. If somebody fired a gun at you, you would probably be very frightened and feel very alone. But a bomb affects dozens or even hundreds of people, all of whom have a sudden common bond.

A few hours before the explosion I had been to the Dome Theatre in Brighton to attend a concert John Wells had arranged to mark his new book *Fifty Glorious Years*, a mock tribute to Mrs Thatcher and especially to her husband Denis. Wells appeared in the military costume of a Ruritanian Prince Consort, and acted as MC for a series of short musical items.

Every time one sees his performance one believes that it cannot be lifelike; the real Denis cannot be such a caricature. Then you hear of a genuine conversational snatch.

While Wells was depicting him on stage, Denis was having a drink half a mile away, and talking about Left-wing infiltration of our broadcasting services.

"When Margaret wants to know what's on the BBC, I don't tell her; instead I say, 'It's on Mafia 1' – you know, as in Marxist Mafia 1 and Marxist Mafia 2."

"Sorry, He doesn't do toasters."

The **Banquo at** the feast was, this year, Cecil Parkinson. He didn't show up at all, though my guess is that he will return next year and will be cheered to the gilt roof of the Blackpool Winter Gardens. At least half the Tory Party seems to want him back. I saw a very old gent in a battered tweed jacket, slumped half asleep over his walking-stick. On his lapel was a badge which read: "Torquay Young Conservatives Say Bring Back Cecil."

The role of Resident Spectre used to be filled by Ted Heath, though people don't seem to notice him so much these days. He has certainly lost none of his gossamer sense of humour. At a reception he marched straight up to Lord (David) Young, who has just been appointed to the Cabinet with the job of stirring up British Industry.

Heath announced: "I used to think you were intelligent. But you've taken a job where you'll have no influence in Cabinet, without a political base in Whitehall and with no chance of achieving anything at all. As I say, I thought you were intelligent – that is, when I found out who you were."

Was it a joke? Heath's friends say it was, but then it must be extremely hard to tell the difference.

Another social straw in the wind: your modern youthful Tory is equipped with one of those digital watches which make a beeping noise on the half-hour and double beep on the hour. I suppose this is because it makes them appear terribly busy, too important even to find time to look at their watches. The effect at meetings was that every thirty minutes there would be a mass squeaking of these tiny noises, like a protest rally by shrews.

But Tories love buying things. Among the objets achetés available at Brighton were marzipan busts of Mrs Thatcher, four inches tall, guaranteed to last six months and costing only £2.50. Who could actually put such a thing in his mouth? You'd feel like a pervert. One of the nastiest things I saw was a large red sticker marked "Cancelled due to lack of public support." This was for gumming over posters which advertise events organised by your political opponents.

To return to Mr Jopling. He is, after long consideration by the panel of judges (me), the winner of this year's all-conference Foot-in-Mouth award, though in the case of the farming Minister, I suppose it should be called the Foot and Mouth award. There were many remarks better left unsaid during the conference, though Mr Jopling is the only Minister I heard who made two in the same speech. He announced first of all that "the thresholds are beginning to bite". Then later he ringingly declared, "There are no sacred cows in British agriculture." Of course there aren't; they're all being killed because of EEC regulations. ☙

A LETTER FROM SIR KEITH JOSEPH

Dear Santa,

Gosh, it seems a jolly long time since I last wrote, it must be a year, I wonder why I did, was it about my shoe, did I leave my shoe in your GET OFF! no, it wasn't the shoe, it was about GET OFF, THIS IS A NEW SUIT! it was about my Christmas list, I remember now, I wanted little porters for my train set, little porters with little flags and those titchy trolleys with little bags on an ALL RIGHT, YOU BASTARD, YOU HAVE BEEN GIVEN FAIR WARNING, NOW IT IS STRANGLING TIME! and little brown suitcases, I apologise for the interruption, Santa, but if there is an auk on your shoulder, do not ask me how they get in, we have had the chimneys blocked, we have written to Claire Rayner, it does not seem to stop them, there is no other course when they are standing on your shoulder, when they are looking to see what you are writing even when you have got your hand curled round the paper, even when you have told them cheats never prosper, there is no other course but to throttle them with your bare hands.

Its eyes have come out, Santa.

Thank you for the porters, I did not see you bring them, they put me to bed very early here, but there they all were on Christmas morning, at the bottom of my IF THAT IS ANOTHER BLOODY AUK, I SAY IF THAT IS ANOTHER BLOODY AUK RINGING THE DOWNSTAIRS BELL, ASK YOURSELF THIS, DO I WANT TO BE STRANGLED? of my stocking, with my tangerine. Also, I got a new rubber spoon with holly and a little gold bell on it from my loyal staff, and a canvas dressing-gown, and a big 2lb box of Black Valium, they are my favourite!

Where was I, Santa? Oh yes, the Bombay Test Match, well don't ask me, how would I bloody know, I do not have ears in the back of my head, you have got elves up there, ask an elf, they know about cricket, I have things to do, I have paperclips to fix on my lip, I have flies to count, I have to keep getting up and touching each wall and running back to my bunk before I have counted up to thirty-seven.

Sorry, Santa, I did not mean to be rude, it is just that things get on top of one sometimes, e.g. auks, PLEASE DON'T FORGET ME THIS YEAR, SANTA, I want a little tunnel and a set of points and some little sheep for the *Duchess of Carlisle* 4-8-4 to run over and a box for keeping a frontal lobe in that plays *Rule Britannia!* when you open its lid, I mean the box plays it, not the lobe, I do not think the lobe is the bit with *Rule Britannia!* in it, I think the lobe is the bit with shoe information in, I can never remember anything about my shoes, and I want thirty-nine million pounds in a big bag.

I have promised it to the scientists. I like the scientists, they have white coats and they sit on my bed and they say they could do anything if only they had thirty-nine million pounds, so I have been trying to get it for them, but YOU THINK I DON'T SEE YOU IN MY INKWELL YOU BASTARD BUT I DO, TAKE THAT! but people are trying to stop me, they think I do not know what I am doing, but I know what I am doing, if the scientists get their thirty-nine million pounds I will have jelly every day, I will have a television in my room, or a live tortoise.

Please bring me the money for the scientists, Santa, I will unblock the chimney, I will not peek, I will not giggle or tell anyone. You know where to find me.

Your friend,

Keith

THEATRE: HEWISON

THE LONELY ROAD   RUPERT FRAZER *as Dr Franz Reumann*   ANTHONY HOPKINS *as Julian Fichtner*
SAMANTHA EGGAR *as Irene Herms*   ALAN DOBIE *as Stephan von Sala*

AREN'T WE ALL   NICOLA PAGETT *as Hon. Mrs W. Tatham*   REX HARRISON *as Lord Grenham*   CLAUDETTE COLBERT
as Lady Frinton

SHE STOOPS TO CONQUER   DORA BRYAN *as Mrs Hardcastle*   TONY HAYGARTH *as Tony Lumpkin*
TOM BAKER *as Mr Hardcastle*

THE DEVILS   ESTELLE KOHLER *as Sister Jeanne*   PETER McENERY *as Grandier*
TIMOTHY KIGHTLEY *as Mannoury*   GEOFFREY BEEVERS *as Adam*

LAURIE TAYLOR

Teacher's Pets

I ALWAYS favour the *Times Educational Supplement* for Friday evening reading. It is so refreshingly unsensational after the usual week of shocking news that it prepares the spirits for a weekend's relaxation. But it begins to look as though my pleasure may be short-lived. Last Friday I had barely finished a longish fashion article by "Mortarboard" on the Do's and Don't's of Patching Corduroy, and was turning with languid anticipation to a piece by "Tawse" on "How to choose a playground whistle", when I was distracted by a large headline which announced the shock findings of a sizeable investigation by the paper into teacher-pupil affairs. Affairs of the heart, that is.

It appears that romance "flourishes" in today's classrooms. Many schools "circulate unofficial danger lists of flirtatious or precocious girls who must be kept at arm's length at all costs". For good measure, there was also a lesbian on hand to confide that she suffered agonies when seduced by a fourth form girl, and that in her experience, "there is much more sexual activity between pupils and teachers than meets the eye."

Now, of course, like every other student of English character, I've read any number of stories over the years about how our leading artists, statesmen and bishops were sexually seduced at their public schools by practically anyone who enjoyed a degree of authority over them and had a moment to spare. But if the *TES* survey was accurate, seduction was now not only spreading to day schools in the comprehensive sector but was also being practised by pupils upon their teachers.

It was all quite disturbing enough to send me off first thing on Monday morning to Brantbury Heights Comprehensive in North London to see my old friend Stan Duxbury, now headmaster there, and of course even better known nationally as the Presenter of Channel 4's late night controversial education programme, *Red Easel*.

Had he seen the report? What was his reaction? What were his first thoughts? How did he feel? (I've found from past research that this intense interrogative style helps put media people at their ease.)

"Oh yes. They've got it absolutely right."

"All that seduction?"

"No doubt about it. Seduction in schools has got completely out of hand."

"Really?"

"Believe me. You can't turn round in today's classrooms without someone trying to seduce you – or in some cases two or three of them – what the psychologists call 'pack seduction'."

"But who's behind it all? Who's to blame? Who really is responsible? Where does the buck stop? Who are the guilty people?"

"You certainly can't blame the teachers... erm... *I'm so sorry.* Could we possibly do that bit again. I'd rather like to get the emphasis a bit stronger."

"Of course. I'll just say 'Well, who's to blame?' again. Well, who's to blame?"

"YOU CERTAINLY CAN'T BLAME THE TEACHERS. All over the country they've gone out of their way to make themselves look as unattractive as possible. They've rummaged through Oxfam shops and jumble sales until they've found sports coats which are three times too big for them, trousers with a crotch which hangs down well below the knees, and battered suede shoes which you wouldn't ask a dog to retrieve. And then for good measure many have gone in for a prematurely bald look, developed a shambling walk, and even – and here you're talking about a detumescent few – taken to smoking large pipes filled with St Bruno."

"But it's made no difference?"

"None whatsoever. We knew we were losing our own local battle in 1980, when the Deputy Headmaster – you may remember old Drewitt, about 35 but tried to look 60 – when he was well and truly seduced in A-Level British Constitution. He's more or less a passenger now. Just sits there in his office scrawling 'I Love Julie Sangster' over the uncompleted timetable, whimpering to himself, and occasionally singing snatches of some Anglo-French melody which seems to contain the phrase 'Zank Heaven'."

"Are there any other tell-tale signs?"

"Pardon?"

"Are there any other tell-tale signs?"

"Oh yes, indeed. As I speak to you, there's at least a dozen senior teachers off with love-sickness; we've got three diagnosed broken hearts; and we had to cancel Sports Day last Thursday because half the PE staff were sitting in the middle of the games field making daisy chains. The national picture is even worse. In Shropshire there are reports of some teachers being seduced twice or even three times a term."

"I suppose it tells sometimes."

"It tells sometimes. You can watch a down-at-heel, middle-aged geography teacher leaving the staff room in the morning, a stack of marked essays under his arm, a fresh piece of chalk in his hand, wife and two young nippers back at home, and you know, you just know, that one mid-morning break, he's going to walk back along that corridor with an ominous jauntiness."

"Seduced?"

"Exactly."

The light in Duxbury's study had faded as we talked, and now, through the long Triplex windows I could see the children beginning to leave for home, smiling and chattering as they'd done for centuries. But how many, I wondered, were now animated not by age-old childhood interests – hopscotch, conkers, hide and seek – but by thoughts of how many teachers they'd seduced that day. In some ways I supposed it was a comment on our times. But more to the point, what exactly did Duxbury make of it all? Not just his own experience of course, but his reading of the national situation as exposed by the *TES*? What did he really think? What was his absolutely honest opinion? What did he feel deep down inside?

"I suppose it's a comment on our times." Somehow that says it all. ℮

"And now Dr Haskins here is going to tell us how to avoid industrial injury."

HOLTE

SCHWADRON M.D.

"Your 50 minutes are up, Mr Orshatzky."

"He beat me mercilessly in the golf tournament. Let's hope this operation will put him out of commission entirely."

"Your X-rays came back. But they didn't tell us anything we didn't already know."

"There isn't any such symptom, Mrs Duderwader."

"Dear Constituents, I would like to share with you a breakthrough I experienced today in my psychiatrist's office . . ."

"Thank goodness you're here. There's no snow on my TV picture."

Go Tel It on the Telly

TERRY WOGAN: *(Standing modestly in front of blow-up self and half-smirking with feline insinuation as the applause rises to fake-satirical hysteria)* Ah! Such fake-satirical hysteria! *(Audience heckling)* I never knew Les Dawson was here tonight!! *(Audience applause)* *(Sudden new tack:)* "Tel . . ." *(meaningless pause)* I quote from Sharon of Tadcaster who wishes to tell Tel owt about – oh no – not more on the reluctant sausage, Sharon? I thought we'd swept that one under carpet for good and all. Under the Axminster with it, or the Arding and Obbs wall-to-wall come to that. Sharon wants to know if I know that sausages curve in the other direction if you fry them in Australia. We've got Guy the Gorilla on tonight. *(Audience is roused to something like the required incredulity)* We have though! We have and all. Indeedy. Without a word of lie. *(Meaningless pause)* Avaunt Sharon, I do not wish to know that. *(Pause)* Which way do they curve if you fry them in England, though, Sharon? Answer me that! It's somewhere before nine o'clock, on a Saturday evening, and I am required to inform you that the southbound carriageways, all three of them, of the M1, that is, are completely blocked. Know why? They've all come to see me legs. They have! It's a well-known fact that when you transfer from radio to TV you get wonderful ratings because they all want to see your legs. Sorry, I seem to have lost me brogue *(Calling out)* Has anyone seen me brogue? Guy the Gorilla will be here in a minute. Not to mention Raquel and Rick Mayall. I'm lucky with the ladies. Sorry Rick! Seriously though, here's some traffic news: the southbound carriageways of the M1 are blocked between junctions – and you make them up for yourselves because Ian Botham's here on the great new Benson and Hedges label – don't libel that label! – and with his great new single, "Great Set o' Lads!" Seriously though, you don't mind me calling you Guy the Gorilla, do you, Ian?

IAN BOTHAM: No, I don't mind, Tel. I picked up the nickname from the England team and they're a great set o' lads basically, Tel.

TERRY WOGAN: And here's a woman who says that yodelling while frying sausages in Australia makes them split in no time. Thank you, Charmaine of Kettering, for that charming piece of information, and it's nearly nine o'clock and nearly time for some racing tips. Roulle brothers, Charmaine, do not rule, am I right now? It'll be the great new one from Grievous Bodily Harm in a minute. Did you come from a sporting family, Guy?

IAN BOTHAM: My Dad was a bit sporting I spose.

TERRY WOGAN: *(Rolls his eyes and raises his eyebrows)*

IAN BOTHAM: But basically I picked up a few sports and concentrated on cricket after a while which I'm glad about because I'm with a great set o' lads.

TERRY WOGAN: It's just coming up to somewhere in the region of nine of the old clock and nearly time for *The Diddlin' Song* with Maimed for Life, that great performer singing away as if there was no tomorrow which there probably isn't. Why did you, you prehensile ball-thrower you, whap Ian Chappell on the nonce with a half-full can of Foster's – or if not exactly that, you indulged in *(execrable accent but he knows it and wants us to love him for it)* a *contretemps* with him?

IAN BOTHAM: Don't get me wrong – the Ozzies are a great set o' lads if you don't rub them up the wrong way . . .

TERRY WOGAN: Which way ought you to rob them up?

IAN BOTHAM: About middling leg I'd say. *(They both waggle their eyebrows at each other and titter. Audience applause, leading to standing ovation as Wogan shakes his hand frankly and sincerely and smiling with slightly reserved impishness)*

TERRY WOGAN: Ian Botham, put it there. *(New tack:)* "So!" I kid you not. That's what it says here, and this is no relation of EJ. "So!" I repeat, from Eileen of Cleethorpes, "jackin' it, Tel?" Jackin' it in! Certainly not! I'm here, aren't I? Mind you, that Botham put his foot in his mouth often enough. Still, you don't want to discourage the young. I'm only goin' on me holidays for a couple of weeks. Then I'll be back. Oh yes. Eileen of Cleethorpes has got a lot of stuff here about splitting bangers on the southbound fast lane of the M1 while yodelling through a self-propelling bollard – you know the type that walks down the motorway on its own bedad – but we won't bother with that because it'll be time for Assault and Battery's great new single and anyway someone called Rick Mayall is here.

RICK MAYALL: *(Sidling out from behind a flat with asinine expression and manner)* *(Audience applause, verging on hysterics)* Yaow, loik, y'knaow, naow! *(Reassuringly)* It's alroihht, it's a'roight, cos I got this *(audience giggles)* – smash yer fice roight? – *(he stares and waggles his eyebrows aggressively)* *(audience hysterics)* *(New tack:)* Seen my spots? *(Audience hernias)* Loo' a' tha'! Ere! Go'! erch! Disgustin, y'knaow?

JAMES WATSON

I've troid everythin'. Paint-stripper . . . embalmin' fluid . . . Araldite . . . Acriflex . . . still won't come off. Terrible. *(Audience standing ovation. Close-up of Wogan holding out his hands and clapping in a gesture of reverence, his face a rictus of sincerity)*

TERRY WOGAN: Beverley of Gosport has been on at me about me meaningless pauses. "Could it be that he is transmogrifying into a cat?" she asks. I never knew that word could mean so much. Transmogrifying indeed. And what sort of mog would I resemble, Mrs? Hm? Do I talk like a cat? I might look like one, but why would I pause to change into one? I pause because I'm thick! Oi'm Oirish, y'see . . . no offence. Here are some racing tips. Heroin Addict 9-1 at Chepstow. Irretrievable Brain Damage 3-1 at Kemptown, and finally Parkinson's Disease 2-1 at Doncaster, and don't ask me the times as it would spoil me lovable vague Oirishry begob. Am I right Rick? but first:

MANIC VOICE: It's all in the great new *Radio Times* with so much more to enjoy and so much less to read, bingo, fun pictures, page three style artistes, and much, much more! And of course there's, but don't tell Tel, Raquel Welch's new book coming up, and how!

TERRY WOGAN: Did you come from a very *(funny-serious voice)* dramatic family, Rick?

RICK MAYALL: Mnyeah. *(Squirms and writhes) (Audience titters)* Smash yer face, roight? *(Stares at camera. Audience applause)*

TERRY WOGAN: We've got Raquel in a minute with her great new sound, "This Book I've Got Out Now" – how about that for a nice easy to understand title, ladies? Beverley of Gosport? That'll be after the fabulous sound coming from Taking and Driving Away and it's from the LP, *Multiple Pile-Up*. JY will be in in a minute, fresh from an interview with His Holiness, I shouldn't wonder, or The Queen Herself bedad. A bit after nine fifteen or so. Rick, put it there. *(Wogan takes Mayall's hand and shakes it)* It's been a privilege. Apparently there's this Latin cove, name of Terence, according to Enoch of Antrim or is it Down? Fella with a moustache. Do you like moustaches, Raquel? He penned ditties, says Enoch, just like me.

RAQUEL WELCH: In *And God Created The Dinosaur* I made my debut as a dumb blonde, the archetypal earth-mother and I'm picked up by this pterodactyl –

TERRY WOGAN: It's a libel surely. Terry Spondee. Terry Dactyl, never!

RAQUEL: Whatever. I married my childhood sweetheart on account of a pregnancy experience and now I have this daughter who is charming. And just beautiful. And Talented. And just amazing. She's making her second movie right here in England right now. I said to her, honey, you are this one terrific lady an you should get out there and get it and hit them with it, okay? This book I've got out now –

TERRY WOGAN: – has made you some enormous assets?

RAQUEL: – whatever. I have this book out now which just kind of says it all about getting your feet wet and how you can't clone anybody – you know? – and how we are all in these terribly messed up times, and even if you have a nice body and figure you still wake up one day and say, hey, you know.

TERRY WOGAN: This is true.

RAQUEL: Listen, Tom –

TERRY WOGAN: She's had a busy day folks.

RAQUEL: I have this book out now which says we have to get our heads together –

TERRY WOGAN: *(Rolls his eyes and waggles eyebrows)*

RAQUEL: Whatever. The art of being a woman isn't just sitting on your fortune but saying, look, I'm not going to take any bum raps, and I'm going to explore the whole goddam nature of selfhood and the interior person and I'm going to get shot of any male vibrations that get laid on us.

TERRY WOGAN: The onus is onus. Kind of t'ing. That's what Sophia said.

RAQUEL: If anybody talks to me about Sophia I shall smash his goddam face.

TERRY WOGAN: There's a lot of it about. You've both got enormous assets though, Raquel, and thank you very much indeed for talking to likes of me. *(Shakes her hand and covers his eyes)* Help, JY! Where is he? Should be in be now. He usually comes in about now and we exchange stories about reluctant sausages and pregnant pauses . . . ♋

If you are one of the hundreds of parachuting enthusiasts who bought *Easy Sky Diving*, please correct page 8, line 7; the words "state zip code" should read "pull rip cord".

M. Miller (*The Advertiser*, Bournemouth)

Research conducted on 400 impotent men revealed that the one thing they had in common was that they all smoked. A spokesman for the anti-smoking group ASH said today: "If this study puts someone off smoking, that's all to the good, but we're not really sure whether it stands up".

E. Makin (*Liverpool Echo*)

The soldiers stepped in to help when fire threatened the Redesdale Arms, Otterburn. They formed a human chain to salvage the drinks from the cellar and then freed cattle from a smoke-filled barn.

E. Holmes (*The Journal*, Newcastle)

A piece of coal which fell from a living-room fire is believed to have started a £3,500 blaze at a Norland farmhouse yesterday. Firemen think the piece of scorching coal set fire to an armchair at Upper Spark House Farm, in Spark House Lane.

D. Wheeler (*Halifax Evening Courier*)

A jobless teenager who threw an egg at the Prime Minister, and missed, was fined £50 yesterday.

W. Duff (*Glasgow Herald*)

INTERNATIONAL SECTION

NAPPIES FOR LAMU ASSES
The Lamu administration might ask donkey owners to have nappies tied on donkeys to collect their dung so as to keep the town clean, it was revealed during a leaders' meeting at the Lamu Social Hall.

D. Patience (*The Standard*, Nairobi)

A 32-year-old man, picked out at an identification parade by a robbery victim, allegedly protested to police that he could not have been seen at the scene of the crime because the lights were off and the room was dark, the High Court heard yesterday.
A seven-man jury yesterday found Fan Ping-sun guilty.

J. Robinson (*South China Morning Post*)

"No, no, say it after me."

BILL TIDY
GENTLEMEN PREFER BLONDS

"They think they've trapped a Russian Nancy class submarine off Kronstadt!"

"If Copenhagen can have a mermaid . . ."

"I remember when an open sandwich was an open sandwich."

"Doesn't it ever get dark here?"

"God, at last – someone who thinks Volvos are brutishly butch!"

ROBERT BUCKMAN
DOC BRIEF

Hello. This week I thought we'd take a look at some parts of the alimentary system (or "guts") and at some of the common trouble spots that keep on coming up.

FLATULENCE

Flatulence is the word we use to describe the passing of collected air from the large bowel into the atmosphere, though not often the word we use when other people do it. Chemically speaking, the gas itself is largely derived from the enzymatic activity of bacteria living in the colon and can give scientists valuable information about their metabolism. Particularly in a lift or phone-box. Colonic gas is rich in methane and low-molecular weight sulphides and many other ingredients commonly found in acid rain. These residues represent unconsumed energy and it has been calculated that under controlled conditions the average burst of flatulence could illuminate a large ball-room, or under other circumstances empty it. The formation of large quantities of gas is encouraged in the context of a high-fibre diet, and is discouraged in the context of a public library. Harley Street dieticians have worked out a way of coping with habitual and excessive flatulence. They stare at the person standing next to them and blame it on them.

STOMACH

The stomach is really a biochemical cauldron for mixing food with digestive juices and is named from the Spanish word "estomach" which means "disgusting". The stomach contains very strong hydrochloric acid though no one knows how it manages to smuggle it in without dissolving the teeth. As you probably know, gastric acid is strong enough to burn a hole in a carpet. This was discovered by doctors

treating a man called Alexis St Martin whose stomach just happened to be lined with Axminster Floral. We now know that stomach ulcers are caused by worry and a recent survey of 320 Italians being investigated for ulcers revealed that the commonest cause of their worry was the thought that they might have an ulcer. Behavioural therapists are now working on a positive-thinking approach to the condition in which people are trained to believe so strongly that they haven't got ulcers that the problem disappears. Mind you, they tried that with unemployment and look what hap-

pened. Ulcers used to be status symbols. So did Anna Ford.

OESOPHAGUS

The oesophagus is a flexible muscular tube leading from the outside world via the mouth to the stomach or vice versa as in being sick. It conducts food downwards by a movement called "peristalsis" in which one bit pulsates and then stops and then the next bit pulsates and then stops and so on. This is basically the same mechanism that snakes use when they walk, only slower and noisier. The oesophagus is divided into three parts or "thirds" but fortunately they're all joined together. The bottom third (or "bosphorus") is joined to the stomach and is thus able to participate in many of the exciting functions of gastric mucosa, eg, catching ulcers. Birds have very inter-

esting oesophaguses which have a bal-looned bit in the middle which is full of stones which grind up their food for them which is just as well since they haven't got any teeth. In Man the middle third of the oesophagus (or "sarcophagus") can also become filled with stones or it certainly feels like that after you've been drinking vodka.

DUODENUM

The duodenum is a thin piece of gut named after the "duodena", an attic or corridor in an emperor's villa usually filled with boxes of winter clothes or odd boots. In the gut, the duodenum leads from the gastric antrum (or "pantry") to the jejunum (or "garage") via the ampulla (or "front-porch") to the mesentery (or "rose-garden"). The main function of the duodenum is to allow the digested food coming from the stomach to mingle with pancreatic juice and bile in an intimate and informal environment with exciting decor, cheap wine and ethnic atmosphere. The duodenum, like the stomach, can develop ulcers but is less inclined to do so, probably because it's generally less tense, takes more holidays and spends most weekends at the cottage. The contents of the duodenum are not acid but alkaline, and far from burning a hole in a carpet can actually be used to remove ink stains from rayon and machine-washable

fabrics. Using modern fibre-optics it is now possible to look right down into the duodenum but to be quite frank it's hardly worth it since it's not exactly Sophia Loren's boudoir down there. All things considered, the duodenum is the least attractive part of the gut with the possible exception of the haggis.

PHARYNX

The pharynx is situated right at the back of the mouth and is the bit that we doctors can't quite see when patients say "ah". The walls of the pharynx contain over nine hundred separate muscles whose job is to make sure your food doesn't go down into your lungs, though they're not so good at stopping it going up your nose if someone makes you laugh while you're eating trifle. The back of the pharynx is rather badly designed and food and stuff, eg, meat, can often get lodged there, sometimes causing respiratory embarrassment in a situation

known in America as "sudden death". This can be dealt with quickly using something called the "Heimlich manoeuvre", I think, or maybe that's the practice they've just outlawed in Utah. Anyway, if the Heimlich manoeuvre is the thing for getting meat out of throats or horse's hooves, and if you're interested in finding out more, please send me a stamped addressed envelope and I'll give you full details and some pieces of meat rescued from sudden death in this way.

THE DOCTOR ANSWERS YOUR QUESTIONS

Q: Am I overweight?

A: No, of course you're not. Stop moaning and come to bed.

FOOD – FASHION, FAD AND FASCISM
A Selection From A Gastroenterologist's Travel Diary

HI-TECH MEETS HOMEOPATHY ▲
Racing fan and playboy Patrick Double-Barrell (*seen centre after a marvellous party*) was the first client at the Esher Homeopathy Clinic and Racetrack. Doctors Angela Pasteur (*left*) and Thomas Lister (*right*) are seen demonstrating the new homeopathic carbon-monoxide colonic irrigation unit.

SCARSDALE REVISITED
The new North Scarsdale Clinic certainly produces impressive results in crash-course weight-reduction and rejuvenation. Among recent satisfied famous customers are the Everly Brothers (*left and right*). ▼

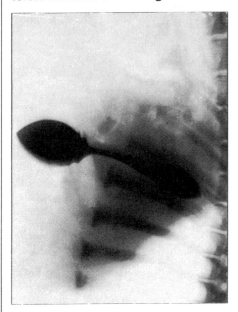

ARISTOCRACY AND THE PYLORIC ▲ SPHINCTER
William, Seventh Earl of Deptleigh-Beauhunkers (*pronounced "Deeply Bonkers"*), is the only person in the world proven to be born with a solid, silver spoon not in his mouth but in his stomach, his lawyers claim. The Savoy Hotel prosecuting counsel will reply tomorrow.

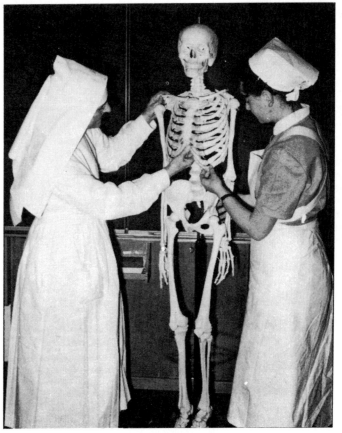

◄ THE TRADITIONAL NURSING SKILLS
In the Vienna nursing school at the resort of Bad Minton, modern nurses are taught the old skills in the fundamentalist way. Here Sister Ober-lautenant Schwinkler (*left*) and Nurse-Gruppenfuhrer Shriek (*right*) welcome pupil-nurse Anna Endelbaum (*centre*) back from the punishment block.

The SHADOW OVER GREYFRIARS

By E.S.TURNER

"Oh, crikey! Oh, haddocks!"

"Stop pushing, you uttah wottahs!"

The chums of the Remove jostled round the school notice-board, seeking confirmation of the dreadful rumour.

It was the worst rumour yet. It was worse even than the one that said Greyfriars was to be moved to an old warehouse in Cork, to protect it from the politicians.

The notice-board announced a meeting of the Society for the Prevention of Christian Knowledge, to be addressed by the Bishop of Durham. There was to be a rally by the Greyfriars League of Young Patels. There was the latest appeal for help from the parents of Coker, who had been kidnapped by the Moonies. And that was all.

"What is this fearful fuss about?" demanded Arthur Augustus D'Arcy, who was on a friendly visit from St Jim's.

"Haven't you heard?" said Harry Wharton. "They say Greyfriars is to be shut down."

"Oh, Kinnocks!"

Gussie's monocle fell. Marjorie Hazeldene, one of the girls recruited into the Sixth, in an attempt to avert financial ruin, laid a comforting hand on his arm. Gussie, after all, was very good at "lacwosse".

"They cannot do it, deah boy. What is the reason for this dweadful folly?"

"The first reason," said Harry Wharton, "is that there are not enough decent chaps like us to keep the place going. And the second is that, even if there were, our people can no longer afford the fees."

"My people can," said Hurree Jamset Ram Singh.

"And mine," confirmed Vernon-Smith.

"And I am expecting a five-shilling postal order," began William George Bunter.

"What I want to know," said Bob Cherry, thoughtfully, "is why there aren't enough decent chaps like us."

"I blame the parents," said Harry Wharton, blushing crimson. "They're failing in their – er, duties. To – er, breed."

Marjorie, Clara and Shirley hardly knew where to look.

"*How* do they breed us?" demanded the Fat Owl. "You beastly cads will never tell a fellow."

"Bump him! Bump the Fat Owl."

Bump! Bump! Bump!

They were still bumping Bunter when the call came for Morning Prayers.

"Oh, my sainted aunt!" exclaimed Nugent. "What are we today – Christians, Buddhists or Hindus?"

"Rastafarians," said Winston Winston, the new boy known as the Terror of the Antilles.

"Why don't you slope off to Ethiopia?" grumbled Johnny Bull. "And take Bunter with you. They'd slim him down a bit. Or better still, put him in a pot."

Mr Quelch, the form master of the Remove, overheard this racialist taunt.

"After Assembly, Bull," he said, "you will wait on me in my study."

At Assembly the Head, Dr Locke, wore a waxy frown.

He ordered the girls of the Sixth to remove their "Coal Not Dole" badges. Once again he warned both girls and boys against the use of do-it-yourself tattooing kits. He said he hoped it was not glue he smelled.

Then he gave them the news for which they were waiting. Three hundred years of greatness were to be extinguished, like a candle in the wind.

"For my part," he said, "I am glad the end has come. These times of rapid change have been deeply unsettling. We have seen schools as old as Greyfriars closed down in mid-term for lack of funds. We have just seen five boys from another school sent down for burglary and every day there is the spectacle of sons of gentlemen being expelled for trafficking in cocaine. Worse than that, we have seen even headmasters disgraced for allowing themselves to be photographed in – ah, undress, while engaged in –"

Dr Locke broke off. The Famous Five looked at each other bewildered.

"But here at Greyfriars we have held our heads high. My *Daily Telegraph* assures me that the introduction of girls in the Sixth will have done much to eradicate 'ancient vices' in public schools. Everyone knows that no such vices have ever existed at Greyfriars."

"Yaroooooh!" yelled Bunter. "Stop it, you cads!"

Bunter had been the victim of the ancient vice of pin-sticking. Dr Locke had no desire to hear his side of the story. Bunter had made an unseemly interruption and that was enough. "Come here, wretched boy," he commanded.

Bunter waddled forward and the tightest trousers in Greyfriars received six of the best.

"And this one," said Dr Locke, administering a seventh swish, "is for the Court of Human Rights, which in its wisdom seeks to end corporal punishment."

"Yow-ow-ow-ow-wow!"

Bunter's howls did much to disperse the gloom which had descended on Greyfriars.

Now he was blubbing that at his next school he would get his people to see that he was excused punishment.

"Ha! ha! ha!" yelled the Famous Five. The Fat Owl was really priceless!

Shirley Williams, who had stuck the pin in Bunter, felt no guilt. Everybody hated her because of her name and she hated everybody. It was true that Bunter had once rescued her from drowning, but he was really trying to save her purse.

It was the eleventh hour. The chums were packing their trunks. The latest rumour was that Greyfriars was being taken over by a man called Rowland who had failed to seize Harrods.

Vernon-Smith, the Bounder of Greyfriars, and Marjorie Hazeldene had already left, under a cloud. Marjorie's people were taking her to Switzerland for a short holiday.

"I–I–I–I say, you fellows," wailed Bunter, "I'm most frightfully sick."

"Well, you didn't have to empty the tuck-shop single-handed," said Johnny Bull.

Suddenly came a frenzy of cheering from the Quad. It was unbelievable. Greyfriars had been saved!

The hero of the hour was Hurree Jamset Ram Singh. They chaired him and sang, *For he's a jolly good fellow.*

"The jollygoodfellowness is terrific," agreed the dusky nabob.

"How did it happen?" everyone wanted to know.

"You have heard of the most excellent and ludicrous Bhagwan, with 68 Rolls-Royces. My revered father in Bhanipur saved him from drowning and the admirable and impossible Bhagwan has given my sainted father half his esteemed and imperishable motor cars. When they are sold the esteemed wealthfulness will support Greyfriars. It was my inestimable idea. There is only one condition."

"What's that, Inky?"

"The excellent and preposterous Bhagwan will be the next Head of Greyfriars."

"So much for Virgo."

KENNETH ROBINSON

Expert Licence

A BOOK coming out soon will "celebrate the fiftieth anniversary of the British Council". But why wait for a mere book when the fifty years of annual reports and catalogues make such good reading? Or, at least, good skipping. Anyway, I've had a nice disenchanting browse.

To begin at the end. In this, its fiftieth year, the Council has sent works by Bill Woodrow to Portugal. They include a fish in an electric fire, which the sculptor calls "Fish In Electric Fire"; a dismantled vacuum cleaner, which he calls "Dismantled Vacuum Cleaner", and eight bicycle frames.

I shall not bother you with the title of that last one. But you may like to know that Mr Woodrow has told the Portuguese, "I do like bicycles very much you know, and this is a whole new angle on bicycles, cutting them up and straightening them out."

I have no idea how well the Portuguese take to this sort of thing. But I imagine the Japanese are inscrutable enough to survive any sort of invasion by British Council artists. I do hope so, because in Tokyo they have been confronted by the photographs of Michael Parr, who takes all his pictures in the rain. By using an underwater camera, he shows very clearly the habit of Londoners, wearing newspapers or boxes on their heads.

These pictures were shown in Japan, beside the sculpture of David Nash, who says he never needs to take any finished work abroad with him. Wherever he is going, he just stands under a tree when he gets there. If a couple of branches fall off and land on top of each other, he puts them on show in a gallery, with the title *Cuddling Twigs*. Or he picks up a piece of bent wood, stands it against a wall and calls it *Lazy Log*.

This, I suppose, is what the Council means by its aim "to promote an enduring and understanding appreciation of Britain".

If so, it seems a much cheaper method, at a time when the Council's administrators are grumbling about their poverty, than some of their more unnecessarily ambitious projects. My browsing in the files tells me that the Council has even exported a Chinese version of *Romeo and Juliet* ("Lomeo, Lomeo, wherefore art thou Lomeo?"). And there was also a production of *King Lear* on a Japanese ski slope, where the audience had to walk downhill for each new scene. Doubtless with merry cries of "Break a leg, Sir John!"

Perhaps the British Council needs to be reminded of its more humane and economical events. Recently, for instance, "practical help" was given to a girl in Cyprus when she was researching the eating habits of the green turtles. And there was that much-publicised film showing the explicit activities of two consenting budgerigars, in Nottingham.

A lot has been said in the press about this two-and-a-half-minute production. Especially about the cutting of ten seconds from the Islamic version of the film. So much so that a Council spokesman has commented on media misunderstandings. "We do not want to give offence," he says, "to religious laws and customs of other countries. In fact, this just shows how, on a much larger scale, we find it difficult to cope with other countries on our small budget."

How small, do you suppose, *is* a small budget? The government grant is now "only" (says the council) £78m. This, together with other forms of earning, totalling £130m, makes the Council feel very shaky about its future. In fact, the current annual report complains fearfully about "a perennial threat to the budget".

I really do feel sorry about this bleak poverty, because anxiety seems to bring out the very worst in the British Council. The latest annual report is filled with dull-looking graphs and depressing pictures of deeply-committed elderly gentlemen. Worse still, there are some tiny bleats of encouragement from Mrs Thatcher. And these have frightened the Council into a frenzy of highly-emotive words we never associate with our cultural mentors. Words like Ethiopia, Lebanon, Poland and Iraq. In fact, a lot of fun has gone out of the amusing, irrelevant and always-ambiguous British Council.

It seems such a short time ago that it was all such fun. *Hamlet* was performed in Icelandic; football was encouraged in Gozo; Venezuela had an exhibition of British Railways, and *Midsummer Night's Dream* appeared next to the Sphinx.

Then, as you may remember, the sculptor, Richard Long, made a line in a field by walking across it. When he later took a picture calling it *Line in Field by Walking*, it was rushed to an art gallery in India. With it went Michael Craig-Martin's work entitled *Oak Tree*. This was, in fact, a glass of water. Some people, said Mr Craig-Martin, might think the glass of wa-

"Pssst, Harry, what's it like?"

ter was *merely* a glass of water, and that the oak tree existed only in his mind, but not only was the glass of water *really* a glass of water, it was *also* an oak tree.

It is not fair, I know, to write principally about the Council's adventures in art. In 50 years it has done so many other light-hearted things. Like sending Anthony Blunt to Italy to lecture on William Blake (who else?). And it was in Venice that the Council quite seriously displayed "an electric cardiagram of a couple celebrating intercourse". And who will forget that C. Price Thomas once trekked off to Lisbon to natter about "Diseases of the Chest"?

All this is going back quite a bit. To the time, more than thirty years ago, when the Council kept saying self-consciously that it was "reaching out to the artisan class – to the merchant seamen who arrived so frequently in Britain". These men were often shown a Council film called *Surgery in Chest Diseases*.

I'm sorry to keep harping on the subject, but it was something that kept the Council excited for some years. Not only because the film wowed audiences, apparently, in Swansea, Palestine and Madrid, but also because it was thought to be the greatest in a series which began with *The Life Cycle Of The Newt*; *The Development Of The Rabbit*; and *The Onion* (all 1942).

If you have ever wondered how *exactly* our cultural image is helped by all this, and by, say, the production of an all-Bengali *Macbeth* in Bangladesh, the Council once gave a useful definition in an annual report. "The most valuable basis for cultural exchange," it said, "is not in the arts, but in a common human need." Such as chest surgery.

Like all organisations that have survived for 50 years, the British Council has inevitably lost its early naïvete and charm. I was delighted to find that it was begun as a means of "stemming the tide of Fascism", and that great annoyance was caused when "its work was interrupted by the flood of Nazism." It is nice, too, to find that, in 1941, the annual report rebuked the British "for not always realising the high intellectual quality of foreigners."

But best of all, in 1943, the Council could solemnly believe that "the British have a body of thought that the world must need to prise from us like pearls from an oyster."

Just occasionally a pearl is revealed today. Before he gave up the job of Director-General, Sir John Llewellyn made what must surely be the most truthful and the most tactless definition of the British Council's aims.

"We are not do-gooders," he said. "We believe that the more other countries know about us, the more they will want to trade with us."

Maybe we should be careful what we do with our bicycles, our vacuum-cleaners and our electric fires. And maybe we should know a hawk from a handsaw. Or, at least, a glass of water from an oak tree.

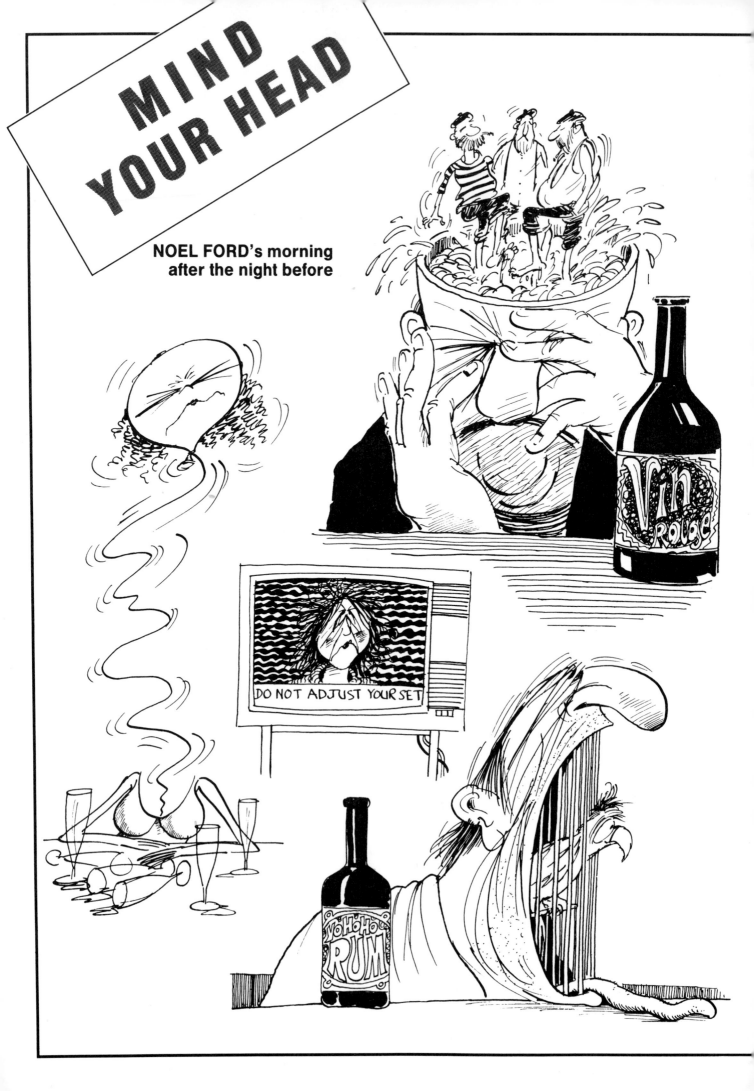

MIND YOUR HEAD

NOEL FORD's morning after the night before

CHRISTOPHER MATTHEW

Celebrity Squares

An unusually bulky postbag in recent weeks prompts me to a further selection of notes and jottings From Among My Press Releases.

The Jeffrey Archer Award for self-promotion goes this month to Knight, Frank and Rutley whose large, stiff-backed envelopes have produced more delights and surprises than even Savills, Humberts or Jackson-Stops and Staff have managed to muster – although to judge from recent form, even they might soon be forced to relinquish the title in favour of Hamptons. But I'm rushing ahead of myself.

My thanks first to Mrs Felicity Hoare of Robert Fraser International who wrote to me concerning the Marbella Hill Club, the luxurious private estate in southern Spain currently being developed by Prince Ferdinand Bismarck and Count Rudi von Schönburg, and whose letter began with the words "I am enclosing a black and shite photograph and press release . . . "

And talking of household names, as every agent knows, there is no better way of getting a property mentioned in the press, or indeed in some cases of pulling the punters in, if only out of mild curiosity, than by lacing the mundane diet of particulars with the occasional zest of celebrity.

The fact, for instance, that Gordon Honeycombe, the well-known TV personality and brass rubber, has asked Benham and Reeves to unload his upper maisonette in Primrose Hill for £74,950 is bound to have the fans hurrying NW3-wards, especially in view of the fact that the price includes some of Gordon's most cherished rubbings.

Keen two-wheel men will doubtless be equally interested to learn that Hampton & Sons have been instructed by eight-times world motorcycle champion Phil Read MBE to sell Pine Glen, his secluded woodland retreat near Newdigate in Surrey for a sum not unadjacent to £185,000. The Read spread comprises two reception rooms, a sun lounge, a snooker room with bar, four bedrooms, two bathrooms, and seven acres of grounds including a swimming pool, tennis court, stables, schooling paddock and two ornamental ponds, and makes me wonder if I've really made as full use of my Honda C50 as I might have done.

Chestertons give good journalistic value for money as always by not only informing the property writing fraternity that they are selling the 86-year lease on David Essex's luxury penthouse maisonette with its ninth-floor conservatory in Manchester Street, W1, but also by providing a fascinating in-depth round-up of David's plans for getting his musical of *Mutiny on the Bounty* onto the stage before the end of the year.

Whatever misgivings David may be harbouring, Chestertons would seem to be in little doubt about the outcome.

"He . . . will be starring in it himself as Fletcher Christian," they declare, "whilst Captain Blythe (sic) is being played by Frank Finlay."

One supposes they are equally confident of getting the asking price of £235,000.

Only marginally less intriguing was the headline in a Humberts' press release: "FOREIGN CORRESPONDENT AND PILOT WIFE TO SELL COTSWOLD HOME."

They were, as I'm sure you will already have guessed, referring to "author and former foreign correspondent Iain Adamson and his air pilot wife Zita" who had instructed Humberts' Chippenham office to find a purchaser for Littleton House, their 16th-century home, for around £97,000.

Knight, Frank and Rutley felt no need to resort to coyness in the case of Burgh Island off the coast of South Devon, for which they are asking over £650,000 – not only thanks to the fame of its luxury hotel with its natural sea pool, with the dais in the middle where bands used to play for the guests, and its Ganges Room which incorporates the stern of the wooden flagship *HMS Ganges*, but also because in its time it has welcomed such guests as Noel Coward, the Beatles, Agatha Christie,who wrote *Evil Under the Sun* there, and the Dave Clark Five – though not, as far as I know, Frank Sinatra, whose erstwhile third-floor pad in Glendore House, Clarges Street, W1 has now been turned into a tasteful three-bedroom show flat and is currently on Hamp-

tons' books at £495,000.

Properties with rather more tangential associations with the famous include a six-bedroom, two-bathroom, Victorian house in Mount Gould Road, Plymouth, called Herriot House, built by Michael Foot's dad and now on offer through Fox and Sons at £49,950 ("there is still scope for further updating"); No 20 The Vale in Chelsea, a large studio house owned for thirty years by Sir Alexander Korda's set designer brother Vincent and now for sale through Knight, Frank and Rutley for a sum in excess of £950,000; Netherby Hall, the Graham family seat in Cumbria which Young Lochinvar entered so boldly "among bridesmen and kinsmen and brothers and all" and whose 7 recep, 19 beds, 3 baths, 2 self-contained flats, 6 garages and 32 acres of gardens and grounds you too can now enter with equal boldness through the good offices of Humberts' Landplan and a cheque for £50,000 for the 125-year full repairing and insuring lease; and Gilmilnscroft House in Ayrshire whose former owner, the justice who officiated at Robbie Burns's marriage ceremony, must be shaking his celestial locks in disbelief at the thought that Knight, Frank and Rutley are asking over two hundred grand for the 4 recep/5 bed/3 bath 17th-century house, 114 acres of land, stables, flat and lodge.

Incidentally, just for the record, if things have gone according to plan for Jackson-Stops and Staff, you've just missed the farm in Worcestershire where *The Archers* were in-

"Nip in the air! Is it potassium or nitric acid?"

vented and Walter Gabriel wrapped his choppers rustically around some unlikely sounding vowels and committed his very first "Me ol' pal, me ol' booty" to the sound waves.

Ooh dearr, ooh dearr, ooh dearr.

Never mind, you can still assure yourself of a minuscule footnote in agricultural history for a mere half a million by becoming, like Winston Churchill and Eileen Joyce before you, an owner of the 26-acre Chartwell Farm at Westerham in Kent.

Nothing quite as historic as the first recording of *The Archers* ever took place at Kilcott Mill at Wotton-under-Edge in Gloucestershire, unless you count the day in 1979 when the journalist from Milling Feed and Fertilizer came down to interview the present owner about how he devoted his retirement to restoring the mill to its former glory as a fully operational watermill. That, or the day in 1086 when the local area census officer knocked on the door and informed the miller he'd made it into Domesday Book, and that, if he was any judge of the way property prices were going, he wouldn't be surprised if by the year 1984 people weren't looking at figures in excess of £175,000 for the 2 receps, 3 beds, 2 baths and the waggon shed which, as he'd mentioned before, would convert very nicely indeed into a three-car garage. Provided Knight, Frank and Rutley were still going, that was.

As it happens, there's quite a little glut of

"Waiter, there's a man eating my soup!"

mills on the market – wind and water. Humberts have one – Cole Manor near Bruton in Somerset which could apparently "with some effort" be restored to working order. Savills have a couple: The Old Mill at West Farndon in Northants and Windmill Hill Farm at Hellidon near Daventry, also in Northants, from which it's possible to see four counties. And in addition to Kilcott, Knight, Frank and Rutley can show keen milling aficionados either the superbly restored 18th-century Pentlow Mill, which straddles the Stour at Cavendish near

Sudbury in Suffolk, for £300,000 or alternatively for £39,000 the wonderfully remote little World's End cottage at Staunton-on-Wye in Herefordshire, whose windmill still provides some of the electricity for the house.

For downright quaintness, though, nothing that's come my way lately can compare with Pineapple Spa Cottage at Lower Swell, Stow-on-the-Wold in Gloucestershire, for which Jackson-Stops and Staff are inviting offers based on a paltry £36,000.

Built in the early 19th century as one of a row of cottages near a carbonated chalybeate spring, the eastern facade with its fir-cone and honeysuckle finials and its carved pineapple over the front door seems curiously out of place until one remembers that it was designed by Samuel Pepys Cockerell at about the same time as his brother Sir Charles was busy at work along the road, building that forerunner of the Brighton Pavilion, Sezincote.

That's it. Time's up again. I had been hoping at this fascinating stage in the article to contrast this tiny touch of India in the Cotswolds with the neo-Gothic grandeur of Sheffield Park in Sussex, now being offered by Humberts in seven lots; but this, like the second largest house in Kent and one of the biggest tourist attractions on the island of Mull, will have to be consigned to my pending tray for a week or two. ॐ

COUNTRY LIFE

SUNDIAL FOR THE BLIND
The centrepiece of the scented garden for the blind could be a sundial.
N. Stevenson (*Peeblesshire News*)

Downstairs also is the luxury family bathroom with three-piece coloured shite and knotty pine panelled ceiling and trim.
K. Davidson (*Mercury & Eastwood Advertiser*)

A police sergeant had a ringing noise in his head after being hit with a telephone thrown by a twenty-year-old woman, magistrates heard on Thursday.
C. Woodward (*Ellesmere Port & Neston Pioneer*)

Woman quizzed after death.
C. Schutte (headline in *Western Morning News*)

On Friday, when he retired, Mr Reber was presented with a portable colour television and a pair of binoculars.
A. Jowett (*Essex County Standard*)

SWOOPING flocks of cockatoos have begun attacking the suburb of Woronora in Sydney, Australia and devouring houses. Flying in flocks of 30 or 40, the sulphur-crested cockatoos eat wooden roof-tiles, railings, wall cladding – in fact, much of a house. Insurance companies will not pay for the damage. They say cockatoo attacks are an Act of God.
E. Wilson (*Southern Evening Echo*)

Geldings: Ball's in Jockey Club Court.
J. Fitzpatrick (*The Sporting Life Weekender*)

The committee wants a mandatory national licence fee determined by the Secretary of State, with exemptions granted for jeepers of guide dogs for the blind and hearing dogs for the dead.
S. Apted (*Solihull News*)

Cllr Thomas said it was the ratepayers' job to criticise. Councillors tried to do their best, but ratepayers could always vote them out if they were not satisfied. He received a round of applause.
I. Slee (*Hampshire Ratepayers Journal*)

Only a handful of heros and heroines have been entered for this year's Gloucestershire Medal for Courage Award. The county council blame the low figure on natural Gloucestershire modesty.
C. Kay (*Western Daily Press*)

INTERNATIONAL SECTION

Two youths die after consuming heroine.
R. March (headline in *SUR in English*, Costa del Sol)

The fire in the public bar toilet was put out by fast acting patrons and did not spread.
W. Simms (*Auckland Star*, New Zealand)

President Banana has at his disposal the 1950s Rolls-Royce Phantom which carried Queen Elizabeth when she was here in her teens in 1947.
P. Sternberg (*Sunday Mail*, Zimbabwe)

GEORGE MELLY

Death on the Road

"**W**EBSTER," wrote T. S. Eliot with prim relish, "was much possessed by death," and so, increasingly, am I. At 58 I am aware not only that my life is probably at least twenty years nearer the tomb than the womb, but that the Great Reaper may swing his scythe at any moment; 7.25 this evening for instance. Until I was about forty, death was almost an abstraction. It happened either to old people, or because of an accident, or an unlucky wager on the terminal roulette wheel. Then the number of my near contemporaries who had died would scarcely have made up a respectable tea party. Now it's a large cocktail party with gate-crashers showing up by the minute. Soon I'd need to hire the Albert Hall.

The intimations of my personal mortality are, as yet, modest: two teeth capped, reading glasses and a hearing aid, thickening toe nails, a painful stiffening of the thighs after a mile walk. I'm beginning to feel like an old car, perfectly serviceable but a bit hard to start on cold mornings, heavy on petrol, and a gear box with a knack to it. Years of life in it still, of course, and yet it's sobering to remember those old cars. There's one in the lane in Wales. Someone drove it down from London without much trouble but then, two days later, it just wouldn't start again.

Yet, rather to my surprise, none of this makes me feel gloomy. On the contrary, my reaction to a memento mori – the abandoned car in the lane, a dead hornet in an empty bath, the meaningless generalities of the crematorium clergyman over someone he didn't know – is a kind of euphoria. Death, I believe, is the apt punchline to the meandering joke of life. How we struggle to make good, to know everything about computers or the life cycle of the black ant, to play the bassoon better than anyone else in the world, to make millions through the skilful movement of currency from country to country. Then, in a single moment, it's all over. Sir James Goldsmith is no richer than the cheerful old black tramp, hung with pots and pans, clattering about the environs of Paddington. Arthur Scargill and Ian MacGregor will find themselves in total agreement. There will be no difference between the future work of Philip Larkin and E. J. Thribb (17).

I feel I might be less sanguine if I were not a convinced atheist. Belief in personal immortality would, I imagine, be far more worrying. As it is, the idea of non-being is no more disturbing than the thought of a dreamless if endless night.

None of this applies, of course, to the deaths of others. Here, if I was fond of them, I feel a probably selfish deprivation. Even the death of an enemy, while not exactly upsetting, unravels the edges of one's own life. After a funeral I find myself resenting the inability of the person I've just seen burnt or buried to experience not the rare great joys or griefs, but the humdrum and banal activities I can observe through the windows of the post-funeral car: slipping into a public house, waiting for the green man to light up at a traffic light, collecting a suit with a note pinned to it apologising that a stain couldn't be removed "without serious risk to the material". On the other hand, I find the unscheduled but ever closer approach of one's own death intensifies the pleasure of everything – banishes boredom. To hook a trout, to catch a certain effect of light on distant hills, to swallow the first oyster on September 1st, to make love – all these have become again as marvellous as the earliest remembered experiences of childhood. Then things were marvellous because they were without precedent. Now it's because it might always be the last time.

These thoughts, fairly commonplace I dare say, are much less concentrated than this piece might suggest. Only now and then am I aware, like Eliot's Webster, of "the skull beneath the skin". Nevertheless, as Auden advocated in relation to poets (why not plumbers and taxidermists? Come to that, why not jazz singers?), it's useful to think of one's death at least once a day. Recently, several deaths have ensured that I do: a much-loved interior decorator of genius, dead of a stroke at 63, his witty tongue and repertoire of facial mannerisms still widely if unconsciously reproduced by a large circle of friends; Alberta Hunter, the great blues *chanteuse* and the composer of the first blues Bessie Smith ever recorded, dead in her eighties after a remarkable late renaissance in New York.

Also, I feel obliged to add, I had a nasty shock myself recently. I got up one Sunday morning and was crippled by an excruciating pain across my back, the only relief to pace the floor like a caged tiger, grey with anguish and bathed in cold sweat. It was only a kidney stone and, after twenty-four hours in a cheerful public ward floating on pethodone, it "passed". Before my injection though, the agony was what my mother called "exquisite". I can do without that at my end. I can do without angry senility too; biting the nurses and totally incontinent. Federico Garcia Lorca asked for a quiet death "in clean sheets". In the event he was shot, probably by the Falangists, during the Spanish Civil War. Better that though than the fate of his childhood friend Dali, senile, burnt and anorexic at 83. If there is to be pain I hope they'll turn me into an instant junkie.

Sometimes, after a fast number with a lot of prancing about, I imitate someone in the audience turning to a friend.

"If he goes on like that at his age," I say, "he'll drop dead!"

They usually laugh, but I mean it. ℰ

"Anita, this is Mr Craxton. He says he's blind."

100 Years (or so) of the Motor-Car

CONCERNING the four most important inventions that affect 20th century life, everybody except Russia accepts that Bell invented the telephone, that the Wright brothers pioneered powered flight and that Baird invented television. But who invented the motor car? This burning issue may not interest everyone, let alone those who wish it had never been devised. However, whether you like it or not, you are going to be deluged in the next two years by articles, books, television specials and exhibitions of all sorts to celebrate 100 years of motoring.

A few years ago, it was a fairly simple situation. Motoring historians and museum academics accepted that in 1886 Gottlieb Daimler and Karl Benz, working independently in the German province of Swabia, both patented their internal combustion engine vehicles, founded companies to market them and had vehicles running on the road. This epoch-making year was not questioned by anybody, especially when Daimler Benz, who merged in 1926, celebrated their 50th and 75th anniversaries in 1936 and 1961. I well remember taking part in the 1961 event, driving a Mercedes sports car slowly but constantly boiling around the streets of Munich under the fierce supervision of Herr Neubauer, the famous Mercedes racing manager. The slow speed was due to the oldest running Daimler leading the procession, an 1887 model from our own London Science Museum, proving that we keep historic cars better than anyone, no matter where they come from.

However, the 100th anniversary has caused a flutter of jealousy and activity. If Daimler Benz had not existed today, I suspect that everyone would be happy to pay fulsome tributes to the two inventors. But Daimler Benz is still one of the world's great motor manufacturers and, what is more, they are German. After all, everyone in the US has always believed that Henry Ford invented the car but actually he did not come onto the scene until 1896. And similarly in the past Austria made claims concerning a vehicle made by one Siegfried Markus, who was supposed to have had a car running in Vienna in 1875. This claim has been disproved. Austria was further embarrassed in 1936 as Markus was a Jew and so his name was removed from the caption in the Technical Museum in Vienna to placate Hitler.

However, the dream of a self-propelled vehicle goes back to the 15th century, when it was devised as a weapon of war and even Leonardo da Vinci came up with some ideas. The first actual self-propelled machine was produced by a French army engineer called Cugnot, built in the 1770s and driven by an enormous steam boiler with a speed of $2\frac{1}{2}$ mph and running for 15 minutes at a time. History certainly recalls that it ran in the grounds of the Artillery Arsenal in Paris, "where it proved so violent and difficult to steer that it knocked down a solid wall."

After that somewhat unsatisfactory start, steam vehicles of many types were constructed and Hancock and Gurney in England ran a successful steam coach service until public prejudice, the vested interests of the newly emerging railways and the odd unfortunate boiler explosion hounded them off the road.

The first man who offered road vehicles for public sale in England was an iron founder from Buckinghamshire called Thomas Rickett. In 1859 he built three light steam cars, one of which was demonstrated to Queen Victoria and another was sold to the Earl of Caithness, who made a memorable 145 mile drive from Inverness to his seat in Thurso,

▶

which is now the Castle of Mey, the Scottish home of the Queen Mother.

But 1986 is the year we will be celebrating the motor car as we know it today. Although Daimler and Benz, who never met although they lived only 50 miles apart, one near Stuttgart and the other in Mannheim, can certainly claim credit for demonstrating what could be done, it was the French who really developed the car in the late 19th century. So it is the French who are most annoyed at being upstaged by the Germans and, to everybody's amazement, suddenly produced out of a hat a hitherto unknown inventor called Edouard Delamare-Deboutteville, a textile manufacturer from Rouen, who they claimed had a car running in 1884. It turned out that it was an entirely primitive attempt to put an engine into a horse break and, after one or two unsatisfactory trial runs, it was abandoned and the patents lapsed. However, the inventor was also an expert in the culture of mussels and oysters and later became famous as the compiler of the Sanskrit dictionary. So the French claim cannot be taken seriously, although the enterprising Automobile Club de France this year constructed a replica which, with the benefit of modern know-how, enabled the vehicle to be driven down the Champs-Elysées.

Italy, too, has tried to get into the act with the claim that in 1884 one Enrico Bernardi, a professor of Agricultural Machinery at Padua, designed an engine which eventually powered a sewing machine and later was fitted to a tricycle for his 5-year-old son.

So what are we all in for now? I shall be attending a big international veteran and vintage car rally in Germany in 1986, hopefully driving the 1899 Coventry Daimler which, driven by my father, was the first car to be allowed to enter the House of Commons yard and the first British-made car to race on the Continent. Generally, we are in for an 18-month ordeal, as the celebrations start with a mammoth curtain-raiser at Silverstone next May, called "Motor 100", and will relentlessly go on until the end of 1986. Museums will have special exhibitions and we will, of course, play our part by having a very special one at Beaulieu, where visitors (at no extra cost!) will experience the history of the first 100 years of motoring in four minutes, travelling in motorised carriages past a series of tableaux and experiences, magically presented by the most up-to-date audio-visual techniques. I only hope that the public will not get too bored with the centenary celebrations and feel heavily relieved that they will not be around in the year 2086, when who knows whether by then the only cars might be in museums, going out once a year for the Brighton Run. Gluttons for punishment can always celebrate the first long-distance journey in 1888, when Bertha Benz, wife of Karl Benz, got up secretly at 5 o'clock in the morning and, taking their two sons, drove without her husband's permission from Mannheim to Pforzheim and back without major troubles – an incredible distance for conditions in those days. She can rightly be called the first lady driver; rumours that she created the first traffic accident are quite unfounded.

Alarmed Motorist (after collision): "Are you hurt?"
Butcher Boy: "Where's my kidneys?"

Nervous Passenger: "What's that queer sound?"
Irish Chauffeur: "'Tis the foot-brake, Sorr, is out of order and the hand-brake won't work.
But don't be onaisy, Sorr – the hooter is all right."

P.C.: "You were doing forty miles an hour, Sir."
Motorist (whispering): "Make it seventy, I'm trying to sell him the thing."

STARTER MOTORS

BROTHERS IN ADVERSITY
Farmer: "Pull up, you fool! The mare's bolting!"
Motorist: "So's the car!"

Constable (to motorist who has exceeded the speed limit): "And I have my doubts about this being your first offence. Your face seems familiar to me."

Motor Fiend: "Why don't you get out of the way?"
Victim: "What! are you comin back?"

"And do I have to keep on holding this?"

T can strike, like hay fever, in middle life. Over 30, anyway. And it casts no warning shadows before it: when I met the victim, he lived up a Kensington mews and thought cabbages were born shrink-wrapped. Within five years he was wearing a tweed flowerpot on his head and reading *The Joy of Compost* over breakfast.

The Good Life, self-sufficiency, countrification – call it what you will, once it gets a grip, you've had it. No point worrying, might as well go along with the tide. It may not go too far: with most men, the whole thing seems to stop at a spot of gardening, a Barbour jacket, and a wistful running fantasy about Felicity Kendal's bum, wriggling beneath patched dungarees while the owner does photogenic things with a pig-bucket.

In this scenario (one of the most brilliant fantasies of compromise ever produced) only one stray, damp, irresistible blonde curl is permitted to fall across the face to indicate sweat and weariness; and Margo and Jerry stand forever by with a reviving gin. The fantasy is safe enough. It is only in rare cases (a doctor writes) that the patient ends up fleeing from Kensington to live in something gnarled and Tudor and read *The Good Fencing Guide* in bed. Rare, but incurable.

While he is occupied with his order for lambproof stock-fencing, hesitating deliciously between the Corax patent floating-pawl universal ratchet-winder and the bargain set of straining-posts with galvanized droppers, I reflect that, at least, the advantage of this obsession is the way it covers every aspect of life.

You don't have to go to a football ground to indulge it, or buy a pair of expensive skis; any commonplace of life can be seen through the magic lens. I am married to the only man who watched the entire television *Mansfield Park* with breathless attention, hoping for another glimpse of a particularly fine wheelbarrow.

A desultory chat about turning the garage into a laundry-room will suddenly take a wild plunge into agricultural fantasy when the plans for a harness-room are suddenly included behind the ironing-board. There is a huge shepherd's crook suspended in the kitchen where the baby's bib used to hang; now the bib hangs on a tormented chunk of ram's-horn handle. When I passed my driving test and began to speak of a runabout, some docile little Mini, well on in years, in which to throw bags of groceries, a mad, distant look came into his eye; days later there materialised in the drive a huge khaki Land-Rover of advanced age and horrible aspect. It is a showstopper, down the baby clinic; its implicit promise to save the day in wild rural winter emergencies has at least been fulfilled once, when only its trusty four-wheel drive was able to plough through the drifts to take the yeoman farmer in for an emergency appearance on *Blankety-Blank*. Still that is not the sort of thing we Good Life wives would ever make unkind cracks about. Perish the thought.

Come to think of it, I don't know why he is reading so very attentively about stock-fencing. We have no stock yet. Yet? Ever since the mysterious telephone call from a man arranging to "bring they beehives around for 'im", I have lived on a knife-edge. I did not like the way he drew that red ring round the advertisement for an Ideal Pig-Tethering Harness; nor do I know whether that banging noise in the garage of nights has anything to do with the leaflet titled "BUILDING A RABBIT UNIT".

I have, you understand, nothing at all against animals; after the first shock, indeed, I have grown quite fond of the Muscovy ducks. Out there with my scoopful of corn, I feel quite like Felicity Kendal after all. They line up like hideous draggled chorus girls, and follow me down the path in strict formation. I quite enjoy it; it is, after all, my first taste of Leadership since the sixth form (unless you count a brief spasm of editing the *Tatler*, only there they didn't follow me around adoringly all day on flat, webbed feet. Not in an orderly line, anyway). No, beasts are all right in their place. It is just that I have been sneaking the odd look at his copy of *Home Farm* magazine (formerly *Practical Self Sufficiency*) and I know that they never do stay in their place. As the disease progresses, matters inevitably and inexorably go beyond mere ducks.

The cover-lines on this horrifying publication put the wind up the escaped townie straight away. "CHOOSING A RAM. . .WHO'S WHO AT GOAT '84. . . THE TRACTOR EXPOSED." They are serious farmers, these smallholders, operating without the clinical protection of machine and battery-unit. You can trundle comfortably through domestic articles on cabbage soup and pickled damsons, then suddenly be plunged into the murk of husbandry - PREGNANCY TEST YOUR OWN COWS. . . Blushing to the roots, you turn a tender and sentimental eye to the promising cross-head ORPHAN LAMBS. Aaaah! No, Aaarggh. *"The lamb must empty its bowel of the foetal plug of dung. The ewe usually licks out the anus."* No, no, of course the editor is not suggesting that you – but there is no guarantee. He might be. They are tough birds, these smallholders; in the last issue, which I incautiously picked up on an empty stomach, there was a letter from a cheery woman who makes her own catfood. All you have to do is boil up tons of pigs' melts (I looked it up. Yes, innards) and chicken-necks "on the Aga overnight" (next week, *The Perfumed Kitchen*, yech) then in the morning: "Just pick the bones out of the chicken necks. . ." Considering I can't stand downwind of a tin of Whiskas, even before 9 a.m., the outlook seems bleak for the cats when he goes 100% organic.

Here he is, back from the garage. Oh, from

Rough Husbandry

beyond the garage: he nipped over to Peasenhall to fetch a trailerload of something. The something is steaming, eight feet high, outside the back door. "Two years old, mixed sheep, goat, and cow; lovely and rich!" He regards his midden with devotion. "I can feel my leeks growing fatter, just looking at it!"

I smile enthusiastically, and carefully spill tea over the advertisement for *Caring Home for Bunty and Petal middlewhite gilts*. One must, of course, do one's bit as a potential smallholding wife – there are countless Felicities dying to step in, they advertise in HOME FARM as *Attractive agriculturalist seeks similar male with own land* – but a pig called Bunty I will not share my life with. Nor Petal. Nor will I lick a lamb's —

"Just off to Eastern Counties Farmers." That'll be a while then. Time to hide a few more mail-order catalogues for huge boots and revolutionary tractor attachments. Eastern Counties Farmers is the perfect shop for the agricultural fantasist; he wanders dazed between displays of calf ear-tags, BOARMATE spray, and ranks of jellied marmalade and best creosote in identical five-gallon drums. He may run into a fellow-spirit and discuss deep-beds for half an hour.

Meanwhile, I can ring the husband of the female goat-herder and beekeeper down the road; he and I have formed an underground organisation called SSDL, the Smallholders' Spouses Defence League. It was convened when the same week saw the arrival of two unscheduled beehives in our garage, and an unannounced runt in his beer-brewing shed. I doubt if either of us will, or can, do much about it; but there is always moral support. Outside, across the darkening fields, things are mooing and gnawing at fences; they are trying to get in and live with us. And as far as the eye can see across the fertile flatlands, there is no Margo or Jerry to save us now. 🐛

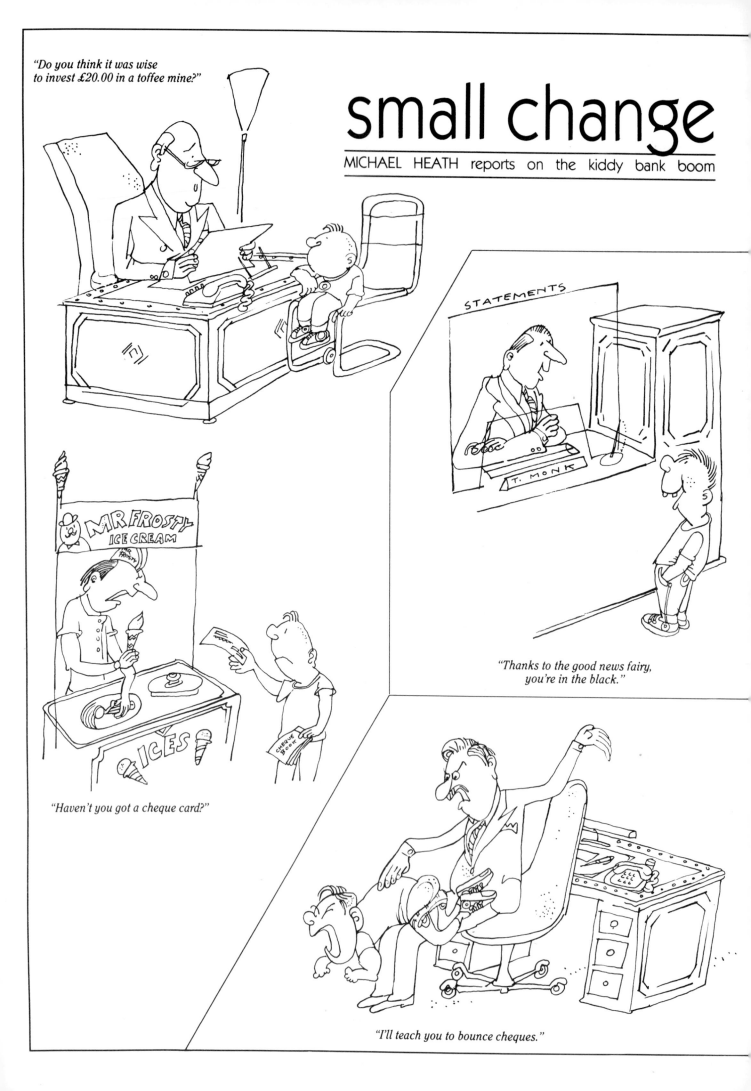

Spelling it like it is

I (nominative) have been enjoying (present perfect continuous) boning up (help! gerund? gerundive?) on my grammar. If our children are going to be taught two of the three R's, after all, I do not wish to be caught out in a hung participle.

HM Inspectorate of Schools has decreed that reading and writing, grammar and spelling are to be re-introduced into the curriculum. It is an ambitious plan, with the ring of haplessness about it: rather like abolishing umbrellas and then discovering that rain can be wet.

It is too late anyway for a whole generation which has been unforgivably deprived of that valuable mental resource, language; not to mention the fun of parsing. Parsing! The very word reveals one's roots in the last generation but one (even the *Telegraph* was clearly stumped, and changed it to *passing*).

Irene Thomas of *Round Britain Quiz* maintains that a letter reveals at once its writer's age. "If the letter inside is clearly written, well expressed and punctuated, the writer is over 35."

So to be caught indulging in furtive scansion or prosody, spotting a spondee or identifying litotes or synecdoche, is a dead giveaway. It is like scattering one's conversation with affectations such as *anent*, or *yclept*, or *hussif*, when all around the Daleks are talking of bytes.

For 20 years we have been instructed that punctuation would confine the child writer, and prosody constrict the Penguin Modern Poet, and we have been encouraged to jettison these vain useless skills. Now the grammarian in the closet can safely come out.

Hence my feelings of happy release. Perhaps now someone will invite me to a Spelling Bee. Spelling bees had joined the farthing, the bushel and the apostrophe as archaic emblems of a childhood from which my generation was amputated. But I could still secretly spell – and what a painful, uncongenial affliction that has proved to be. It makes me blimpish and schoolmarmish as I blue-pencil *miniscule, discernable, terrefied, embarassed, extravagent, expatriot, concensus, supercede, flaunt* for flout and *flout* for flaunt again. In one week my paper managed to call poor Russell Harty both *unctious* and *oleagenous* and made him Russel too (triple *sic*).

Once I was being shown round a primary school of high repute in media-land. The headmaster informed us newspaper folks that before he took up headmastering he'd been a printer himself. That should have warned me. The top drawer of his filing cabinet was labelled: *"Catologues"*. Then we were shown into the Remedial Reading Room, pride of ILEA. There on the blackboard in round bold primary teacher's hand was the word: *"Telivision"*. When I rather nervously pointed it out, both the remedial teacher and the ex-printer headmaster stared hard at "Telivision" but plainly neither of them saw anything wrong with it.

Not many people can spell and it has become a kind of boast not to care. At Eton I believe it has long been considered infra dig: on my first day in the *Evening Standard* office the Old Etonian next to me asked: "How do you spell 'slope'?" It is odd how often those who are congenitally unable to remember how a word is written choose to become writers and publishers. A divine insouciance presumes that some ancient greybeard in shirt sleeves, someone who went to elementary school and does the *Times* crossword on his way in from Petts Wood every day, will correct all solecisms. But the greybeards are a dwindling species, so newspapers and books are now riddled with *humourous* and *insistance* and *jodphurs*. Foreign words always get this cavalier treatment. Nobody can manage *aficionado* or *de rigueur*. Why use *bête noire* if you can't spell it, cry I; what's wrong with "black beast"?

(Mis-spelling remains acceptable in certain spheres, indeed obligatory. *Mackeral* and *vichysoisse*, for instance, are the accepted forms in menu-ese, and it is a poor greengrocer who deviates from the standard RIPE ADVACADOE'S.)

As it is considered so pedantic to pay any attention to how people spell their names, I might as well change my name to Valary Groves, then my tormentors could distort it back to its original. Sometimes I wonder how Mr Hugh Montgomery-Massingberd can stand the strain; also David Mlinaric, Pete Townshend, Adam Fergusson, Nigel Nicolson, Bernard Donoughue (don't omit the *ugh*) and all others whose names are minefields. I once knew a chap fired for putting a "t" in Lichfield but that was way back in the olden days of 1972.

Schools are now so timorous about any distinction between the apt and the inept pupil (learning by heart, we are told, is invidious because some are naturally better at it) that the revived curriculum is bound to come as a shock. Since many do not write so much as spray (Ron woz ear) how can they be expected, at 16, to read whole books?

"It is a tall order," according to John Thorn, the headmaster of Winchester. An O-level candidate would have been made to read a whole book, he said, but we must remember most children do not take O-levels. "Even in our

"I know it doesn't make you feel any better, Mr Pendleton, but it makes my job infinitely more bearable."

school," he added, "it is quite an uphill struggle to get a child to read Dickens."

And where will Winchester and Grange Hill find the traditional teachers? "Miss Groby taught me English Composition 30 years ago," wrote Thurber. "What she loved most of all were Figures of Speech. You remember her. You must have had her too. Her influence will never die out of the land. A small schoolgirl asked me the other day if I could give her an example of metonymy. . ." Hard to re-impose an understanding of metonymy, without re-suscitating the extinct Miss Grobies.

"Already," wrote Kingsley Amis in his "More will mean worse" essay of 1960, "a girl who has literally never heard of metre can come to a university to study English literature; what will her successors never have heard of – rhyme, poem, sentence?"

There was also a professor of English in Michigan a few years ago who wrote to a literary journal complaining that his work had been *plagerized*. This could not happen, as was noted at the time, if the professor had been acquainted with the Latin (plagiarius, a kidnapper.) But then, polysyllabic words must seem more and more a whimsical jumble of letters now that Latin has all but vanished. It is only to be expected that privilege will get an extra *d* if nobody is told about lex, legis, f. Without roots all words are mysteries. Only last week a new novel out from Heinemann contained the phrase "in the hall-*come*-dining room". But then its author is an Etonian.

I have been looking at an old family copy of *School Certificate English*, or "Bayliss" as it was doubtless known in the 1930s and 40s. The first sentence in the book (The Noun) reads: "Servants are a problem." Its essay-writing advice is excellent but its topics (Food Rationing, War Memorials, People One Meets in the Bus, Spring Onions, National Pride, the Home Guard) might fail to inspire Grange Hill and Wykehamists alike today. When it comes to the ground rules of grammar, however, Bayliss is uncompromising, severe and dashed hard. I can't see it catching on, honestly.

In hoping that all children of 11 will learn to conduct a telephone conversation HM Inspectorate is on safer ground.

The English Speaking Board, a sterling organisation, has already established an Oral Assessment aimed at the youth population who will never attempt a written exam. Telephoning is part of it, described as a "life skill". The test includes: How to answer, how to dictate and receive telephone numbers, how to ask the caller to wait, how to use words and phrases that are polite (please, thank you, I'm sorry), etc. Life skills which used to be thrown in, as it were, with Life. In another 20 years we may expect tests in breathing, nail-filing, and tying shoe-laces, so that everyone gets a prize.

In last week's *Sunday Times* there was a poignant story. A poor Czech-born Derbyshire miner was forced by penury to go back to work. A picket went to daub "Czech scab" on his house, but couldn't spell Czech, so he daubed "Polish scab" instead. With the help of the new curriculum a whole new generation of miners might be taught at school how to spell Czech: now there's a cheering thought.

"Once on the outside I intend to pedal like crazy!"

"Next, my impression of Beethoven's Sonata in D minor, Op. 31, No. 2, as played by Humphrey Bogart."

BANX

"Not much of an elephants' graveyard though, is it?"

"Tell me, has he always been so childish?"

"I've pencilled in a blemish on your record, Henshaw."

"... And I say, having to queue for Terry Wogan's autograph is taking Purgatory too bloody far."

"Of course, he's not the plainclothes man he was in the Sixties."

"Bloody hell, we were vandalised last night."

"Of course, in a perfect world we'd both be sex symbols."

CAPTION COMPETITION
WINNER

YOU'RE RIGHT, MRS THATCHER—THESE'LL TAKE A BIT OF LICKING.

C. Thomson
of Glasgow

1933 caption—"THE FACT OF THE MATTER IS, MADAM, WE'VE GOT NO SHOES THAT ARE BIG ON THE INSIDE AND SMALL ON THE OUTSIDE."

Le Cracker de Noël

Bob: Un cracker, M. Scrooge?
Scrooge: Pourquoi pas? J'ai toujours du temps pour un peu de fun.
Bob: Right! Tenez votre bout . . . tenez étroitement . . . Tirez!
Scrooge: Je tire encore. (*Soudain, le cracker se divise en deux.*) Mais, il n'y avait pas de crack!
Bob: Peut-être il est dud. Ah non, regardez. Le petit strip explosif est toujours intacte. Vous voulez tirer encore?
Scrooge: Avec mes mains nues? Pas sur votre nelly. Je ne veux pas être brûlé le jour de Noël, comme un turkey.
Bob: Mais non, il n'y a pas de danger. Regardez, je vais tirer le strip moi-même, un bout à chaque main. (*Une explosion.*) Ay ay ay! J'ai brûlé les cheveux sur mes mains. Ouf!
Scrooge: C'est de votre faute. Vous ne m'écoutez jamais. Maintenant, inspectons le booty que j'ai gagné.
Bob: Que *vous* avez . . . M. Scrooge, c'est moi qui ai gagné!
Scrooge: Fair enough. Inspectons *votre* booty.

Bob: Premièrement, la riddle. "Qui étaient les deux Premiers anglais inférieurs à tous les autres?"
Scrooge: Je ne sais pas. Qui étaient les deux Premiers anglais inférieurs à tous les autres?
Bob: "Pitt the Elder et Pitt the Younger. Parce qu'ils étaient vraiment les Pitts."
Scrooge: Très bien! J'aime cette riddle.
Bob: Je ne la comprends pas.
Scrooge: Mon vieux Bob, vous n'avez pas une sense d'humour. Quoi next?
Bob: Une model plastique de la State Coach.
Scrooge: C'est joli!
Bob: C'est cheapo cheapo. Il y a aussi une moustache fausse.
Scrooge: Bravo. Mettez-la.
Bob: Inutile. J'ai déjà une moustache naturelle.
Scrooge: Bon, je vais la porter moi-même. Voilà! Vous croyez que je rassemble au Prince Albert?
Bob: Oui, comme je rassemble à la Reine Victoria, moi. Et finalement, le châpeau de papier.Qui est trop grand pour moi.
Scrooge: Mais pas pour moi.
Bob: Well, comme un cracker, c'est un wash-out.
Scrooge: Bob, vous êtes un vrai Cratchit. Un party-pooper. Un blanket mouillé.
Bob: Il est difficile d'être cheerful tout le temps, spécialement maintenant que vous êtes une caractère réformée. Je préfère vieux Scrooge, presque.
Scrooge: Mais non, mais non! Cheer up! Prenez un verre! Bottoms up! (*Etc, etc*).

ORIGINS OF JAZZ

1 **Where did jazz come up the river from?**
 a Eel Pie Island
 b Waco, Texas
 c Eugene, Onegin
 d Down the river

2 **Who composed *Maple Leaf Rag*?**
 a Jelly Roll Maple-Leaf
 b E. L. Doctorow
 c Margaret Trudeau
 d Ragtime Cowboy Joe

3 **What was the baptismal name of 'Bix' Beiderbecke?**
 a Huntley N. Palmer
 b Aubrey Beiderbecke-Smith
 c the least of his troubles
 d Wernher Von Braun

4 **Which would you rather die of?**
 a Darktown Strutters' Ball
 b Viper's Drag
 c The Flat Foot Floogie with the Floy Floy
 d The Way You Look Tonight

5 **Who was the first Trumpet King of New Orleans?**
 a Henry VIII
 b Louis XIV
 c Joshua Fitt
 d Wild Walter Gabriel

TRANSLATION

(*N.B. Marks will be awarded for consistency of Period Flavour.*)
Translate into **HIPSTER ARGOT:**

"Hallo, Fats," cried Doc, on entering the flat. "Shake me by the hand, old chap, I have not seen you for a long time! How are you, my dear fellow, still smoking that excellent marijuana?"

"Oh gosh," replied Fats mournfully, "I no longer concern myself with that despised effluent nowadays. The last time I invested in a supply, an unpleasant policeman surprised me in the act of enjoying some, and boot was applied to bottom all the way to the Precinct House. I am not exaggerating. So do not inquire about that waste material where I am concerned. Are you in regular musical employment?"

"Fortunately, yes. I am enjoying an extended nightly engagement at the Ubangi Club. We have an extremely peppy aggregation, I assure you, much appreciated by the clientele."

"What instrumentation are you employing?"

"Two woodwinds underpinned by the stan-

DOCTOR JAZZ
Exam Paper set by Russell Davies

Candidates **MUST** attempt the Translation Paper and **TWO** other sections.
Candidates attempting the Brass Section may not also answer the Rhythm Section, and vice versa.
No candidate need attempt the vocaliste, as she is already spoken for.

---

dard propulsive unit. The percussionist is Sticks Pugh. Believe me he is one thermally scalding juvenile, no excrement.''

"I do not disbelieve you. I say, have you seen Miles?''

"Miles Kington, the bass viol plucker?''

"No, you oaf, Miles Davis. *Miles*.''

"Ah Miles, yes certainly I have seen him, I accosted him yesterday in the recording suite where he was consigning to posterity no niggardly outpouring of his art.''

"No excrement?''

"It is the case, I emphasise it.''

"No excrement.''

"Well, I like your company, but your hours do not suit. I must be on my way. It was nice to see you, old boy. We must meet together and exchange stories of the old times again as soon as possible. Do you remember the occasion when Shorty was introduced to Princess Margaret of England when he was plainly inebriated? Haw, haw, that was a funny incident. Shorty is still living locally; you should bestir yourself from off your bottom and go and see him. In fact sundry felines into whom I bump are longing to share an illegal cigarette with you and perhaps play some repetitive rhythmic phrases in your company. Come on, old fellow, leave these over-quiet surroundings and rejoin the general polyphony!''

"No excrement.''

ESSAY QUESTION

*Write an **ESSAY** on one of the following subjects.*

1 "I don't know what they sound like but by God they frighten me'' (Duke Ellington). *Discuss.*

2 To what extent is it true that if Engelbert Humperdinck had not been invented he would have had to exist?

3 "Winifred Atwell". *Do you agree?*

4 Compare and contrast the careers of Martha and the Vandellas.

5 "Blind Lemon Jefferson is the father of acid rock.'' *Discuss.*

6 Is you is or is you ain't my baby? *(Give examples.)*

GENERAL KNOWLEDGE

Which of the following are related by blood?

1 **Sir Harry** and **Estée Lauder**
2 **Oliver** and **Françoise Hardy**
3 **Tony** and **Herbie Hancock**
4 **Tennessee Ernie** and **Anna Ford**
5 **F. Scott** and **Ella Fitzgerald**
6 **Marvin Hamlisch** and **HM The Queen Mother.**

COMPREHENSION

*Read **ONE** of the following passages carefully and answer the questions.*

1 Hi teens and tinies it's grrreat to be back with you on the Top Fifty Smasheroo I've been on holiday as you know having a gggreat time too listening to all the tip-top sounds that ARE around hope you have too so let's crack on with the first of to-day's terrrific tracks it's that grrreat outfit Sedentary Gro-Bag with Tomato Rhumba wheee . . . Sedentary Gro-Bag there with er what was it it was of course it was Tomato Rhumba grrreat track talking of which there'll be some unbelievable sounds on 299 tonight when Andy Rajneesh presents Nostalgia Time and this time Andy'll be looking back over those grrreat old sounds from the year of 1982 remember those? Wow, will we ever forget you know you know I get you know, little tear in the corner of the optic when I hear this one again no prizes for guessing it's the late grrreat Jim Catastrophe with Razor Party, yeeahhh . . .
Hard to believe it's only three years since Jim stuck his head in a blender in that horrific accident don't you try it now teens and tinies it ain't worth it take it from your Uncle Tone well maybe Jim Catastrophe was kinda anodyne in his way so here's one from the King himself, you know who I mean, it's Gary Unattractive . . .oooh . . .

a What is the age of the speaker (years and months)?

b How many times altogether does the speaker pause for breath? ("Too many'' will not be accepted as an answer.)

c What is the speaker's favourite adjective? What does he mean by it?

d What is the most surprising word the speaker uses?

e Why does he bother?

f What evidence is there that Andy Rajneesh's show is better than the speaker's? Are you sure?

g Are you satisfied that the speaker is, as he claims, a sentimentalist?

h What advice would you give the speaker with a view to improving his presentation? (Not more than FOUR words.)

OR

2 *Baby I'm a vampire – oooh ooh ooh ooh buzzin' round the camp fire – oooh oooh ooh ooh*

Sinkin' my teeth into your knee
Goin' to the toilet at half-past three
I'm a vampire

Baby I'm a vampire – aagh aagh aagh aagh
Sittin' on a damp wire – aagh aagh aagh aagh
Sick an' tired of hangin' round in caves, caves, caves,
Don't tell me Britannia rules the soddin' waves
I'm a vampire.

© 1984 Tommy Streptococcus

a What is the speaker's trade or profession?

b For whom, in your estimation, would the speaker vote?

c What is his attitude to women?

d What is their likely attitude to him?

e Are the prevailing weather conditions the same in both verses?

f Write a short story accounting for line 4

MAHOOD Curiouser and Curiouser

FRAZER NASH

Nothing to lose but your chains

Next up the hill, the Tannoy declared: *N. Arnold-Forster in his 1917 Becquet-Delage Special with the 11,959cc V-8 Hispano-Suiza engine, bringing to mind memories of First World War Spads and SE5s, and a fine motor-car which of course has a 1923 G.P. Delage chassis. With his vast experience on the hill, G. Smith must nevertheless be the favourite for fastest time with his Alvis-engined Frazer Nash, But W.D.A. Black's 1934 Monoposto Alfa Romeo Tipo B, E.M. Dean's 1937 Bugatti T/59/50B and the 1932/37 Giron Alvis of R.N. Jolley could all run him close.*

Doctor Bee's affections were with the Frazer Nash. A retired GP from Lincolnshire, Dr Bee may fairly be described, along with the rest of the fieldful here today, as a stark-staring motor-car enthusiast, come to Shelsley Walsh to watch old-timer thoroughbreds blast up a hill-climb under the auspices of the Midland Automobile Club and Vintage Sports Car Club. People such as Dr Bee do not miss Shelsley Walsh. People such as Porsche dealers AFN see to that, sitting him beside their caravan half way up the climb, by the S, providing curly sandwiches and lukewarm beer and atmosphere. It's all atmosphere. AFN is atmosphere.

The doc bought his first chain-drive Frazer Nash from AFN in 1936, used it on his rounds. Then for twenty years his passion was the first Fast Roadster manufactured by Frazer Nash, registration number VMF 974, chassis number 421/100/005, built at AFN's Falcon Works, Isleworth, in 1948. It looked like the BMWs it sprang from, very shapely two-seater, built on the superleggera principle of a small diameter tubular framework with steel and aluminium panels wrapped round the tubing. A bit different from the channel iron chassis of the chain

> ## "Dr Bee's specs mist up at the mention of Fane. What it must have been like at the '37 Shelsley. . ."

gangs. He should say so. Same car, of course, that in 1953 went up the Stelvio Pass like blazes to take 6th place overall, and 2nd place in the 2-litre class, of the Alpine Trial through the mountains of Switzerland, Italy and France. At the wheel was Alex von Falkenhausen, engineer, formerly of the Bayerische Motoren Werke, and a jolly sound chap.

I know this, too, because I have just driven the car up to Shelsley and there's a plaque on the dash with the details, not of my epic drift through Crowmarsh Gifford and heel-and-toe change through the staggered crossing at Kingston Bagpuize, never mind stalling in the centre of Evesham, but of von Falkenhausen's more Dornford-Yatesian run. People like Dr Bee know it all anyway, because everyone who knows Frazer Nash knows all about the Fast Roadster, just as they know all about the chain gang, the Meadows engines, the Gough engines, supercharged for the '34 Shelsley, the Blackburne engines, the very first side-valve Anzani, or all about deer old Archie himself, and Ron Godfrey, characters like Aldy, Tommy, Gripper, and the legendary Fane. They'll tell you all about it if you ask, and often if you don't ask.

Dr Bee's specs mist up at the mention of Fane. Those jackets he wore. Those hats. What it must have been like at the '37 Shelsley. . .

To open the afternoon programme, H. L. Hadley (works o.h. camshaft Austin single-seater) and A. F. P. Fane (blown single-seater Frazer Nash) were chosen by reason of their performances at the last climb. Hadley's effort literally brought gasps from the crowd. A perfect start, determined wizardry through the awkward Kennel bend, and he was at the famous S at what looked like an impossible speed – even for Hadley. But the Austin mechanic-cum-driver had a way of bending a dancing, slithering car to his will and fighting every inch of the way he was somehow through the corners and away to the top – 40.74 seconds.

The crowd took a deep breath and held it as Fane arrived at the same spot at very nearly the same speed, cut across the grass on the inside of the left-hand corner, held a series of slides and was gone; but this time the timing apparatus was not equal to the occasion and the time of the climb will never be known. It was just very, very fast.

Actually, Dr Bee knows, it was probably a shade over 50mph, but then that was going it in 1937, the year the inestimable Fane broke Shelsley's record up the hill. He was a hill-climber's hill-climber, Fane. A remarkable Spit pilot, too, a couple of years later when war came. That was a dreadful business, because of course it completely disrupted getting cars from BMW across to AFN. Still Fane got the first pictures of the *Tirpitz* hiding in Aasfjord. That caused a flap. Fane adored a flap, always made him laugh. He bought it in 1942, routine sortie, came down near Duxford. Terrible shame.

Funny thing about that Fast Roadster, it

had the engine cover split transversely in the middle, one flap forwards, the other flap back. And the spare wheel mounted at an angle in the nearside of the engine compartment, you got at it through a flap. Dr Bee sold it back to AFN. They gave him a new Porsche 944, well he couldn't turn that down. And it's right it should go back to AFN.

Before the war, when Aldy was proposing to BMW that he bring in their cars, the funny thing was the Bavarians thought AFN stood for Aldington Frazer Nash. They'd probably never heard of old Archie. Of course, Aldy had been in control since the early 1920s, proper chain gang days, though the enthusiasts didn't get called that until *I Am A Fugitive From A Chain Gang* was shown in the 1930s. It appealed to their sense of humour. You needed a sense of humour, too, to drive a chain gang Frazer Nash, a stick over the side, simple dog-clutch, you had to feel for it.

They did the job, though, Dr Bee remembers. The chains were in their own little oily world underneath the floorboards, behind the seats. There were only two seats. The back, of course, was the famous back-of-a-bathtub shape, with the petrol tank behind, they called it the TT Replica, not that Frazer Nash ever did as well in the Tourist Trophy as they did at Shelsley or as they did later on in the Mille Miglia or the Targa Florio. At that time they had drivers like Stirling Moss and Mike Hawthorn. In the 1930s, Aldy and his brothers were up against Dick Seaman and Prince Bira. It was very different, then.

They only used to build about thirty a year in the 1930s and there weren't two exactly the same. They looked pretty much the same, but there were often little detail differences. It's all there in the Falcon Works records. Dear old Jenks, I might (but don't) know Jenks, he's just done a book on the AFN history. Some chain-driven Frazers had a door on the passenger side. The spare wheel was usually mounted on the nearside of the scuttle, but some had two. Dr Bee can remember those. There were different arrangements with lamps on some cars, and of course you could tell a Frazer Nash with the firm's own 4-cylinder, it had four external exhaust pipes, whereas the Meadows-engined cars only had the three. There were some saloons, but there aren't any left.

And we're just waiting now for T. J. Threlfall in the 1913 Theophile Schneider GP to begin his climb in the Class 6 Edwardian and early Vintage Non-Front-Wheel-Brake Racing Cars Class, the record here of course held by N. Arnold-Forster with 47.30 seconds in the 1912 Bugatti Chain Drive, then after the Panhard Levassor we'll be able to see the 1915 Vauxhall Prince Henry.

Funny to think that after the war it was the Frazer Nash connection that helped get BMW started again, and of course they got Bristol Cars started besides. Porsche involvement in the UK is down to them, too, you could say, and AFN do. The old works atmosphere still seems to be there, even if it is really a Porsche showroom now, because a few Frazer Nashes are still there as well, brought out now and again for a run up to Shelsley, for instance. You meet people there who never forget a Frazer.

CAPTION COMPETITION
WINNERS

1900 caption—CHEAP JACK. "I WILL MAKE A PRESENT OF THIS GENOOINE GOLD WATCH — NONE OF YOUR CARROTS — TO HENNY LADY OR GENTLEMAN FOR FIFTEEN SHILLINGS AN' SIXPENCE. WHY AM I DOIN' THIS? TO HENCOURAGE TRADE, THAT IS WHY I AM GIVIN' IT AWAY FOR FOURTEEN SHILLINGS AN' SIXPENCE. LOOK AT IT FOR YOURSELVES, FOR FOURTEEN SHILLINGS! IF YER DON'T BELIEVE IT'S GOLD, *JUMP ON IT!*"

1932 caption—THE LAST FISH, BEING HOPELESSLY OUTNUMBERED, SURRENDERS.

1986 in View

Benny GREEN

JANUARY

The Government, stepping up the intensity of its thirty-year war against the BBC, suggested that the Corporation might sell advertising space on certain channels and selected programmes. Were the Corporation to take up this kind, far-seeing, magnanimous offer, then its reward would be an increase in the licence fee of 10p, to take effect automatically for the next ten years. Once this offer was announced, producers of religious programmes began making attempts to contact the spirit of Anthony Eden, in the expectation of watching a ghost contorted with glee. The best-selling song of the month, featured for 76 consecutive minutes on *Top of the Pops*, was called "Suez casts a long shadow".

FEBRUARY

Toyah Wilcox was offered the role of Henry V in a prestigious new production of *King John*. After careful consideration Miss Wilcox turned the offer down on the grounds that the play was a male chauvinist tract, and that the songs were not much good anyway. Marti Caine, deciding to start another new career, was swiftly drafted in her place. Harry Carpenter signed to fight Frank Bruno for the Wood Lane Heavyweight Championship. When told of the vast weight difference between the fighters, Bruno said he was prepared to face up to that. Promoter Terry Lawless will be in both corners.

MARCH

Julie Walters went through the entire month without making any appearances on chat shows. The Chancellor announced plans to sell *Coronation Street* to Granada TV. The money raised from the sale would enable him to remove from the tax structure all single men earning more than £1,000,000 per annum. On being informed that Granada TV already owned *Coronation Street*, the Chancellor admitted that there were a few wrinkles still left to be smoothed out. The Lord's Day Observance Society lodged an official complaint with the IBA that Brian Walden's *Weekend World* was too comical to be compatible with traditional sabbatarian principles.

APRIL

The producers of *Panorama* were given a severe reprimand for having put out a programme which, by failing to suggest that the world was due to end next month, had failed in the aim of the series, which was to make as many people desperately depressed about as many things as possible. The culprits, threatened with demotion to *The Money Programme*, apologised and promised it would not happen again. Nor did it. After Chelsea fans, attending a televised FA Cup semi-final, had wiped out the Manchester area, Sir Matt Busby said he thought that violence was not football's problem, but society's. Jimmy Hill ran Sir Matt's statement in slow motion. Tony Palmer announced plans to produce, direct, write and star in a sensational new film about the private life of Ken Russell.

MAY

The BBC, responding to the Government's offer (see January), announced plans to sell advertising space in the Chancellor's next Budget speech. Mike Yarwood was said to be considering sponsoring a national competition to find someone who could write him a line worth saying. On BBC *Sportsnight*, Harry Carpenter was seen defeating Frank Bruno in the second round, when the fight was stopped by the referee Terry Lawless. Sir Matt said it was society's problem.

JUNE

Channel Four announced plans for Alec McCowen to do a one-man show of the works of Marcel Marceau. The Opposition spokesman for Employment said that one-man shows were not job-productive. In the First Test between England and Australia, a group protesting on behalf of the Greenham Common garrison held up play for over an hour. None of the spectators noticed. Julie Walters, appearing on three chats shows simultaneously, said that a) she probably wasn't a genius; b) who could say; and c) on the other hand. . .

JULY

BBC announced plans to screen Frederic Raphael's cycle of short stories, *Camford Blues*, in which various members of the Boat Race crew sit and discuss whether or not Wittgenstein would have made a good cox. In *Bookmark*, a female reviewer suggested the passing of a Government Act forbidding men from writing about women. Brian Walden was quoted as asking, "Who is the Lord's Observance Day Society?" Ken Russell begins shooting *The Life and Music of Tony Palmer*, with massive interpolations from himself.

AUGUST

Toyah Wilcox failed to appear on a chat-show. *The Money Programme* suggested that all self-employed people should be put in prison for not less than five years, just to make things a bit easier for the Chancellor, who spent most of the month on holiday, having a haircut. The commercial companies complained of imminent bankruptcy. The BBC announced plans to screen a 96-part musical version of *Tenko*.

SEPTEMBER

Steve Davis offered the part of Rhett Butler in a new production of *Tess of the D'Urbervilles*, to be directed by Roman Polanski. Tony Palmer's new folk-opera, *Palmer in Love*, was postponed owing to the unavailability of Ken Russell.

OCTOBER

National television strike imposed by walkout of Terry Wogan.

NOVEMBER

BBC announced its acceptance of the Government offer (see January), and said that the experiment of selling space on some programmes would begin with the Party Political Broadcasts.

DECEMBER

Mrs Thatcher decided to take television away from the British. Julie Walters led protest. The Chancellor decided to offer shares in MI5 to the nation. There were no bidders.

"The commercial companies complained of imminent bankruptcy. The BBC announced plans to screen a 96-part musical version of *Tenko*."

NICK

"The panoramic grandeur of the Rockies is the setting for this towering epic . . . ."

"You're new around here, aren't you?"

"Guess this must be kind of embarrassing for you."

"The stewardess has collapsed – anybody here know how to mix a Harvey Wallbanger?"

"Say, where did you get that super sunscreen lotion?"

"Von Richthofen seems to be having a pretty good war."

CINEMA: FFOLKES

BROADWAY DANNY ROSE WOODY ALLEN *as Danny Rose* MIA FARROW *as Tina Vitale*

GHOSTBUSTERS BILL MURRAY *as Veukman* DAN AYKROYD *as Stanz* HAROLD RAMIS *as Spengler*
SIGOURNEY WEAVER *as Dana Barrett*

THE COMPANY OF WOLVES SARAH PATTERSON *as Rosaleen*   ANGELA LANSBURY *as Granny*

NINETEEN EIGHTY-FOUR JOHN HURT *as Winston Smith*   RICHARD BURTON *as O'Brien* and *BIG BROTHER*

The Rolling English Road

" . . . And 'ave one for y'self."

"Oh good, we're going on somewhere."

"Fancy a pint?"

"Oh, yeah, and bring a bottle."

"A new breathalyser, gentlemen.
It recognises the grip of fellow masons."

"That's the Chief Constable's
sixth tonight."

"I see the prosecution have produced
their expert witness."

COLLECTING
ALISTAIR SAMPSON

A Guide for Dealers

1. Good gracious I seem to have left my cheque book behind.
You might get paid by Christmas.

2. I will send you the dollars from the States.
Unless the pound improves, in which case I'll send you the pounds. The rate of exchange looks pretty volatile at the moment so I may wait quite a while. Heads I win and tails you lose.

3. I am doing a bit of pruning at the moment.
Remember that horror you tucked me up with last year? I won't buy another thing from you until you take it back.

4. No. Please don't reserve it. I'll just take my chance.
I hate it. I just said I'd think about it as a polite way of getting out of the shop.

5. We're just looking, thank you.
We are complete time-wasters.

6. No, we are not looking for anything in particular.
We are even more complete time-wasters.

7. I will have to talk to my husband.
I am having a nervous breakdown, as he will explain when he telephones.

8. May I try it for the weekend?
We are giving a party and I want the house to look its best.

9. If I may say so, it was a pretty silly place to leave it.
My loutish nine-year-old has just knocked over your Ravenscroft vase and I have no intention of paying for it.

10. What do you mean by seven fifty? Seven pounds fifty or seven hundred and fifty pounds?
That should cut you down to size.

11. Can you tell me the price of the piece in the window?
I have one at home just like it and I am dying to know what it is worth.

12. Don't worry, I'm quite happy on my own.
I am a shoplifter.

13. £3000? Perhaps it has the wrong ticket on?
I am a German Dealer. I think this a good joke.

14. What's the real price?
I love a good haggle. When I have reduced you to ashes I shall look at my watch and say "Good gracious, I had no idea it was so late" and be gone like a puff of smoke. Think of all the bookwork you could have done. But it was fun, wasn't it?

REMARK — A series of ripostes to remarks made by Customers — RIPOSTE

1. Will you take a personal cheque?
2. What is the Trade Price?
3. I suppose there is no chance that that Hepplewhite commode I bought from you the other day could be Spanish?
4. You know that Corner Cupboard I bought from you two years ago?
5. I bought this in: Kensington Church St,
   Kings Road,
   Fulham Road,
   Mount St,
   Stow-on-the-Wold,
   Bath,
   Tunbridge Wells,
   Bradford-on-Avon.
6. Are you just closing?
7. May I use your telephone?
8. May I use your boys' room?
9. We are staying at: Strand Palace, Regent Palace, Metropole. Claridges, The Connaught, The Berkeley. The Stafford, Browns, The Hilton.
10. We are just browsing.
11. May we look round?

12. Gosh you've had this a long time.
13. Heavens: why is this piece of pottery six thousand pounds?

14. I have come here to lodge the most solemn protest about the iniquitous price you charged my wife/mistress/mother/daughter for that worthless vase/picture/table/chair/candlestick.

1. Yes, Mrs Rockefeller.
2. Quite, Mrs Rockefeller.
3. You have a nasty suspicious mind. Just because I have a flat in Marbella.
4. Your house does not have any corners in it either. I give up. I am going to throw in the sponge and sell boomerangs.
5. You have only yourself to blame.
   I admire your courage.
   There's one born every minute.
   A fool and his money.
   Easy come, easy go.
   That is why you are cleaned out.
   That is why you are disgusted.
   You realise they buy it all in London.
6. As you are covered in mink and diamonds, no.
7. Yes, but only for making telephone calls.
8. Sorry, I have three daughters.
9. Do you mind showing yourselves out?
   Of course we'll reserve it. When can you come to lunch?
   Maybe we could reserve it. Cup of tea?
10. Only giraffes and zebras browse. Get out.
11. Yes, but do take off those frightful plastic pixie hoods. It's not raining in here.
12. Quite right. When I first bought it, it was not an antique.
13. Because it has substantial repairs. Were it perfect, it would be *much* more.
14. *Gotcha.*

"Nice to see no-one's beaten six days yet."

ROY HATTERSLEY

Local Interest

WHENEVER you read of a "largely unreported event", beware. For the occasion about which the journalist goes on to make a world exclusive revelation probably never happened. Indeed, the likelihood is that the introduction was written as a coded message which semaphores – at least to drinking pals at El Vino – that what follows is allegory, fantasy or parable. However, the largely unreported event which I go on to describe really happened. Fantastic it certainly was and some readers will construct a parable around it. But it took place on Wednesday, October 3, at Blackpool.

The event was a meeting organised on the fringe of the Labour Party Conference by the Campaign for Broadcasting and Press Freedom. The subject under discussion was "Should We Talk to the Press?" We met in a cafe-cum-coffee-bar which was decorated either in the style of Dante's *Inferno* or as a tribute to those episodes of *Dr Who* which seem to be set in a science fiction coalmine. Strobe lights flashed red and green. Dark passages disappeared through crevices in the *papier-mâché* walls. I believe that a plastic crocodile lounged in one corner, but that I may have imagined. I am, however, sure that the speakers at this *soirée* were Tony Benn and myself.

I – as readers of this column would expect – answered the questions concerning the Labour Party and the Press in a way which was both simple and obvious. We should speak to them whenever it was in our interests to do so, since the alternative policy of unremitting kindness would gain us no greater favours than the cynical hostility which I advocated. Tony Benn, on the other hand, proposed not so much a boycott as a posture which can only be compared with Louis XIV's assertion that "henceforth there will be no more Pyrenees". We should behave as if Fleet Street no longer existed. Its powers, he insisted, were being eroded and its influence replaced by all sorts of alternative newspapers and magazines.

He did, however, admit that he regularly read two papers which more or less represented "our" point of view. Since one of them was the *Morning Star*, a news sheet which is actually owned by a party which challenges "our" candidates at general elections, I found his definition of consanguinity somewhat difficult to follow. But as he went on to say that

no national daily really mattered, I turned my attention to his alternatives. He listed the "jolly good papers which are now available" – *Militant, Labour Weekly, Socialist Worker, Newsline, The Yorkshire Miner* – the roll of honour went on and on. He added that all this essential reading could be supplemented by the dozens of community bulletins which now flourish in our towns and cities.

As regular readers of this column would again expect, I made the obvious comment. It seemed to me, then, as it seems to me now, that *The Yorkshire Miner* (no matter how admirable its views) is unlikely to persuade the marginal voters of the southern suburbs to rally to Labour's cause, and that in consequence, we ought not to write off the *Daily Mirror*, which is generally on our side, or serious newspapers (like *The Guardian* and *Financial Times*) which do try to report our affairs with a degree of objectivity. This caused minor offence to Mr Benn's supporters in the audience. My addendum that we ought to buy newspapers for more than their political analysis and editorial opinions was regarded as deeply shocking. Apparently book reviews and football reports do not adequately represent the class struggle in which we are all engulfed.

By now you will have realised that I was out of sympathy with at least one section of our audience. But last week I began to realise that in one narrow particular they were right. Com-

munity newspapers can and do fulfil a function which neither national dailies nor local weeklies can adequately perform. It is not a political rôle. And it is carried out largely because of their limited size and restricted area of circulation. But they can speak for a locality in a way which is denied to more orthodox publications. It is happening in part of my Birmingham inner city constituency.

Within that earth, that realm, that Sparkbrook, the problem of prostitution has – in one limited district – reached literally intolerable proportions. In one small group of roads, girls parade the footpaths, stand on the street corners and accost passers-by so blatantly that the local residents will tolerate their behaviour no longer. The local press are in on the act. The *Birmingham Mail* (which insists, by the way, that I under-estimated its circulation in this column six weeks ago) published detailed and restrained reports. Even the nationals have made passing reference. The *Mail on Sunday* (with typical vacuity) revealed that I had myself been accosted by one of the miscreants – a story which had first appeared six months earlier in the *News of the World*. But only *The Heathan* conveyed the true horror of living in a red-light district and the full strength of feeling of the families in the area.

I doubt if either Rupert Murdoch or Robert Maxwell will make a bid for "Balsall Heath's Own Newspaper, published by the St Paul's Project Ltd". But many of their journalists could learn a lot from the way in which *The Heathan* has dealt with crisis within the community it serves. Its October issue carried a double-page spread of pictures identifying individual prostitutes plying their trade. In October it promised that its cameras would catch and identify some of the kerb crawlers and claimed to possess "film evidence that at the time of . . . conventions . . . businessmen who ask 'where can I find a woman?' are directed by Exhibition Centre and hotel staff" to the blasted heath.

It may be pure coincidence that the police have now begun to prosecute kerb crawlers under the 1381 Justices of the Peace Act. Perhaps the feature in the *Sunday People* – "Sex for Sale at the Motor Show – optional extras in top class hotels" was not sparked off by *The Heathan*. But there is no doubt who sensed the mood and got the story first. There is more to community newspapers than recipes for lemon cake. ℮

"Despite our faults I still think we're the finest cross-section in the world."

OOPS! IN CENTRAL PARK

Spring has reached

· S U S A N · J E F F R E Y S ·

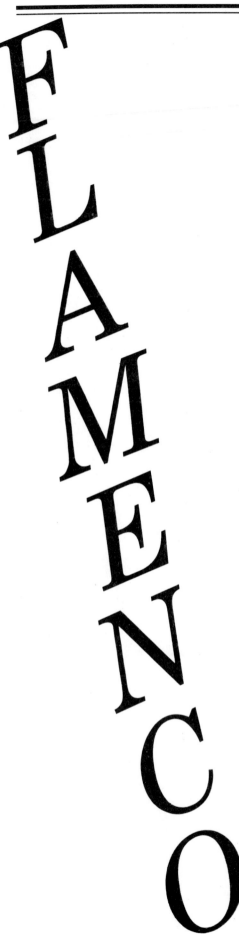

WHEN I got to the *Instituto* I was sweating like *un puerco*. It was hot that summer and I had run with the buses. That thing with the buses when you run for one and do not catch it so you run to the next stop and do not catch another bus until, in the end, you have saved yourself the fare.

"The courses started last week," said the official one behind the desk. "If you wish to do Cake Maintenance, Smocking for Weight Control or English as a Second Helping, you are too late. These classes are all full."

"I do not want such classes, *camarada*. I wish to learn the flamenco."

"Do you reap the bitter harvest of *los giros* or are you on *el regular earner*?"

"A bit of this, a bit of that," I answered.

"Then you must pay the full fee."

"Take it," I said and threw the money at him, "but I will do only the summer course."

"That is what they all say," he replied as he swept the money into a drawer and locked it. "But you will become like the others. Obsessed."

I went to the hall where they did the flamenco, it was empty. From the room above came the urgent, rhythmic hammering of the upholstery class. Terrible gaspings came from the courtyard below where unfit men played five-a-side football. The evening sun streamed in through the windows, blood red across the sand in the *balde de fuego*, the fire bucket.

An *inglés* came into the hall, he was pale and wore glasses. He unbuttoned his shirt so that his string vest showed. He took out a handkerchief and tied a knot in each corner. He put the handkerchief on his head.

"*¡Madre de Dios!*" I said. "Is this how you dress for the flamenco?"

"Well, I get sweaty," he said and rolled down his socks.

Two more *ingleses* came into the hall. They carried plastic bags from Waitrose.

"*Salud*," said the one in the string vest.

"*Salud*," they replied and took out shoes from the bags. The woman's shoes had steel on the heels and toes. The soles of the man's shoes were studded with small silver nails.

"Do you practise much?" I asked.

"*¡Nah! ¡*Leave off!" they said. "We live in a maisonette."

More people came into the room; they greeted each other and were friendly and pleasant.

My heart sank. I was hoping for blood feuds, card reading and perhaps a knife fight. I had hoped for hooped ear-rings, tight trousers and yards of black lace but these people shopped at Marks and Spencer. They were *gente bastante regular*, ordinary people.

I got up to leave; as I did so, three *hombres* came into the hall. They carried guitars and reeked of garlic. Their cheek-bones were sharp

as blades and their sideburns met under their chins. My heart rose and I sat down again.

They began to tune the strings of their guitars. One of them took a thin *cigarito* from the corner of his mouth and parked it on the neck of his guitar. He leaned towards the others and hissed, "I see that Arsenal have signed Charlie Nicholas."

"*¡Mierda!*" I thought. "I will learn *nada* here, I have thrown away my money for nothing. I obscenity on your Adult Education." In disgust I turned to look down into the courtyard where the unfit men were playing five-a-side football. One of them seemed to be dying, with little dignity and no priest.

When I turned my head again the *profesor de flamenco* had arrived. He wore flared trousers and plimsolls. He looked Welsh. Again I got up to leave. If I had left the room then I would still be *una mujer libre*, a free woman. But the way was blocked, I was trapped in the room and now am trapped in an obsession.

What happened next was like that thing with Clark Kent and the telephone booth. The class barred the doorway, very straight and still. The *profesor* clapped his hands, the guitarists struck a chord and the *gente bastante regular* were transformed. Smouldering fire burnt in the eyes of women who had entered the hall respectable matrons. *Macho* arrogance oozed from every pore of men who had seemed mild-mannered. The man and the woman with the steel-bottomed shoes looked as if they slept in the cold, open field and had never been in a maisonette in their lives.

As for the *hombre* in the string vest, he was like a tiger. Every movement he made seemed fierce yet graceful, he looked lithe and dangerous. Even his string vest looked virile.

With a rhythmic *zapaedo* the class swept across the floor past the fire buckets, drowning out the noise of the upholstery class and the five-a-side football. Their fingers snapped and their eyes flashed. They clapped their hands and slapped their thighs. They were not the *gente bastante regular* who had first come into the hall.

I stood on my chair and shouted "*¡Ole!¡*Triff and brill! ¡Keep it up, chaps!" as the dance reached its climax.

When it was finished I went up to the *profesor de flamenco*. I approached with great respect, he was no *hombre regular*.

"Can you teach me to do that?" I asked.

"Well, it's a bit tricky, see," he said, "but we'll have a bash. You need to practise, mind."

And he was right. You must practise often if you wish to clap with the dry, sharp sound of the *palmada* and at the same time stamp out the rhythm with the feet. I practise much, usually in bus queues. I keep warm and soon get the stop to myself.

I am not good at the *pito*, the finger-snapping. All the fingers on both hands must make a loud sound if it is to be done well. With the right hand it is not too bad but the left has the resonance of a bunch of bananas. I practise all the time even in bed and now live a life of great solitude.

For me the *caída* is nothing. It is that moment in the dance when the rhythm is at its most furious and the dancer falls flat on the face. For me this is easy, but I have much work to do on the *getting up again in the same breath-taking moment.*

I like to do the hammerstep. For this you must jump forward on to your left toe and slam the right heel down behind it. It is a powerful step and banned above ground level in all Adult Education *Institutos.* It pulls the floor away from the walls. A team of flamenco anarchists could destroy every bridge in London. I practise it wherever I find a parquet floor.

But there is one thing I can never master however much I practise: *el haughty look.* For this you must stand very straight and look over the cheek-bones to the proud swell of the bosom. I practise all the time but all I can ever see is my feet.

Why do I do this thing? Why spend all my spare time stamping and twitching and my spare cash at the shoe menders? Why do the rest of the class do it?

There is a printer who started so that he could keep his back from stooping and some nurses who find it gets rid of the tension that comes from being nice all day. There is a man who joined because he could not get into the photography class and some more who joined either because they saw *Carmen* or take their holidays in Spain. But these excuses are not the real reason.

I pretend I learn the flamenco for that time when I am an old one and take the Senior Citizens Winter Break to Spain. In those times I will wear tweeds, thick stockings and sensible shoes. The flamenco dancer who will be brought in to entertain the old *inglesa* will see me and choose me to be his partner to make a fool of me. But I will be magnificent. I will whip out my false teeth and as they chatter out the rhythm, my stout brogues will stamp out the *taconeo.*

But this is also an excuse. It is not the truth. For the truth is that the flamenco is a drug and once you have spent an evening sweating, stamping and oléing you wish to spend all your evenings doing it. Every time you master a step you have an appetite for a harder step. Each dance you learn makes you all the hungrier to learn a new one. It serves no purpose. It is an obsession.

But at least it got me off jigsaw puzzles.

BILL TIDY Messing About In Boaters

"In my day a boy accepted a sound thrashing rather than be sent home."

"They're remaking 'Lord of the Flies' or Scargill's Prime Minister!"

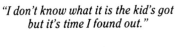

"I don't know what it is the kid's got but it's time I found out."

"Savvy? Anytime I want toast you make!"

"All right, all right, boy, it's a tax haven for most of the year!"

Alan COREN
IF WERNIT COMES

9043 BST 24601984

LOGON
?/Coren 4004

PASSWORD

? ******

OK
HI, ALAN. WELCOME TO GUARNAID DATABANE. GIVE THE NAME OF THE CATE⅝ORY YOU WANT. FOR HELP, TYPE "HERP".

? Winter

OK. SEARCHING FOR CATE⅝ORY "WERNIT".

WERNIT, IN BRIAN AT LEATS, CONSISTS OF FIVE MOTHS.

? Moth

A MOTH IS A SMALL WINDED INSERT. A MALE MOTH IS A FATH. A MOTH LAYS UP TO TED MILLION ERGS. A MOTH DOES NOT OF COURSE HAVE TO BIRNG THE ERGS UP. IN A MEANINGFLU RELATIONSHIM, THE FATH SHOULD BE AN EQUAL PARDON.

? Pardon

A MOTH IS A SMILE WINKED INVERT. A MALE MOTH IS A HAT. A

Delete.
? Winter

OK. SEARCHING FOR CATE⅝ORY "WIRNET".

WIRNET, IN BRAIN AT LAST, CONSISTS OF FIVE MOANS.

? Moans

OK. MOAN ONE: OF 6500000030 MEMBERS OF THE MOUSE OF COBBLERS, ONLY 234058009 ARE WIMMIN. THIS SITUATION IS QUIME INTOLERABLE IN A PARK RANGERS 3, MANCHESTER

UNTIED 5, AFTER EXTRA TILE. TAKE IN EXTRA COPY SHRLLGGLLBBB PLAYED A BLINDER IN MINEFIELD, FACED WITH THE TARDITIONAL 4-2-8-5½ FORMATION. ALL IN ALL, A GREAT MATHC, DESERVING A NIGGER CROWD.

? Pardon

A MATHC IS A SMART SINGED INSEVT. A MAIL MOTH IS A FART

Delete.
? Nigger crowd

OK. SEARCHING FOR CATE⅝ORY I DO NOT KNOW THIS WORM. DO NOT USE THIS WORM, ANAL. PLEASE RUN AGAIN.

? Worm

OK. SEARCHING FOR CATE⅝ORY "WORM".

THE THIRD WORM. MILLIONS OF PEOPLE IN THE THIRD WORM HAVE NEVER HAD ENUOGH TO MAKE A HOLEMEAL VEGAN FLAM USING ERCYCLED LINTELS, KIDLEY BEANS AND CARBAGE CORRECTION GARBAGE: BIRNG YOUR WOK UP TO 3 DEG FAHRENHEIT, MELT 2, MANCHESTER UNTIED 5, AFTER EXTRA TIT. ALL IN ALL, A GREAT MARCH, DESERTING A BIGGER CLOWN. MILLIONS OF BIGGERS, CORRECTION MILLIONS OF I DO NOT KNOW THIS WORM CORRECTION MILLIONS OF BUGGERS IN THE THIRD WORM ON EXACTLY WHAT IS THE PERCISE DEFINITION OF AN UNECONOMIC PIG. IS IT A PIG THAT HAS BEEN WORKED OUT OR MERLY A PIG WHERE IT WOULD BE UNERGONOMIC TO MIND THE REMAINING GOAL.

? Goal.

OK. SEARCHING FOR CATE⅝ORY "GOAL".

QUEERS PARK RANGERS 3, MANCHESTER UNTIED 5, AFTER EXTRA MIME.
ALL IN ALL, A

Delete.
? Winter

OK. SEARCHING FOR CATE⅝ORY "WITNER".

NOW IS THE WERNIT OF OUR DISCONTENT
MADE GLORIA SUMNER BY THIS TON OF PORK.

? Pork

OK. SEARCHING FOR CATEGORY "PORN".

PORN IS THE MATE OF A PIG BUT IS IT A PIG THAT HAS BEEN
WORMED OUT OR MERLY A PIG WHERE IT WOULD BE UN

Delete.
? Pig

OK. SEARCHING FOR CATEGORY "PIN".

DONT TALK TO ME ABOUT CHAUNIVIST PINS, I SLAVE MY
BOLODY GUTS OUT
OUT AT THE HOCKNEY WIMMINS AGAINST ROPE CORREC-
TION RAGE ALL MOANING, ALL AFTERNOON I AM RUINING
THE CAMPAIGN FOR KEEPING UNECONOMIC PIGS OPEN, I
PICK UP BABY SALVADOR FROM THE BISEXUAL TENDENCY
CROCHE CORRECTION CROTCH CORRECTION HUT, AND
WHEN I GET BACK TO THE SQUAT THE SEXIST BASTARD
EXPECTS TO SEE A HOG DINNER ON THE $ABLE, I HAVE HAD
ENUOGH OF THE SILLY CONT FOOT OF COLUMN FOUR TAKE
IN THREE LINES OF POPPY STARTING: WAS GOING LIKE A
DRAIN IN MIDFIELD, DELETE PLAYED A MINDER CORREC-
TION MINER, FINE AT FIRST BUT WINES FROM THE SOUTH-
NORTH-EAST TOWARDS EARNING AND LIGHT GRIZZLE.

? Grizzle

OK. SEARCHING FOR CATEGORY "GRIZZLE".

GRIZZLE FALLS ON YOU IN WERNIT.

? Wernit

OK. SEARCHING FOR CATEGORY I DO NOT KNOW THIS
WORM, LANA.

? Winter

OK. SEARCHING FOR CATEGORY "WERNIT".

WERNIT, IN BRINIAT AT LEAST, CONSISTS OF FIVE MYTHS,
INCLUDING BLEAK SEPTOBER, FREEZING CLOD NOM

? Bleak Septober

OK. SEARCHING FOR CATEGORY "BLEAK SEPTOBER".

BLEAK SEPTOBER IS A GORILLA MOVEMENT UNTIL THEY
GET CUAGHT. AFTER THEY GET CAUGHT, THEY BECOME
POISONERS OF CONSCIENCE. POISONER OF CONSCIENCE
NUMBER 83467.33, WEST BORMWICH ALBIONONI 4, REPLAY
THURSDAY AT MALE UNECONOMIC PIG, IS ABOU BEN
WARRISS, EARLESS LEADER OF THE DAMASCUS 9 SODDING
TRACKSUIT OFFER.

? Tracksuit offer

OK. SEARCHING FOR CATEGORY "TRAPSUIT OFFER".

THIS WERNIT, GO JODDING IN A BRUSHED KITTEN
"GURDNIA" SACKSUIT, PLEASE DO NOT STATE GENDER
WHEN ORDERING AS A REFUSAL SMOETIMES OFFENDS,
CHUST SIZES 32 – 7980/A/62, £17.99, GUARANTEED NITTED IN
THIRD WORM CONT FROM PAGE SIX BRESTFEED UNTIL AT
LEAST NINE MOTHS THEN ADD THE MELTED PARMISAN,
COVER THE WOK, AND LINK HANDS AROUND THE BASE, THE
WIMMIN UNTIED SHALL NEVER BE DEFEATED IN YESTER-
DAY'S EDITIONS DR MARIE STOAT SHOULD OF CURSE HAVE
READ DR MAISIE DOATES.

? Parmisan

OK. SEARCHING FOR CATEGORY "PARMISAN".

A PARMISAN IS ANOTHER NAME FOR A GORILLA BEFORE HE
IS CUAGHT AND BECOMES A POISONER OF CONSCIENCE.
GARY BALDY, TO QUOLE $\frac{1}{4}$ EXAMPLE, WAS A GRATE ITAL-
IAN PARMISAN, ADD PAPRIKA AND ORIGAMI TO TASTE,
TOSS LIGHTLY IN YOUR WEEK, COME BACK IN A WOK, AND
TELL ME TO MY FACE WHY WE SHOULD SUPPORT POLICIES
DESIGNED TO ENCOURAGE FASCIST JUDGES TO UPHOLE
THE NEO-NAZI FILTH IN THEIR CAMPAIGN OF GENOCIDE
AGAINST PORSTITUTES, MAKE THAT TWO EXCLAMATION
MARKS, TAKE IN CROSS-HEAD QUOTE JAW-JAW NOT
WHORE-WHORE UNQUOTE, COPY CONTINUES WHAT IS A
PORTSITUTE I ASK YOU EXCEPT A PERSON DETERMINED TO
KEEP OPEN AN UNECONOMIC PIT IN THE FACE OF INCREAS-
ING PLEASURE FROM THE GOAL BOARD, ACCORDING TO A
NUMB SPOMESPERSON TODAY. IF WE ARE IN FOR A LONG
HARD WERNIT, THEN SO BE IT, HE CONCLUNED.

? Wernit

OK. SEARCHING FOR CATEGORY FOR DOG'S SAKE, LANA, IF I
HAVE TOLD YOU ONCE I HAVE TOLD YOU A THUR A THUM A
THOG I DO NOT KNOW THIS WORM.

? Sorry, I do not und

OK. SEARCHING FOR CATEGORY "SOLLY".

SOLLY? IT WILL BE A BIT BOLODY LATE FOR SOLLY,
SUNSHITE, WHEN THE CURSE MISSILES ARE RAINING DOWN
ON HUMANPERSONS ALL OVER BRIAN, WHAT WE DEMAND
IS ACTION NOG BEFORE WE ARE ALL OF US PLUNGED INTO
UNCLEAR WERNIT, SIGNED A BISHOP, NAME AND DIOCESE
SUPPLIED, COMES IN GARY, BULE, AND NERGE, PLUS £1.20
FOR POTS AND PARKING, PLEASE MARK YOUR ENVELOPE
CLEARLY WITH THE WORM "TATSUIT" TO AVOID CONFU-
SION AND DELAY.

? Unclear wernit

OK. SEARCHING FOR CATEGORY "UNCLEAR WIRNET".

UNCLEAR WIRNET WILL BE THE LAST WIRNET OF ALL. IT
COULD HAPPEN BY DESIGN. IT COULD HAPEN BY MISTAKE. IT
CUOLD HAPPEN BY ACCIDENT. WHO KNOWS, LANA, IT
COULD EVEN HAPPEN BY COMPUTER ERROL.

MERRILY HARPUR

SINGLE BELLES

"The boring thing about you international playboys is that one could be anywhere."

" . . . But will we still be together when our tans are old and faded?"

"I'd better warn you – there are no hidden extras."

"I think I've forgotten how to do this."

"My eyelids slam down over my eyes in case she sees the pound sign pinging up like a cash register."

IT started with swapping: my set of jacks, one missing, for a tennis ball which was still impressively hairy but bounced like an apple; three crayons in yellow, pink and a reluctant burnt umber for a little wooden donkey on a pedestal, whose base, when depressed, caused the donkey's legs to give way, only some of the elastic had perished; a bra, all cotton, size 32A, for *Bamalama Bamaloo* by Little Richard (hellish hard, that last one, but the bra was a status symbol I couldn't be without).

Particularly strapped for cash one summer term, Mary Steele and I emptied out our desks and top drawers and arranged the – well, frankly – the detritus, the gubbins on to a tray, priced it, and trotted round the corridors selling the stuff. We displayed half-eaten erasers, broken pencils, lids off lost jars, bottles with no tops, Italian stamps, elastic bands, three sheets of crumpled airmail paper – nothing was too shabby or dingy for our sales push. In an hour we had sold every last gew-gaw and were the richer by £1 0s. 2d. As our whole term's pocket money was one pound, we were in a frenzy of wealth and excitement. We particularly congratulated ourselves on the sale of half a pair of scissors, which we told a junior girl "would be useful for something" (she was

a jumble addict if ever I've seen one). From my share, I paid 2/6d for a Parian ware figure of a boy picking something out of his toe at the school fête, but that takes me down a different track of serious collecting which doesn't concern us here. However, I have never forgotten the feeling of mild disappointment at the end of the tray sale: we had money, certainly, but our desks gaped too tidily, our blazer pockets were strangely uncluttered. I never want to know again that kind of gnawing emptiness (and indeed I never have). I decided to change sides: vendor into emptor.

I should like to introduce my parents at this stage. As with many married couples, one is a Normal and one a Jumblie. Brought up to see into both camps, my sister and I have worked out a kind of compromise: throw away regularly the real rubbish we have accumulated to make room for the next influx of life-enhancing bargains. It would not be untrue to say that the Jumblie in us has been handed down through the female side. Indeed, my mother has developed a spectacular new approach which involves "feeling sorry" for things and "giving them a kind home". This theme has emerged since the "bound to come in useful" or "almost the same colour" myth has been exploded. We now know, from her untiring example, that the jumble cup matcheth not any saucer neither shall the button ye purchase for a snip ever find a fellow. She plays a kind of cosmic Kim's Game, trawling in destitute knick-knacks, and no item is too large to escape her friendly compassion. Thus we have managed to train our own families to recognise the delights of differently patterned plates and the unparalleled thrill of wearing secondhand clothes. What is a whole Rockingham tea-set compared with one exquisite Rockingham milk-jug? Simply this: the second is easier to store, easier to admire (excess can glaze the eyes of appreciation; think of a roomful of Mona Lisas and you get the picture) and very much easier to buy.

My first chance for self-expression came when four of us shared a flat in Earl's Court in the first half of the Sixties. Since I was salaried at £8 a week before tax, there was not much boodle over to make the home Ideal. I shared with three other open-handed clutter addicts, however, and in no time we had chambers

fascinating enough to rival the British Museum. Our skilfully exhibited possessions included an ostrich egg, tin advertising signs, an old-fashioned camera, peacock feathers, long patterned pieces of cloth and a set of brass scales.

Readers growing restless will want to know our contacts, our sources. Nothing fell off the back of a lorry, although some things looked as though they had, and as though the lorry had been travelling at some speed when they did. We visited junk shops and street markets, of course, but the sight to raise blood pressure (be still, my beating heart) was a hand-drawn notice reading "Jumble Sale Church Room Today".

You see, in a street market the laser-eyed dealers are about; they will have snapped up the aces before you have stumbled from your bed, and re-priced them and put them into ritzy curio boutiques (but I once won a Tiffany lampshade in oyster-coloured glass, some beads missing, for £4 in Brick Lane). In a jumble sale you have only the organisers to outwit; if they don't know their onions they will sell them to you for peanuts.

Example given: a straining grey November afternoon near Chelmsford, a charity jumble sale, jolly few people about; my fingers sifting in the old cardboard box full of broken jewellery; suddenly I am holding a dirty pink and black brooch marked 3p ("It's only plastic, dear"); my eyelids slam down over my eyes in case she sees the pound sign pinging up like a cash register; I give her 10p (it *is* a charity) and I own a perfect eighty-year-old cameo, palest cream and shell pink, set in solid silver. In the same sale, an excellent dinner jacket and trousers for £2. It was only when I got them home that I saw that they must have belonged to Fat Daniel Lambert, as they would have hung loosely on Cyril Smith. So it's swings and roundabouts and which gambler could resist it?

At a good jumble sale, there will be a trestle table groaning with home-made cakes and pots of elderberry and rhubarb jelly, cheese straws and shortcake and stoneground, husk-whiskered, underfelt biscuits. There will usually be a fruit cake of immense proportions whose leaden weight you are invited to guess. This stall empties the quickest so many people

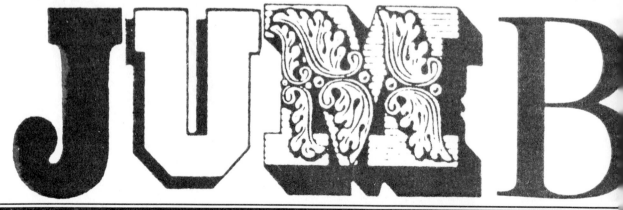

visit it first. Then there is a Soft counter selling peg-bags, small cushions, shoe-bags, cloth dolls, knitting-bags, aprons and bags. These, as they are all clean and new, are good Christmas presents as they can be received, kept in a drawer and sent off to another sale next year. Some bags have been doing the rounds for many years and have forgotten their original purpose. There is a Bottle stall where you will fix your eyes on a bottle of whisky and win some tomato ketchup or a dandruff shampoo. There is a Tombola, where you will win nothing. Then, on table after table, rack upon rail, the jumble itself.

There are several views on how it should be displayed. Some feel happiest when it is all thrown together, like a Russian salad: I prefer books here, records there, bric-à-brac further along, but I have a suspicion that if it is too well-sorted laser-vision will have had a look-in. Taken from their natural surroundings, each object assumes an incandescent desirability. Decide swiftly: don't ponder and wander on, for it will be gone when you return. Have as many arms as the goddess Kali and remember that the good-natured punters are in fact grasping fanatics, as untrustworthy as a short spit. Only when the fever is dying and the pocket is empty can you afford to be magnanimous ("Oh, that's lovely, well done, what a find, pity about the stain"). Drained, you take a cup of tea in a thick china mug. Such a feeling of achievement swarms over as you have never felt before (since the last time). Later, you will pore and gloat over your booty, polishing and washing and boasting.

I am sometimes asked to officiate at charity jumble sales or fêtes, or Fayres as they're occasionally called. I warn them with quiet insistence that I will not be making a speech, no, cannot be persuaded. Two reasons (which I do not give) are these: first, I am awful at public speaking; and second, and far more important, once when I did attempt a few words ("Great pleasure . . . worthy cause . . . blah . . . do spend . . . "), I saw at the far end of the hall a stout, tweed-coated woman had jumped the gun and was negotiating in whispers over the price of a Coalport tureen. So now, barely pausing by the microphone to shout, "Good afternoon it's open," I hurl myself, elbows out, into the crowd of human locusts.

"Oh, the little people still come at night, but they'll only do stick-on soles nowadays."

"It's funny, really – when your father's at home he never says a word."

NB

DRESSING DOWN

My friend (some might say *Doppelgänger*) over there shares with me a certain incredulity regarding the Style section earlier in this organ. Why? What do you mean, Why?

Oh, for heaven's sake. Look: on the one hand you have all these people writing about style or advertising their stylish goods, and on the other you just have to poke your nose out of the window. The British of 1985 are the most slumped, shuffling, depressed, ill-dressed, grubby, seedy looking bunch you could see. One wouldn't want to tread in them. All the efforts of writers and merchants to put some **visual pep** into the bastards are doomed to failure, as far as I can see, for the simple reason that the British male has absolutely no personal vanity.

People will tell you that **vanity** is a sin, but that is nonsense. Vanity, unless unrestrained, is a treat for other people. It is what makes you easy on the eye. Without vanity, you end up with people looking like . . . looking like . . . oh, we've got one of those awful food joints round the corner and the chap has got, hanging in the window, those terrible, stale, white, German, veal-'n'-dead-pig sausages with blotches on, the sort of things you'd expect to find a broken-off bit of hypodermic needle in where the pig has been injected against something and the injection has failed, and the pig has died and been crammed into the hateful bladder like a Christmas sock . . .

And that's the image of the Briton, really: a **pallid stale bladder of greasy meat**, somehow magically animated, stood on end (retaining, of course, the characteristic curve or slump) and dressed in turd-coloured clothes. Perhaps I have hit upon a philosophical truth here concerning the nature of the origins of Man; perhaps all that stuff about breathing life into the clay was a nice euphemism for an unpalatable truth, in which case can you imagine being God and having to *do* that? Or perhaps not.

The significant thing is not the origins of man but his current state, this being a weekly magazine, and frankly his current state is pretty awful. My friend having kindly bared his all, let us dress him up to take his place among the great mass of the British people.

One starts, of course, with the **skin**. This should be greasy and grey-ish as if from a long immersion in the sort of liquid which collects in the gutters of an East Midlands small engineering factory. It should also not fit properly, being loose round the thighs and distended over the stomach.

Hair comes next. Again, it should be greasy, unwashed and badly cut, unless our Monster is in that mysterious craft called "say-ulss", in which case it should be dry as a bone and rigid. Hair should also be provided in other regions, most notably the **moustache**. Anthropologists

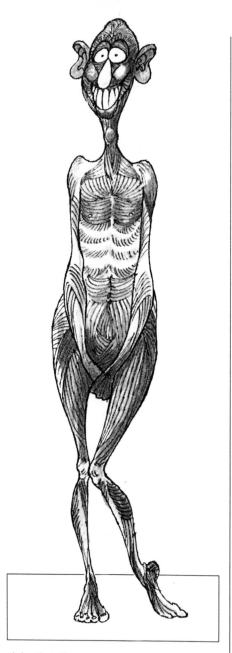

claim that the moustache is a mimic of the pudenda, and quite rightly so; you only have to look around you to see the truth of that. There should also be imperfectly-shaved hair on the face and, inexplicably, a **stubbly patch** behind the left ear.

Spots are being worn at the corner of the mouth this season.

Next comes the **underwear**. This should consist of **nylon ankle socks** (colour: dog-end) with the elastic gone in the top of the left-hand-foot one; a pair of **pale blue nylon briefs** with a hole in the armpit of the left leg; and a **vest** (colour: vest) long enough to tuck into the pants and out of the leg holes again.

This alluring *lingerie* is mercifully covered by the *shirt*. This garment (colour: stain) should wherever possible have a pattern of **little dogs** on, but do not despair: the eye of the Briton is such that, even when he picks out a shirt which does *not* have a pattern of little dogs on, it will,

once worn, look as though it does have. Buttons should be left undone at neck and navel; by a miracle of nature, the vest, though long enough to poke out of the underpants legs, does not cover the **navel**, which is therefore visible through the gaping shirt.

Trousers this season are being worn extra long so that the bottoms drag in the mud as the wearer shuffles along. Preferred shade can only be described as "trousers-coloured", and fashion high points are (a) a prominent darn in the **gusset** region, caused by the modern Briton's habit of nervously scratching at his **privates** and (b) a waistband that turns over on itself at certain points, thus ejecting the shirt, which has no tails.

For street wear, **shoes** are still *de rigueur*, (colour: old meat pie; material: pastry) and for the true British look they should *never, ever* be polished. And, of course, the **anorak** (colour: bogey) is still *the* garment for shambling along in. It has all the characteristics of true British style: it is fundamentally and irredeemably ugly; it accentuates the natural stoop of British shoulders; it has a greasy sheen to it which rapidly acquires that patina of filth so prized by Britons; and, whatever your figure, it reduces your shape to that of an old bin-liner stuffed with curdled blancmange.

Accessories are few but should be carefully chosen: a cheap digital watch, a pair of spectacles lightly dusted in scurf, a plastic briefcase (colour: cheeseburger), a greasy headdress of imitation tweed.

Some of you will say, "What about the upwardly mobile?", to which I reply: they are *not* upwardly mobile at all; they are simply mobile, buzzing round and round like beastly flies. But examine their dress and you will find that on the whole they are spiritually, if not in every detail, as described above. There are exceptions. But the rule holds on the whole. Italian and French men look as if they have taken trouble to choose their clothes in the morning and to wash and shave. We assume it is because they are excitable Southerners looking for sex with women. I don't think it is. I think it's pride and vanity – and good for them. Our pride is in having no pride, and the result is that we walk around looking as if we don't give a toss, don't care, have no hope, enjoy nothing and are just waiting for the rain to stop so that we can squelch home to our cold, grey fried eggs and our cold grey greasy deathbeds.

And yet . . . Savile Row, Jermyn Street, Simpson, Burberry, Gieves and Hawkes, Aquascutum, Herbie Frogg, Paul Smith, Tommy Nutter, a whole litany of stylish names. Why do Britons ignore them and walk around looking like something that ought to be scooped up and chucked in a sack? We ought to be ashamed of ourselves, but we haven't even got the collective balls for that.

Pot and Crucible

Dear Stan,

Well here I am wholed up in my hotel room near the Crucible Thaeter in Sheffeild, according to the Press it is merely a temporary restbite in my unstopable progress to the World Title or something along that pattern, but you know and I know it is a chance for a bloody good snort up so cheers Stan and thanks, this stuff is the berrys as they say.

Well I have had an easy tornament so far you probably saw where Dingo Yatterbury the Australion International showed up yesterday with his eyeballs hanging out due to you know what and I polish him of by 10 frames to 2, I don't know how many balls he was seeing at a time but he certinly didn't pick the right one to hit. I had some laghs in the game i.e. the 2nd Frame when Dingo asked the Ref Len Figgis to clean up the cue ball where there is a speck of dust on it, well of coarse Len put his little percepex marker on the spot and picks up the ball and polish the ball round and round in his fingers with his white gloves on, then he replaces the ball and here is the funny part Stan. As he steps back from the table without thinking about it he pinches his nose and sort of sniffs like you do and boomf, you can see he have blown the top of his head off nearly. I seen it on the play-back and you could see day light under his wig for a couple of 2nds, and the Commontator goes "the cue ball must of picked up a speck of chork or dirt in the coarse of play", ha ha some speck of dirt Stan you will of laght if you seen it.

We have got a lot of Press a-round in Sheffeild all sniffing a-round wanting to know about Drugs and asking daft questions i.e. "Is it true Pot Black is named after this special mariwhana the snooker players smoke" and etc. But in any case most of the Press are too pissed to know weather they are looking at a Junky or not. They don't sit near the players in the Thaeter so they don't even smell Ty-Phoon Tony Clegg when he starts up. The Ty-Phoon have got a new dodge where he comes in and start smoking the sponsers snout, puff puff drag drag big breaths you know and that soleful look on his face while he does it becos he reckons the sponseres will bung you a nice little sweetenor on the side if you do that. But anyway as soon as there is something happening on the table like Taffy Prosser having one of his tan-trums then the Ty-Phoon swiches the packets of fags substiting the one he brung in which have got the sponsers name on the packet but you know and I know the cigs is all crammed with Lesbianese Gold or what ever hi-grade stuff the Ty-Phoon have picked up at the docks. Soon he is sitting there in a flagrant cloud or on one as the case may be. Nobody have objected so far and the sponsers love it becos the Ty-Phoon is sitting there spouting smoke with an even more soleful than usual look on his dyall, it make no difference to his game he is an idiot what ever you give him to smoke.

Did you see the telly coveredge this a.m. well that was another scream Stan they had the Entry of the Gladeaters as usual where Taffy Prosser comes down the steps looking in

"Ty-Phoon is sitting there spouting smoke with an even more soleful than usual look on his dyall"

a better mood than usual probaly becos he have seen what is coming along behind, I mean Wayne Nurberger of Canada with eyes sticking out like Chapple Hat Peggs making the likes of Dingo Yatterbury the Australion International look allmost normal (xcept for the ears). Anyway there is a big smile on Wayne's face but it is soon wiped of when he reolizes that the hyperdermic Stringe is still sticking out of his bum where it have been stuck in by his faithful vallè Ron. You can see the litening calc-u-lation going through his mind – "shall I pretend to be a Die-a-betic, and etc?" – but no he decides against it and back come the smile across his chops and he backs up the stairs sharpish and out of the Thaeter again. The dum TV audiance probaly think the video have gone into reverse so no body is any the wiser xcept us back-stage where Wayne Nurberger is nocking Seven Bells out of his faithful vallè Ron. You have got to have a giggle Stan otherwise this game is nothing but money.

Its Drugs, Drugs Drugs here, I have had lots of Fans ask me what do I think about the Drug Mennis, I never know what to say i.e. something like "Well Im glad you ask me that question while Ive still got a nose" and etc. well I never do say that but you felt like saying it to see what they will do, you get fed up of them going ooh and ah all the time. They go ah if you get it right and ooh if you cock it up and beyond that they dont know the time of day, Taffy Prosser says half the punters think a deep screw is a thinking man's prison officer well he ought to know.

Well Stan tomorrow I have got Flash Nevinson the naturalized South African, I will naturalize him all right, seriously he is no problem. No great shakes I was going to say but great shakes is just what he has got until he gets about a quarter lb bag of Valiums down him, you should see him when he gets there in the morning I mean we all look like death but the way he looks you would not like to burden an under-taker with it. Flash is not all he is cracked up to be, I know a bird here who have spent the night with Flash and she says he would only lay there muttering "Foul Stroke" which she says it put her off hers anyway. Well snooker is a funny game isnt it.

Well Stan I have got that David Vine's Auto-Graph for you, suprise suprise he can right as well as go shopping for pull overs. He is alright realy but you have to get use to him talking to you as if you was a Camra all the time. I tell you, if us snooker players had an Auto-Cue we would all be millionaires eh? You have really

"Take a couple of these pills and I guarantee that you'll fly."

LET'S PARLER FRANGLAIS!

L'Arts Sponsorship

Le bureau du boss de Multi-World. Le buzzer sonne.

Boss: Oui?

Intercom: C'est M. Blitz pour vous voir . . .

La porte s'ouvre. Entre le dynamique M. Blitz.

Blitz: Vous êtes le boss de Multi-World?

Boss: Oui, mais . . .

Blitz: Je suis ici pour transformer votre compagnie! Maintenant, vous êtes un boring, run-of-the-moulin, interglobal firm. Mais avec moi, vous serez un patron des arts! Un symbole de culture!

Boss: Ah, non, ah, non! Vous êtes encore un rep de l'Arts Council!

Blitz: Pas du tout. Je suis un spokesman pour le Midway Theatre Group. Donnez-nous £50,000 et vous serez un homme heureux.

Boss: Look, sunshine. Chaque jour j'ai des spokesmen pour les arts dans mon bureau sur la scrounge. £50,000 pour une théâtre, £100,000 pour le ballet, £1m pour un Vincent van Loony. Je dis toujours: Scram!

Blitz: Moi, je suis différent. Si vous donnez £50,000 pour la production de *Charlie's Tante* par Midway Theatre, je vous donne – un walk-on part!

Boss: Quoi?

Blitz: Oui, vous pouvez jouer un role minuscule mais satisfaisant, comme le manservant. C'est un caméo, mais un caméo brillant.

Boss: *Moi*? Jouer un *manservant*?

Blitz: Vous n'avez pas de confiance? Mais si, vous serez superbe! Je vois d'ici les reviews: "Un tycoon . . . et maintenant un thespien!" "Faîtes garde à vos laurels, Olivier!"

Boss: C'est ridicule . . . mais c'est attractif.

Blitz: Imaginez-vous . . . la camaraderie de la Chambre Verte . . . le gossip de back-stage . . . le back-stabbing . . .

Boss: J'ai beaucoup de ça à Multi-World.

Blitz: Un kit de make-up *personnel*. Une *costume*. Votre photo dans le programme . . .

Boss: J'admire votre cheek. OK, d'accord.

Blitz: Bon! Maintenant, le painting . . .

Boss: Quel painting?

Blitz: Un painting par mon protégé d'un Royal Jardin Party à Buck House – avec *vous* dans le background!

Boss: OK. Combien?

Blitz: £50,000. Et le ballet . . .

Boss: Ah, non! Vous voulez que je danse?

Blitz: Non, non. Mais le Forward Ballet Group présente une nouvelle production, *Le Big Business*. Un ballet interglobal, quoi. Et si on avait "Multi-World" sur les leotards, £100,000.

Boss: Vous êtes un supersalesman. OK . . . Vous ne voulez pas, par hasard, travailler pour Multi-World?

Blitz: Pas du tout. Je suis dans le business sponsorship. C'est ma vie. Et c'est la profession du futur.

Boss: OK. Quand commencent les rehearsals pour *La Tante de Charlie*?

---

got to lagh, Stan.

Will you send some comix I got nothing to read here xcept the hotel Menu and the program from the Cruncible which is lod of tosh i.e. "Tommy Wiggins is a miss spent youth" and etc. which I never said and me Dad will kill me if he finds out. The whole thing gets up my nose which remind methanks again Stan for the nazal spray if you know what I mean it has fit in very nicely with my plans as the Actrice said to the Bishop. It is very boring here, sometimes when I look at the telly and see us on again I think snooker is just two blokes putting on a computer game that you do not even have to play. Call me asinic if you like,

> you probaly will
> You misreable old Sod
> Yours in sport
> Tommy

P.S. I met this old bint at a Reception that plays Crokey for the County and stone me if she dont ask me for some stuff as they have a big Crokey game coming up. Well I flogged her some I just hope she was not married to the Police Fedration or anything, dont worry I will keep your name out of it. Keep on potting. 🌀

Denis Pirie, a civil servant and former member of the National Front, has been allowed to keep his job as an adviser on export sales to the Department of Trade and Industry.

The Needed Civil Servant

"If Hitler were alive today
And he had won the war" –
The smile he managed to display
Was like an oven-door –
"I would have reached a higher rank
And had a Merc to drive;
I should have Deutschmarks in the bank,
If Hitler were alive."

"I might have served the Master Race,"
He heaved a heavy sigh,
"Instead of which, I know my place
And serve the DTI."
Then brightened, "But it's nice to note,"
(His Leader on the wall)
And buttoning his leather coat,
"I'm needed in Whitehall."

Roger Woddis

"Yes, O High One, one previous conviction."

SINCLAIR DYNAMO HAT & Rodent Polisher Set, 1903

SINCLAIR PORTABLE CHANNELPROOF BOOKCASE, personally designed and built for Captain Matthew Webb, who went down with it, 1883

SIR OSWALD SINCLAIR C5 MINIBUS, 1924

JAMES SINCLAIR (fl. 1944) Coke-Fired Stereo TV Set

GENERAL SIR HARRISON SINCLAIR (1847-1919) with the Electric Leg for which he received the freedom of Lerwick prior to his seizure in 1911

Clay miners at work beneath the BRITISH SINCLAIR HEAVY FURNITURE PLANT, Orange Free State, c. 1880

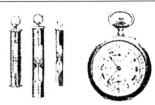

SINCLAIR BROS. BOWEL LAMPS & PANCREOMETER, carried by Dr Livingstone into the Congo, and left there

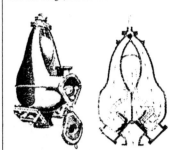

SINCLAIR (GRAND CAYMAN) LTD BULLET-PROOF DICKIE, as worn by Archduke Ferdinand, 1914

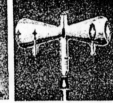

Early SINCLAIRPHONE (1901), enabling people standing next to one another to communicate almost effortlessly. It later formed the basis for the (below) 1903 SINCLAIR HAND MINCER, subsequently withdrawn when it did exactly that

The NORMAN SINCLAIR (1871-1928) Steam Butler

SINCLAIR EXTREMITISER, developed in the early 19th C. to facilitate toenail clipping between nuns on different floors

Two great early Sinclairs, SIMON (called Geoff) Sinclair (1701-1773), inventor of the sprout press, and COSIMO Sinclair (c. 1540-c. 1590), who accompanied Erasmus on his first journey to the bank

The doomed SINCLAIRSHIP PATENT MAST, photographed in 1931 just before it crashed in flames, leaving the R33 to float irretrievably away

The ISADORA SINCLAIR C9 ELECTRIC SLED. The batteries were good for nearly 19 yards, after which propulsion was taken over (below) by a team of Pocket Calculator Salesmen

Ornately decorated lavatory fittings recovered from the wreck of the MARY SINCLAIR

SINCLAIR GENTLEWOMAN'S HELICOPTER, 1919, Gladys Cooper up. She has not yet begun to flap

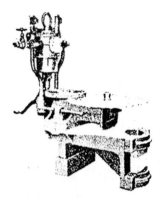

EAMONN SINCLAIR (né Mooney) C3 BIDET FOR THE INSANE, 1893, with (below) EXTENDABLE RESTRAINING SWATTER

SINCLAIR PATENT BECKONER, 1937. When the rubber bulb was squeezed by the left hand, the right forefinger bent

LORD PERCY SINCLAIR OF THAT ILK (1828-1911) with his ELECTRIC VALET, the batteries of which have just run out

HOLTE
TABLE MANNERS

"Come on, Gordon! The Japanese evening was your idea. How do I get the little bastard to let go of the plate?"

"I'm terribly sorry, sir, but it does say on the menu 'with peas' . . ."

"How do you expect to grow up big and strong like Daddy if you won't eat?"

"Excuse me – can we see the vegetarian menu please?"

FRANK KEATING

Trooping the Colour

I HAVE seen Manchester United play twice this season. Both times they wore *white* shirts. The *Red* Devils as lillywhites! Oh dear, oh dear. . . Arsenal trotted out a couple of weeks ago in sickly yellow. Why have the gunners forsaken their cock-robin chests of cherry?

Football teams which still retain their distinctive colours of legend are an endangered species. It is, alas, much to do with the greed of men who know the price of everything and the value of nothing. A decade or so ago, some teams started changing their shirts for the decent enough reason that a colour clash might spoil the enjoyment of television viewers – as in the commentator's time-honoured explanation,"For those of you with black-and-white sets, Everton are in the blue." But now a monochrome TV set is as rare as the beloved ancient monochrome strip of Fulham – I saw *them* playing in garish red last month!

It was fair enough in olden days that visiting trainers packed an "away strip" in the laundry-basket skip if the contest was between identical colours – say when the claret-and-blue of Aston Villa met the identical from West Ham or Burnley. Now it is much more cynical than that. In colour schemes, as in everything else, sponsors want their pound of primaries. Clubs thoughtlessly change their shirts on anybody's whim – usually that of their sponsors or the managers of their own knick-knack souvenir "boutiques" – for a regular new strip, even with the most subtle of changes, means the kids will nag their parents for replicas, all exorbitantly gift wrapped.

Not only have the traditional colours and patterns been changed: Hunter's Hotspurs have shirts now embroidered with *Holsten*, Mr Maxwell's Oxford with Mr Maxwell's *Sunday People*, QPR with *Guinness*, Chesterfield with *Coalite*, and Rochdale, believe it or not, with *The All-in-One Garden Centre*. Indeed, of the 92 League clubs only about a dozen are not in the pay of sponsors now.

Unless it is already too late, hurry, hurry for a last glimpse of the legendary shirts of generations – the stripes of Newcastle's magpies, or the verticals of Albion and both Sheffields, QPR's hoops, Blackburn's "halves", or Bristol Rovers' "quarters", the old gold of Wolves, the canary of Norwich, or the gingery-tangerine of Blackpool that was worn by Matthews and Mortenson and exactly matched the crinkly hair of Alan Ball.

And yet. . . is it all romance once you delve even skimmingly? How long is a legend? When do *traditions* qualify as *history*? For instance, the fact is that time immemorial's Red Devils of Manchester United have, since they were Newton Heath FC, played in the following colours: green and gold (till 1896); white (till 1902); red (1923); white (1927); for the first half of the 1934 season they wore white shirts with cherry hoops before settling on plain red shirts with white shorts. Have Liverpool FC always been the Reds of Anfield, and Everton the Blues of Goodison? *No*, as they say, *way*. When they first played each other, in 1893, Liverpool were in shirts of royal blue and white quarters, Everton in "ruby" tops and black shorts.

Can anyone north of the Border imagine the Scotland International team playing in anything but royal blue? Well, till 1900 they were adorned in primrose-and-pink hoops, in genuflection to the racing colours of the Scottish FA president, Lord Archibald Philip *Primrose* Rosebery!

International rugby union teams have been more historically consistent. When England first played Scotland at Raeburn Place in 1871, Scotland played in blue guernseys, badged, as still today, with a thistle and laurel-leaf cluster. England played in all-white with a red rose at the left breast, as agreed at the RFU's second-ever committee meeting in Blackheath. They have never changed.

One might have expected the British Lions rugby touring side to have remained in the same garb since their first tour in 1888, so obvious is their outfit of red shirts (for Wales), white shorts (England), and green "turnovers" (Ireland) to their stockings of Scottish blue. Not a bit of it, the strip was first used by Karl Mullen's side to New Zealand as long ago in the mists of history as 1950.

The All Blacks of New Zealand were called the Kiwis when they arrived in Britain in 1905. They hired a set of dark blue guernseys to play in. At once they started a string of runaway victories in the South with a style of play which necessitated every man in the side being fast, fit and athletic (unlike the English who picked lumbering forwards and only nippy backs: nothing's changed). For their sixth game, the Kiwis travelled up to Hartlepool, then the stronghold of the union game. The leading Fleet Street sportswriter of the day was a Mr Vivian. On the eve of the match against Hartlepool, his article – describing their play – was sent overnight on the train, accompanied by a set of billboards saying THEY ARE ALL *BACKS*. The local newsagent, unaware of rugby tactics and positions, thought it was a spelling mistake when he was told the colour of their jerseys. He changed the posters to All *BLACKS*. It stuck.

Apart from Edinburgh Academicals (1857), Scotland's oldest surviving rugby club is West of Scotland from Glasgow's Milngavie, which

"OK, lady. Let me see all the pictures of your grandchildren."

decided on its founding in 1865 to play in red-and-gold as some sort of homage to the traditional high tea of the city – eggs and boiled bacon. They remain the club colours.

Arguably the most famous of any club rugby side is Llanelli – the *Scarlets*, as they are known the world over. Their history, written by Gareth Hughes, is far and away the most colourful and comprehensive of its type I have read. The Scarlets use to play in black. Hughes quotes extensively from the *Llanelli & County Guardian*:

Sept. 8, 1881. At the meeting of the Football Club on Tuesday it was resolved that colours be changed from black to primrose-and-rose. Several members seemed dissatisfied. . . . (and) the Gen-eral Meeting was declared null & void. . .

Sept 22. On Saturday last Llanelly [sic] FC made its first appearance of the season on the Stradey grounds. It was expected that the players would have appeared in their new colours, but evidently the choice of the Committee has not met with entire approval. We should like to see that all members play in football costume, not only for the sake of appearance, but for their own sake as the number of shirt sleeves left on the field would clothe a small parish.

Dec 29. On Monday last the Newport team wore amber & black jerseys with stockings to match, and Llanelly primrose-and-red, making a very striking contrast. . . .

August 16, 1883. There was a large attendance at the a.g.m., held at the Thomas Arms, Tuesday evening last, and the tone of the meeting was highly enthusiastic. . . New colours – red and chocolate quarters – were selected for the coming season.

April 17, 1884. Llanelly versus Irish International team. The Llanelly team were first on the ground, making their first ever appearance in full scarlet colours, their scarlet gold-laced caps adding much to their bright appearance. . . .

The Scarlets were born.

Colour had traditionally been woven through Sport before even Tom Brown won his house colours at Rugby School. Even as the flanelled fools of cricket insist on their pristine, Persilled whites, they set mighty store on the lore, emblemism and a precise colour charting of their caps and ties. Pity the clubman who cannot recognise his stripes and quarters.

After one village game, I was almost felled by a withering gaze after remarking to an opponent how quirky and quaint it had been to see him bat with an old necktie serving as a belt and holding up his trousers – rather like WG, I had said. "This tie, sir," he sneered, "predates Grace: do you not recognise the magenta, violet, green and gold of the oldest cricketing tie in the world, sir – the Eton Ramblers, sir, founded in 1862, sir." Er, sorry, sir.

You must similarly never fail to recognise the Harlequin (ex-Oxford) cap of dark blue, buff and maroon; the Incogniti splodge of purple, yellow and black; not to forget the snooty crimson, green and cream of the Free Foresters.

And try not to effect a batting partnership ever with a chap in an I Zingari cap – or with said black, red and gold ribbon about his midriff. He will presume to bag all the slow bowling. IZ is, by the way, the traditional "wandering" side: the name simply means *The Gypsies* in Italian. And if ever you fancy wearing their tie without (horrors) being a member, be certain to make the knot with the gold strip, for they insist their colours symbolise a decent chap's "ascent out of darkness, through fire, into light". They can be rather patronising old fellows, and I wouldn't be surprised if they had a secret handshake. Through their history they have refused to "hire" a pro. One batsman founded the cricketing dictum – "Always run on principle to anyone wearing an IZ cap."

Remember how the cricket establishment gave Mr Kerry Packer an awful coshing when he had his floodlit "World Series" stars dressing up in pinks and powder blues a few years back? Yet nothing's new, Billy Beldham's first cricket club at Hambledon in the 1770s wore "coats of sky-blue, with collars in black velvet; knee breeches, stockings, and shoes with gilt buckles, engraved with CC for Cricketing Club".

Katharine Whitehorn, as she does with most things, puts all the folklore and romance of sporting colours in place. She wrote: "I cannot for the life of me see why the umpires, the only two people on a cricket field who are not going to get grass stains on their knees, are the only two people allowed to wear dark trousers."

"If any man here knows why this couple should not be wed, sit on it."

BASIL BOOTHROYD
Our Next Four Years

REACHING the other Monday's paper off the mat and falling over a bit on my left elbow, I was amused to find the Fleet Street boys, even on Inauguration Day + 1, still sounding off about our great age. Mine and Reagan's, that is.

I call them boys in no patronising way. Or try not to. It's bound to creep in. Most of them weren't born when I was already a grown man of fifty, owning most of a house and several suits, but not yet apt to fall over sideways when stooping.

Come to that, I'd been knocking around for nearly a year before Reagan was born, so put that in your oath and swear at.

No, that's not respectful. Though retaining, in general, more faculties than I know what to do with, I confess to being lost for a phrase sometimes. Let's say put that in your dummy and bubble it.

In any case, I'm prepared to accept Mr President as a contemporary, and forget that seniority carries delusions of superiority, rough-hew them how we will. You can't expect me, at 74, to be serious about some stripling millionaire like Clive Sinclair, say, barely pushing 45, and I shall be surprised if Reagan doesn't feel the same about some of his unfledged FBI men, presuming to warn him about rucks in the red carpet that could trip the sprightliness out of him just when he wants to look his best for prime time.

The fact is that once you accept a proneness to tripping, falling sideways, or wrecking a pyramid of Tesco catfood with a careless movement of the wallet, you adjust accordingly. Those who don't will simply have to get used to being helped up by strangers and asked if they're all right. In the old days – call that young days – you took a bottle of milk from the fridge and poured it without even noticing what you were doing. Later the time comes when you bend your mental powers, if not irrevocably impaired, on ensuring a firm grip on the ridged bit round the top. Every day and in every way, as Dr Coué used to put it, I am holding this milk bottle tighter and tighter.

That's how to manage without dropping it, even if a pushy aide does ask you in the nick of time why you're pouring white wine on her cornflakes, or muesli is now the word, try and keep up, and it's better than forgetting what you'd gone to the fridge for in the first place, such as your other glasses or the car keys.

Don't try and keep up too much, Ronald, would be my advice as a slightly older man. You can master an in word like muesli, and the first time you work it into a conversation it can have gone out, exposing you to laughter as an over-striver. Nor too down, either, throwing names like Dr Coué around, which mean as much to a mere 45-year-old millionaire as fighting on the beaches to a groupie, if people are still saying groupie, and I wouldn't have left him in back there if I hadn't wanted to go on about doctors anyway, who keep worrying about ageing.

Not their own, not yet. Yours and mine, and others aged beyond recall such as J. B. Priestley, who was saying in a near-posthumous announcement that there were some days when it was a triumph just to get your trousers on. Rubbish. Swallow your pride and sit down for it. Feel no shame. No one cackled at Methuselah for that.

Besides, the real trick is getting them off. You haven't adjusted. Just because it's a seventy-odd year routine as natural as breathing you think a smart pull on each leg will do it. When it only does one, and leaves a sock in that, and you're left hopping backwards into the spare room or Oval Office, snatching support from a propped-up feather duster, or Stars and Stripes as the case may be, it's time to remember birthdays past and watch yourself. Do that, and you'll fool all of the people most of the time. They'll think you're as young as you feel even if you don't look it. Breathe naturally.

Check that your flies are done up. This probably doesn't have to be said to an actor, but little things can give you away, and we haven't all been brought up on make-up men and continuity girls.

Doctors – I thought for a minute I'd lost the thread of these remarks, which can happen, and if I had a tele-prompter in the sitting-room I shouldn't always be down there wondering what I was going to say to my aide, and have to come up again hunting the desk for a clue, such as the phone off the hook or no handkerchief –

You can't open a paper these days, though physically it's only a matter of working a finger between the pages, without reading that doctors, then, are trying to solve the mystery of the ageing process. All I say on that is that one thing that rubs off on you as the birthdays pass is a bit of commonsense. Not a lot has rubbed off on me, beyond the odd basic (if you take the lid off a paint can don't stand the can in the lid, you could be searching the whole house), but I can see the foolishness in wasting good laboratory time that could be more usefully spent on finding why my right thumbnail stopped growing around Suez in 1965. 1956. The secret of the ageing process is that people grow older, so stop playing with docs, you rats. Get on to thumbnails, or the mental reversal syndrome that causes senior citizens not only to write 1965 when they were trying for 1956, or transpose rats and doctors, but to switch off any light that's on when they go into their workroom and wonder why it's suddenly gone dark.

Still, not to worry if you're doing that, Mr President. It can come to us all. And you're well placed for aides. Fifty years your junior they may be, but when they see you with things back to front, whether it's trousers or skipping down from a visiting aircraft and saying goodbye to the receiving line, they're in there sorting you out.

If you share my arrested nail problem I don't know what they can do about that. At the risk of seeming pious, it's probably between you and your make-up. Maker. Still, leave it at make-up, which between you and me in this fireside chat, I occasionally use myself for the knuckles. My aide assists. No. 2 barrier cream. This is because we aren't as young as we used to be in the matter of steering dead centre through doorways and never giving a thought to the hand that loses station and cracks itself on the knob.

A small point. But the last thing we want for four more happy returns, apart from some callow 40-year-old leaping up to offer us his seat in a crowded bus or Congress, is any smears about premature decomposition, right?

When we're past it, start mixing up people's names and so forth, we'll be the ones to say, and not read it on one elbow by the mat. And talking of elbows, more power to yours. You're a credit to the whole class of 1910-1911, Jimmy Carter. ✍

"Why, Miss Bates, has anyone told you how attractive
you are without your glasses?"

STANLEY REYNOLDS

A Grubby Business

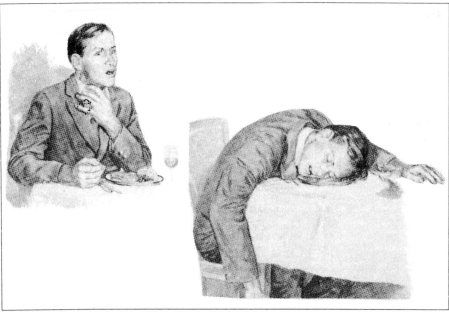

A gourmand pegs down, from **The Official Foodie Handbook** (*Ebury Press* £8.95).

Chomp, chomp, chomp. Gobble, gobble, gobble.

"Oh, waiter, my compliments to the chef. This is the best oeuf poule au caviar I've had since Fernand Point was at La Pyramide in Vienne, or was it Alexandre Dumaine at the Côte d' Or at Saulieu?"

Chomp, chomp. Smack, smack.

Hey, I know this pig. I worked with him, on the *Liverpool Echo* for gawd's sake. Back in 1960. Pints of beer. Wallop, he called it. Somewhere along the line he has become a pig, a gourmand, a foodie. Listen to him now: "Oh, yes, he took over Barthélémy's Les Prés et Les Sources d'Eugénie."

Christ, it's like a foreign language. In fact it is a foreign language. Him, what's his name, from Garsfield Road, Clubmoor, Walton, Liverpool 4, always going on about how you couldn't get thick steamed tripe any more down at the Co-op. Must have gone somewhere to learn all that étouffée of crayfish tails stuff. Gone to some school. Like wine tasting. Probably spit it out on the floor, too, at the foodie school. Taste some grub. Then spit it out. He'd do something like that. Sure he would. Chomp away on God only knows what and then spit it out, go on to something else. Or maybe they actually swallow it at this school and then stick their fingers down their throats. A slice of saucisson de Lyon and then puke. Learn about it that way I suppose.

"*What will you have, sir?*" the waiter asks me.

"*I'll have the thick soup for Chris' sake. What the hell do I look like I'll have?*"

Christ, I hope he chokes to death. Small chance of that. Not when he chomps like that. Chomping like that you don't just pick up on street corners, down the caff, that's high class chomping all right, he learned that at college. Still, there's always hope. Three thousand Americans a year die from choking in restaurants. Choking on food, sixth leading cause of death in the US. We can't be far behind. What's he talking now? Sashimi, sunomo, katsuobushi. He's talking Japanese. Zen Buddhist foodie. Ought to be able just to *think* it. Metaphysical chomping, no cooking, no eating, no bills.

"Yuki at the Kitcho," he says to the waiter.

"I don't know that, sir. Tokyo?"

"No, no, not *Tokyo!*" as if how could this waiter possibly think anyone ever ate anywhere in Tokyo any more.

"Osaka, actually," he says. "23 – 3 Chome Koraibashi, Hi- gashi – Ku ."

Say, that's a hellofa street address, trust the Japs to have street numbers all back to front like that, inscrutable, but the waiter is nodding his head as if he can't wait to get the goddam jacket off and get down to the old Kitcho in Osaka and have some of old Teiichi Yuki's kelp in bean curd.

These new foodies always know the restaurants in places you never heard of before, like Song He Lou in Suzhou, China. I mean, here's a slob who not so long ago thought it was a great adventure, like going on the Trans-Siberian Express or something, walking into the Chinese chippie in Great Homer Street in Liverpool, half expecting to meet Marlene Dietrich there, or, at least, Anna May Wong, and here he is talking about a restaurant in Suzhou in China and he even knows what street it's in, Guanzhe Road, he's forgot the number though.

The Dong Feng in Sichuan, that's another one. The Auberinge in Munich. Whereabouts? No. 5 the Maximiliansplatz of course. Yes, of course, Eckhart Witzigmann's place.

"Curl up at night with a good cook book – I read them like novels."

"Yes, yes, gobble, gobble, yum, yum."

Killed the art of conversation stone dead. They not only talk food, they *think* food. Ought to be a taboo subject. Like women, religion and politics. Most revealing thing a person can do in public, eating. Disgusting. Oughtn't to be allowed. Sinful, really, the way they worship food. Absolutely *worship* it. Food used to be decent. It used to be, well, it used to be brown. Except for peas and Brussels sprouts. Colour now. Like TV. The food's in colour. Symphonies of taste and colour, the new sexual experience, stuffing it up, right up under their noses. Bit much that. Disgusting. Got all these books about it, buy them openly, taking pleasure in food, Keats-like, lyric about it, romantic. The Faerie Queene Cook Book. Ought to have a Milton of food. Ought to have a Bunyon. Sinful. Could walk into a room full of ladies all rigged out in black leather and chains, dangling from the ceiling, strapped to the walls, wouldn't bother me at all, but there's something sinful about all this mucking about with the serious business of meat. And potatoes.

Christ, he's looking at me. Hope he doesn't recognise me. But I recognised him, right off. He hasn't changed. Not physically. Weird that, what with all that eating. No, he's just looking down his nose at me. I'm obviously sitting at the wrong sort of table. Not just good enough going to the right restaurant, you got to sit in the right sort of place. Downstairs at Langan's. By the window at the Tour d'Argent.

"*Jesus! That's it!*"

"*You find something wrong with your, ah, steak and, ah, chips, sir?*"

"*No, no, waiter, great, bring me some more of that wine with a long name. In fact bring me a wine with an even longer name.*"

That's it! He hasn't changed. All those years of eating like he's got six sets of teeth and three stomachs and he hasn't put on a pound. No paunch, no jowls, not one extra chin, starved to perfection he is. He's one of those even newer new foodies. The ones who somehow can eat and *not* get fat. Cuisine Minceur is what they eat. Thin grub. Fellow won a medal in France for inventing that. The Meilleur Ouvrier de France. Disgusting how the Froggies worship food. Us too now. Ridiculous really. But there are, of course, some places in the world where it is not so silly. Not, in fact, silly at all.

"*Brown meat brown enough for you, sir?*"

"*Brown meat just perfect.*"

SIMON HOGGART
Going to the Wall

A CHAP I know writes about travel for several newspapers and magazines, so occasionally he is asked by various tourist authorities to give them advice. In the past ten years or so he has helped both the Chinese and the Russians. The Chinese, he said, were tremendously anxious to please.

"No more tractor factories and collective farms," he suggested.

"Good idea," they said, striking both off the list.

"No more lectures on Marxist-Leninism while showing people round historic palaces and temples," he advised.

"Perish the thought," said his hosts.

"How about a few decent hotels where at least you can get a hot bath and a proper breakfast?" he asked.

"We shall build them immediately," replied the Chinese, and that is just what they did.

The Russians, he reported, took an entirely different attitude. Each suggestion would be met with a glum stare, followed by the rubric: "Ah, but the visitors *must* understand . . ."

The Chinese are terrifically keen to give satisfaction and to have you tell your friends you've had a spiffing trip. Things do go badly wrong on occasion, but then the anguished apologies almost make it worthwhile. If you make a suggestion, so much the better – it is another insight for them into the baffling ways of the occidental mind.

So, in the politest possible way, it is necessary to nag your guide. Say, for example, that the prospect of another evening watching chaps in traditional lion costumes jiggling across a stage to the sound of very small cymbals fills you with a drear foreboding. Simply announce, as we did, that you would prefer to spend the evening wandering around the night markets of Peking. Your guide will probably beam with pleasure, delighted that she (or possibly he) has avoided the embarrassment of taking you somewhere you don't want to go.

If you're fed up with the food (one of the most obvious facts about China, yet it still comes as a surprise, is that Chinese people eat Chinese food three times a day), then you can ask to go to a different restaurant. In Shanghai we requested a "crab feast", a meal several hours long consisting of crab cooked in a dozen different ways, culminating in a pile of steamed crabs. It cost a few pounds extra, but then it would cost far more here, if you could find it, which you can't.

Of course the sights which are on every tourist itinerary are marvellous and, as the French say, each does *vaut le voyage*. They are also very crowded. In the Summer Palace on the outskirts of Peking, reached by the Chinese equivalent of the North Circular Road – one of the most depressing thoroughfares I have ever seen – it was hard to move. The

scores of splendid buildings have equally splendid names: "The Pavilion for Listening to the Orioles", for example. Near The Hall for Dispelling Clouds, I heard a guide who had some difficulty with her English pronunciation explain to an American: "Here is Hall for Despairing Crowds."

"Oh yes, I can see why," said the American, sympathetically.

At the Great Wall the crowds were so thick that you had to queue to get through the watchtowers. Most of the visitors are Chinese, who are nowadays able to travel more easily, and are discovering their own country in a daze of delighted wonderment. Almost all of them carry cheap twin-lens reflex cameras, made in China, of the type which were popular here around the war. They photograph each

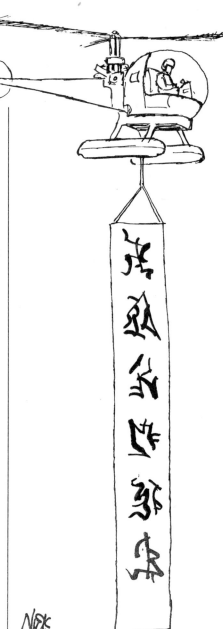

other in their thin cotton costumes against each famous spectacle, with all the passionate precision of Westerners or Japanese.

But the crush cannot spoil the Wall, which marches majestically over the mountain ridges, just as it does on the tea-towels. Incidentally, the belief that the Wall is the only man-made object which can be seen from the Moon is obviously absurd. There are parts of the Wall you can't see from the Wall.

But, as seems to happen frequently in China, the best moments are the unscheduled ones. At the end of the mile or so open to tourists, I climbed unchallenged over a barrier and strolled along a part of the Wall which hasn't yet been restored.

After a while I came upon a couple of workmen eating their lunch. They insisted in sign language that I shared it. So we sat beaming at each other as we chewed hard-boiled eggs and cold duck and swigged a rice spirit I had mistaken for beer and which left one hemisphere of my brain detached from the other for several hours. But through the haze in my head and on the hills I could see the Wall striding over the peaks, climbing, dipping and turning back on itself, looking almost exactly as it must have done four hundred years ago.

There are aggravations too. Expecting a leisurely and even luxurious cruise down the Yangtse, we were told at the last moment that our second-class cabins had been taken over by "big potatoes", agreeably quaint English slang which turned out to mean, disagreeably, senior Communist Party officials. So we spent three days in third class, eight to a cabin, with metal floors, no curtains, and two loos for 72 bottoms. Even here, though, there was one touch of the promised luxury. A steward came in each morning to change the spittoon.

Yet it's curious how you don't, in the end, mind. We relieved our trifling adversity by drinking too much and playing extremely silly games in our cabin. During one of these a big potato came and stared in through the door, his expression both rapt and blank, unable to comprehend the wonders before him.

Two days later we were in Shanghai and again it was a departure from the tour which made the visit memorable. The Peace Hotel on the waterfront was built in the 1930s, and its band of elderly musicians somehow survived the Cultural Revolution with membership and repertoire intact. In the ballroom, the tourists drank forgotten pre-war cocktails and a few danced slowly to *Blue Moon* and *Misty*.

We followed a sign upstairs to the Billiards Room where an old man, far older than the hotel, brought us beer. As we played he sat smiling, nodding and maybe half-asleep. Now and again he would murmur, "Good shot" through the gloom, more to himself than to us, perhaps vaguely remembering the days when the hotel was thronged not with tourists, but with merchants, officers, ticket-of-leave men, lascars and prostitutes – a despairing crowd, if ever he saw one.

BRITISH AIRWAYS

DUNCAN
FLY HALVES

"Do try to remember, pet. Which little girl did you swap your passport with for three marbles and half a Banjo?"

"But where could a small child possibly disappear to?"

"Window-seat, over the wing."

"It's only a security precaution, love. You can be sheriff again when you reach your destination."

"As soon as I saw you, I said to myself, I said, there's a person scared stiff at the prospect of flying. Let me put another Coke in there for you."

"Come on now, dear, give the little boy his pink boarding-card back. You have a nice green one, don't you? Green is a lovely colour too, isn't it? Come on, give the pink . . ."

"Bad news, Miss Ellis – we're fog-bound."

"Hello, Children's Lounge here. I would like to read out a message . . ."

LIBBY PURVES

WHO?

'Who's Who', normally published in March, has been delayed until May by a lazy lèse-majesté computer.

The Observer

Ah, I well remember the day the Call came. It was brought in with the other post, to a silly round marble table where I sat in brief and dubious glory as an Editor. There it was: a form, of legal aspect; a beckoning, bony finger of the Establishment. An invitation to become a Who. Just as if one were Jimmy Savile or a backwoods peer; an MP or a KBE or Greta Garbo (*Greta Lovisa Gustafsson, film actress b. Stockholm 18 Sept 1905*). As if one were Robert Maxwell, or an Emeritus Professor of Applied Geology at Madhya Pradesh; as if one were a Personage.

A little stunned, suspecting some computer error, I considered the options. Did one reply modestly, to the effect that since neither Henry Kelly nor Naim Attallah was yet included, nor Hugh Hudson, nor Bruce-the-sequins Oldfield, one did not feel adequately worthy of precious linage in the big red bible? Or did one hastily slap in the form, first class post before the luck ran out, and go one's way, rejoicing evilly in the knowledge that whatever axes might fall, *Who's Who* never drops your name until you die?

In the event, of course, I did the latter. Most people do. Arthur Scargill and Bernard Levin have never accepted the Call, but both are more than capable of building their own shrines. A few overmarried and over-merged businessfolk refuse it, but seldom for long. A very, very few are genuinely publicity-shy (like the editor of *Vogue*). The rest, frankly, leap at it. Even those shamed in the *Observer*'s cruel list of unasked persons (Anna Raeburn, Anton Mosimann, Audrey Slaughter . . .) could probably bring themselves to forgive, if the Form were to come in the future. We are all weaklings. We even experience a brief, unworthy pang of regret that we shall have to wait until May to find out whether our luck is holding. Some of us, living in obscurity, mopping up Farex, exerting influence and power over nobody except the boy-scout who stacks the logs on Saturdays, find an odd sense of comfort in knowing that we nestle in big red Momma's arms, between Dame Daphne Purves of New Zealand and a warlike Air-Vice-Marshall Reed-Purvis who was the Queen's ADC.

Exactly *why* we find it comforting is a mystery. Real Who-dom is hardly conferred by inclusion in a book of civil servants and pointless peers; the Whos of today are Koos, and Clive Sinclairs, and Whams, and Selinas, and the Tesco Romeo Dad, and anybody at all called Aitken, Sangster, or Grade. Rarely do the Archdeacon of Sarum or Ivo Sarajčić (*Member, Council of the Republic, Croatia*) make headlines. As rarely as do I. But still we are recorded where others fail.

God knows why. It is possible, up to a point, to persuade oneself that one is chosen as an exciting new name of the future; but the argument soon falters into a ridiculous silence. Even at the moment when the magic form appeared, I was regularly being bombarded in my editorial hovel with so many claims to excitingness that the very concept began to seem exhausting, and mediocrity quite an attractive and restful state. Into the office with the giant marble washstand would float one stylish eager-beaver after another, immaculate one and all in hand-rumpled neo-Japanese layered ragsuits; all corking merit in the great media marketplace. "A *very* important, exciting young sculptor, we *have* to have a picture, she's *very* striking . . . and this marvellous novelist, he's nineteen, he's certainly going to win the Booker, I've been very privately told by a close personal friend who's judge . . . Look, we have to clear three spreads for this designer, he's amazing, if *we* don't get him *Harper*'s will . . ." And on it went. Frenzies of avant-garde excitement gripped us daily; but have I heard the name of one single one of these exciting buggers since? I have not.

Sometimes in more reflective mood, one can pull on an imaginary briar pipe, smile patronisingly at the trendy frenzy, and opine that one is In The Book with Dame Daphne and the Archdeacon simply because one has real, enduring, merit. A wide education. The certain depth. What the chaps down at BBC Current Affairs like to call "bottom" (as in "Young Nic is a bright lad, but has he got the, well, *bottom* for the *Panorama* job?"). This very comforting theory, however, got torpedoed in its turn by a consultative telephone call with *the* Mark Boxer, who took over the big cold marble table and the excitingness of *Tatler* from my nerveless fingers two years ago. He happens to be in *Who's Who*; was in it a year before me. Why? What triggered the arrival of his form? Directorship at Weidenfeld's? Remarkable cartooning reputation? Long history in magazine publishing: Boxer is a candid man. After thinking a bit, he said no. "Actually,

"But couldn't you get your speech writer to knock off a little light conversation?"

I rather think it was triggered by my marrying Anna Ford. There were a lot of cuttings, that year. They must have counted them, and decided I was someone who mattered." But hold on: Anna Ford isn't in the book *herself*, for heaven's sake! "Ah. Well, I do wonder if there isn't sometimes a negative message instead of a positive message read into some sets of cuttings, when They consider them," he said, darkly, and did not elaborate. We exchanged pleasantries, one Who to another, and I rang off and continued brooding on the mystique, the comfort, the oddity of the whole business.

Thus it was that after two years and two forms, I finally plucked up courage to ring that staid, unpredictable, uppity publishing house of A & C Black, and ask why the hell they put me in, and whether they weren't as sick as pigs when they rashly chose editors (or anyone else) who then resigned before the first copy could thud off the binding-machine. The anonymous Selector (the panel is as secret as a CIA clam) said No. "That job was only a Contributory Factor." But is obscurity not a problem, when you are stuck with a bore until death? "Well. Certain Ambassadors from Certain Countries do get recalled rather quickly in a coup, and it is hard to find out later whether they have been, well, liquidated." A vision of forms, neatly sealed in antproof boxes, travelling by cleft stick across terrible swamps towards the bones of some 1940s Ambassador, rose compellingly before me. And, by imperial association, another vision. Before I could formulate another question or jeer at the absences and caprices of the book, I suddenly understood where the odd sense of comfort had originated.

In the works of John Buchan, that's where. We have all had a dream, long ago, of that other Call: when the simple soldier or the clerkly solicitor is summoned to an unobtrusive set of chambers off Whitehall; and met by a pair of admirals and a grey-haired man on whose noble, lined features the Highest Authority in the Land sits easily. The secret committee reveals that it knows all about you. "Been following your career for a while now, Hannay. Seems you might be the sort of chap the country needs. Got a dashed queer job for you, but it's a queer old war, and it'll get more dangerous before it's over. Are you game?" And in the dream, of course, we *are* game; and in the dream, the secret generals' following of our career is no more than we would expect of decent and omniscient Leaders.

The real Leaders, alas, are no longer the sort on whose lined features we see anything sitting, much, except the occasional trickle of egg. The old dream is dead. Only the mysterious cabal at A & C Black remain, with their fiendishly irrational judgments, their power to pick and choose capriciously among us, to keep secret files. The Masters.

But then my anonymous Selector broke up the dream. "Of course, the moment comes when a climate is simply created, and someone here says, 'Oh, *he* ought to be in'." So they are fallible, after all. We all know how you create *climates*; it is a low trade. For revenge, I told Selector a little story.

A few years ago, Bill Cotton Jnr was head of Light Entertainment at BBC TV. A man in radio wanted a job; and since all his old friends were working for Cotton already, he hatched a plot. The radio man – who insists I call him Phil Batt, which is not his name – set up a whispering campaign. The brilliance of it lay in the fact that none of his supporters ever did anything so naïve as to praise him. They merely brought his name up, all the time, in passing. Thus, in the Head's presence: "Oh, I'm worried about my dog. Got a dry nose, very hot – think it could be distemper." And the second stooge would add: "Yes, funny, Phil Batt had the same thing with *his* dog." Or: "I like the tie, Bill – a bit like Phil Batt's new one." Or: "Jim? No, sorry, I think he's playing golf with Phil Batt's boy."

After a month, Batt was introduced, for the first time, to Bill Cotton. By a friend. "Oh, Bill, – you know Phil Batt, of course, don't you?" And the unsuspecting, friendly boss said enthusiastically: "Yes, of course – how're you doing, Phil?" Victory. Out of climate alone, a Who was born. ☙

"Bugger, ITV got here first."

HEATH

NEAL ANTHONY

THE 39-PLUS

or where have you been since the war ended?

PAPER ONE

1 Do you have the faintest recollection of: –
Henry Brooke; Patrick Gordon Walker; Nasser; Bokassa; Nkruma; Kenyatta; Katanga; Little Black Banda; Mr Odinga Oginga; King Zog –?

2 Do you wish you could remember: –
Who to blame for Suez; who to thank for Premium Bonds; who did what on Nixon's orders; where the buck stopped; who said who couldn't walk and chew gum at the same time; who stopped the clocks going forward and back; who started them going back and forward again, just like old times –?

3 Examine, discuss and dismiss the suggestion that: –
Zaire used to be called Persia; Taiwan used to be the Belgian Congo; the Gold Coast used to be Ghana; Northern Zimbabwe was Southern Zambia; Abyssinia is still Ethiopia.

4 Which Archbishop officiated at the 1953 Coronation: –
Fisher; Ramsey; Makarios; Durham; Cranmer –?

5 Which do you wish had made it to Number Ten: –
Gaitskell; Grimond; Foot; Thorpe; Mosley –?

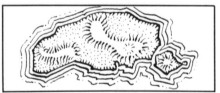

6 Where did Chiang Kai-Shek hole up when Mao chased him off the mainland: –
Formosa; Eoka; Krakatoa; Eureka; Bokassa; Profumo –?

7 Place in order of their exposure: –
Burgess; Maclean; Philby; Blunt; Gerald the Mole.

8 Whom do you recall having seen first on television: –
Richard Dimbleby; Hank; David Dimbleby; Jonathan Dimbleby; Cisco Dimbleby; Sir Mortimer Wheeler; Sir Brian Horrocks; Gilbert Harding; Peter West; Muffin the Mule?

9 Which of the following would you consult over which of the following: –

Dr Beeching;   A dodgy heart;
Dr Spock;   A dodgy rail network;
Dr Who;   A dodgy child-rearing;
Dr Savundra;   A dodgy TARDIS;
Dr Barnard;   Dodgy insurance –?

10 Which of the following was not *really* a Russian: –
Marshal Bulganin; Colonel Gagarin; Josef Stalin; Ilya Kuriakin –?

11 When was Lord Home not, and for how long –?

12 Match correctly the following double identities: –

Lord Stansgate;	Clark Kent;
Sir Percy Blakeney;	Mohammed Ali;
Quintin Hogg;	Batman;
Cassius Clay;	Anthony Wedgwood Benn;
Anthony Wedgwood Benn;	El Zorro The Fox;
Superman;	Tony Benn;
Bruce Wayne;	Lord Stansgate;
Tony Benn;	The Scarlet Pimpernel;
Don Diego de la Vega;	Lord Hailsham;
Mrs T.;	The Wicked Witch of the West.

A CLUE:
TWO OF THE ABOVE ARE ALREADY CORRECTLY MATCHED

13 Who has most consistently got right up your nose: –
The French; Americans: Russians: Argentinians: Northern Irish: Militant Tendency: National Front; Charlene Tilton as Lucy Ewing –?

14 Arrange in order of eligibility for canonisation: –
Billy Graham; Luis Palau; Ian Paisley; Mary Whitehouse; Lord Longford; Cliff Richard; The Osmonds.

15 How many Popes back can you remember: –
John Paul II; John Paul I; Paul VI; John XXIII; Pius XII; Alexander VI; Hadrian IV –?

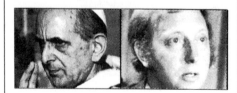

16 Re-arrange correctly: –
HAROLD WILSON – wore a funny hat and carried a fly-whisk;
JOMO KENYATTA – banged his shoe on the table;
NIKITA KHRUSHCHEV – smoked a pipe and wore a Gannex mac;
ARTHUR SCARGILL – never smiles.
(ONE OF THE ABOVE IS ALREADY CORRECT.)

17 Was *Pandit Nehru* a: premier; pundit; panda; bandit –?

18 Identify the correct spelling: –
Picasso/Piccasso/Picaso;
Quadafi/Gadafi/Qadaffi;
Deng Xiao-Ping/Dang Zao-Peng/Dung Zo-Pong;
Zbigniew Brzinski/Zbiegniew Brezhnevski/Zhbgnwgh Brznskhnskz.

19 What fictional police officer arrested a man by bursting into his bedroom, brandishing a revolver and snarling, "Getcher trashers on!" Was it: –
Lockhart of No Hiding Place; Gideon of the Yard; Dixon of Dock Green; Regan of The Sweeney; Barlow of Z-Cars; Commissioner Robert Mark –?

20 At a dance celebrating "Golden Oldies", might it be possible to jive, jitterbug, rock, twist, shake, boogie and do the birdie all in one evening, *without* needing the services of an osteopath afterwards –?

21 Who accompanied Hillary to the summit of Everest: was it –
Tenzing; Ching-Ching; Maudling; I-Ching; Ying-Tong; Suzie Wong –?

22 Which of the following has *not* (yet) been identified as a cause of cancer, heart disease, migraine, plague, tennis-elbow or housemaid's knee: –
Alcohol in tea; nicotine in coffee; caffeine in tobacco; tannin in drink; fat in everything; sugar in everything else; salt; sex; celibacy; water –?

23 Match the marriage partners: –

Philip Archer;	Mrs Dale;
Sophia Loren:	Theo Kojak;
Dr Dale;	Grace Fairbrother;
Arianna Stassinopoulos;	Carlo Ponti;
Mickey Rooney;	Nobody;
HH Pope Pius XII;	Mrs Rooney I, Mrs Rooney II, Mrs Rooney III. . .

24 Which title might suggest the work of which author: –

Dennis Wheatley;	Five Get Reprinted Again;
John le Carré;	Cupid Throws Up;
Barbara Cartland;	A History of the English-Growling Peoples;
Enid Blyton;	The Spy Who Came Over Confused;
Erich von Däniken;	The Right-Winger Rides Out;
Winston Churchill;	Chariots of the Gullible.

25 Arrange in order of prone-ness to malfunction: –
Thermionic valves; stereophonic diodes; printed circuits; integrated circuits; travelling circuits; people.

ROY HATTERSLEY

A Brush with Fox

I MET Samantha Fox sometime between seven forty-five and eight fifteen on the evening of Thursday, November 15, 1984 at the Royal Lancaster Hotel. I worked out the time and place of our meeting when a picture of this Stanley-and-Livingstone type event appeared in the *Mail on Sunday* colour magazine on Sunday, December 30. Why, you are already asking yourself, should any newspaper want to print a six-week-old photograph of a middle-aged politician and a girl who happened to be a guest at the dinner at which he was speaking? The answer comes in two parts. The first is technical in that colour magazines have a gestation period of more than a month, so an earlier revelation was not possible. The second explanation concerns why they should want to publish such a picture at all. The answer to that is that Miss Fox was fully clothed.

Before I explain why Miss Fox's un-undressed state is so interesting, let me describe what I assume to be the circumstances of our meeting. My guess is that we exchanged a word or two at the Annual Award Dinner of the Society of British Magazine Editors. My participation in this event (alas, not as a winner but as a presenter) brought me brief gossip column fame. The *Sunday Mirror* ("they're just good friends") and the *News of the World* pictured me sitting next to Faye Dunaway – whose husband, they both failed to mention, is a distinguished photographer who had been invited along to the dinner to present the "Golden Camera" or a prize of some such risible name. The *Daily Express* caught me as I was leaving for home with – I confess it – my tie undone. The caption under the picture carried the clear implication of "drunk and disorderly".

I make no complaint about any of that. The pictures provoked much good-natured ribaldry in the Sparkbrook Labour Club and a great amount of friendly banter in and around the Hillsborough stadium of Sheffield Wednesday AFC. But they helped me to identify the occasion on which Miss Fox and I met. Lopsided bow tie, hair in desperate need of a trim: a comparison of the pictures confirmed November 14. Elementary, my dear Watson. And anyway, most of the jokes about the Dunaway photograph were the product of obvious envy. The wisecracks about the Fox picture were less endearing. Most were variations on the theme that my middle stuck out

more than her top.

For – as you may know from your own newspaper reading, or have deduced from the extraordinarily subtle clues which litter the preceding paragraphs – Samantha Fox is a nude, or near nude, photographer's model; what is known in modern newspaper parlance as a "page three girl". Indeed, at the moment she is *the* "page three girl", the "Page 3 Girl of the Year" no less. And she is by no means exclusive to *The Sun* and its Sunday sister, the *News of the World.* She appeared in the *Sunday People*'s New Year cartoon with the Prime Minister, the President of the United States and similar international notables. She is so famous that, according to one picture caption, she "knows that she has a duty to her millions of fans." And on Thursday, November 15, 1984 I met her – without realising it till the obliging *Mail on Sunday* drew the fact to my retrospective attention.

Now you would not expect a respectable old codger like me to recognise Miss Fox as Miss Fox. But the blood is not so thin, the eyes so tired or the brain so befuddled that I can no longer be reasonably expected to remember a pretty girl when I meet one. Of course, I recognised Miss. Dunaway. But I suspect that, had I been a member of an obscure sect which prohibited attendance at the performance of moving pictures, and had, therefore, missed *The Thomas Crown Affair* and *Bullet, Chinatown* and *Bonnie and Clyde,* I would have recalled our meeting six weeks later. But not Miss Fox. There is something quite extraordinary about a young lady of eighteen who, with her clothes off, is generally acknowledged to be the object of mass desire but, when fully dressed, turns out to be wholly unmemorable. The fault may lie in me. But I doubt it.

If Miss Fox or her agents and managers feel my reverie to be less than gallant, I gladly concede that of the two blondes who appeared face to face in the *Mail on Sunday* magazine – Samantha ("I enjoy showing off my body") and Roy ("mind your own business") – Miss Fox has enjoyed all sorts of success that has been constantly denied to her temporary drinking companion. On a single morning she appeared in the *News of the World* "Sex and You" feature; in its *Sunday* magazine "Glamour Special" and in a *Sunday People* double page spread covering her intellectual attributes – well, vaguely related to her intellectual attributes.

Miss Fox (such is the price of fame!) was "slated – and hurt by the all-girl pop group, *Bananarama.*" Lead singer Siobhan Fahey told *Penthouse,* "I'm sick of seeing her picture in the papers. She's so stupid, I could slap her." And the *Sunday People* (no doubt feeling parental concern for vertically tiny Sam who sprang to popular prominence after becoming runner-up in the "Miss Sunday People Contest") set out to prove the envious pop star wrong with a Mastermind Test. If your mind is beginning to boggle already, perhaps you should read no further.

"What," Miss Fox was asked, "is the special feature of a cabriolet type car?" Like a flash, the answer came back: "Topless." She was just as quick to identify the "currency note facing the chop" (the "nicker") and, lest you should think that her special subject was *double entendre,* she scored well in the art section. "Who," she was asked, "painted Goya's nude *Maja*?" She got the answer right first time. The *Sunday People* will, of course, say that their feature was firstly an excuse to print some mildly titillating pictures, and secondly a huge joke. Two huge jokes actually. And I suppose that I am getting too old to laugh. ℮

"It's just you and me left, and I'd like to get home."

Ned SHERRIN

Buried Treasures

AS Elizabeth Taylor announces her intention of being laid to rest in the valleys of Wales, with which, of course, she is inextricably associated, and as Richard Burton is already sleeping out eternity in Switzerland, where will all the others go? Is Sean Connery booked into Marbella or the Gorbals? Will Michael Caine end up in Beverly Hills, Windsor, or the Old Kent Road? And Joan Collins?

I have it on good authority that three great actors, Clint Eastwood, Jack Palance and Robert Redford, have all expressed a wish to have their ashes scattered over the little house in Keinton Mandeville, Somerset, on which a plaque commemorates the birthplace of Sir Henry Irving. Nowadays acting Lords are two-a-penny, or at least two (or rather three if you include Lord Graves, certainly a Lord and undeniably an actor). However, Sir Henry first celebrated the transformation of mummers from rogues and vagabonds to gents.* Unfortunately Messrs Eastwood, Palance and Redford were not the first with the idea of mingling their ashes with his. Telly Savalas, Raymond Burr and Larry Hagman have already inserted instructions in their wills (and testaments) to the same effect and the Parish Council of Keinton Mandeville meet next week to consider whether these mass scatterings are more likely to prove a health hazard, a threat to main road traffic to Taunton, or a valuable tourist attraction.

As the brisk autumn breeze blows down the grey limestone canyon of modest cottages which is main-street Keinton Mandeville, the council has to assess the nuisance or novelty value of being able to prise a speck of dust out of a visitor's eye and charge for it as all that is mortal of Messrs Eastwood, Redford, Palance, Savalas, Burr, or Hagman – or others who may follow in their wake. "Wakes a speciality". Was it Emile Zola, or was it Zola Budd, who said, "All I desire for my funeral is not to be buried alive"? More probably it was Lord Chesterfield in one of his rare letters to his daughter-in-law. To be scattered into the skies above Keinton Mandeville is a reassuring safeguard against Chesterfield's imagined fears.

"Burn me and scatter the ashes where they will, and let there be no abracadabra of ritual is my wish about myself", was George Meredith's wish. (Is it Eastwood, Savalas, or Hagman who is the Meredith reader?) Strange how people who will hardly be present feel the need to prescribe the details of their departure. "I direct," wrote Verdi, "that I be given a modest funeral, either at sunrise or at sunset with no pomp, no singing, no music." I shouldn't think it would do for Mr Manilow; but he is not on record as choosing Keinton Mandeville as a resting place so we can discount him. No music does seem a pity though, especially for the fans. You would have thought a drum might have been heard – or at the very least a funeral note. But the Japanese back in 650 were full of the same strictures. "When a man dies no gold or silver or silk brocades and no dyed stuffs are to be buried with him," was the practical dictate of the Laws of Kotoku.

Why such spoil-sports? Thirteen hundred and thirty-four years later cannot the Parish Council of Keinton Mandeville run up a more amusing form of service for all these thespians, dying to smother the walls of the cottage with their ashes – drums, funeral notes, abracadabra of ritual, pomp, singing, music, gold, silver, silk brocades, dyed stuff and all? It's the least they can do for a died stiff.

Charles Lamb had the right idea: "I have been to a funeral where I made a pun to the consternation of the rest of the mourners. I can't describe to you the howl which the widow set up at proper intervals."

What pun? What widow? How tantalising! One pun per internment must be permissable. A grief-laden Welsh voice throbbing across the echoing Alps, "Gone for a Burton"? It doesn't have to be new or funny – just apposite. Or will there be a whispered comment on Miss Taylor's designer-shroud – Taylor Made. Perhaps Keinton Mandeville will appoint a Punster-Laureate to trick out the obsequies with an official pun. Bathos could not be more triumphantly achieved than it was at Victoria's going;

Dust to Dust,
Ashes to Ashes;
Into the tomb
The Great Queen crashes.

"But we're not supposed to look smart, we're supposed to look terrifying."

Fritz Spiegl has published a collection of punning gravestones. Why not punning passings on? Mr Spiegl records a stone in Hornsey Cemetery: "To the memory of Emma and Maria Littleboy", the twin children of George and Emma Littleboy who died July 16th, 1837; "Two little boys lie here, yet strange to say these *little boys* are girls." It gets a snigger in the graveyard so why not at the graveside? Not quite a pun, but definite evidence of levity was unearthed at Nettlebed in Oxfordshire. "Here lies father and mother and sister and I. We all died within the space of one short year. They all be buried at Wimble except I. And I be buried here." And then there is the sexist epitaph in Dunoon. "Here lie the remains of Thomas Woodhen, the most amiable of men. His real name was Woodcock but it wouldn't come in rhyme." What an honest admission of literary shortcomings, "Wouldn't come in rhyme"!

Punning comes back into its own in Tombstone, Arizona: "Here lies Lester Moore. Four slugs from a '44. Now Les no More."

There is bathos in Woolwich where Major James Brush is commemorated: "who was killed by the accidental discharge of a pistol by his orderly. Well done, good and faithful servant." And there is a pyramid of conceits in Dennis Skinner's parish of Bolsover. "Here lies in a horizontal position the outside case of Thomas Hinde, clock and watchmaker, who departed this life wound up in the hope of being taken in hand by His Maker, and being thoroughly cleaned, repaired, and set agoing in the world to come." "Unverified" (in Shropshire) is succinct; "Here lieth ye body of Martha Dias – always noisy, not very pious, who lived to ye age of 3 score and 10 and gave to worms what she refused to men."

Perhaps Keinton Mandeville will cover the walls of Irving's Birthplace with suitable plaques adjoining his own, which commemorate the ashes which swirl above them. The Laureate? (If Roger Woddis is not available). The ghost of McGonagall?

Here blows the dust of Eastwood, Clint,
Filling what was a rural void,
Of human clay he may be skint;
But he lives on on celluloid.

The ashes of portly Raymond Burr, burned
For a while and then were urned.
Each spec's now in the air adjacent
Available to fans of "Ironside" and "Perry
Masont".

Here flies what's left of Robert Red-a-ford
No grander grave could any dead-afford.
As the sun dances make your bid
And grab what's left of the Sundance Kid.

All around is Jack Palance,
So grant dead Jack a backward glance,
A forward glance might bring surprise
And bits of Jack within your eyes.

I would have done Kojak, Savalas, Hagman, and J.R. – but they would not come in rhyme, in time.

* Is this a pity? Discuss.

COUNTRY LIFE

Knutsford Hard of Hearing Club are looking for new members, because they are sure there are a lot of people in the area who still haven't heard about the club.
A. Shorrocks (*Knutsford Express Advertiser*)

Baxters the butchers have axed more than 100 office staff following the sudden takeover by meat giants Dewhurst's.
H. Evans (*Northants Post*)

For sale: Man's sterilizer, nearly new, £4.
Babynest, hardly used, £3.
M. Taylor (*Abingdon Courier*)

A piggy bank containing cash, a video recorder and carriage clock, worth £576, have been stolen from 47 Laurel Road, Blaby.
S. Clark (*Leicester Mercury*)

SPECIAL ANNOUNCEMENT
Owing to popular demand, there
will be
NO LIVE MUSIC
at The Berkley this Christmas
S. Griffiths (*Beccles & Bungay Journal*)

INTERNATIONAL SECTION

In order to involve every member of staff actively in the elimination of red tape and promotion of efficiency, 517 red tape committees were established at all levels within the organisation. These committees hold weekly meetings.
G. Gertsch (*De Rebus* legal journal, South Africa)

The State Commerce Commission has wiped out an ad campaign publicising its ski races for New York businessmen after complaints about the slogan – "Let's see how fast your company can go downhill".
M. Fahey (*New York Magazine*)

The arrest was carried out quietly with the minimum of fuss by 15 policemen dressed in swimming trunks and shorts.
A. Bridgewater (*Sydney Morning Herald*)

Some Mothers Don't Have 'em
DONEGAN'S surrogate parenthood bureau

"You like him? He's yours for twelve grand – that's two grand less than I gave for him."

"Well, he can't have a polo pony – I haven't finished paying for *him* yet!"

"We both want a family, but so far Simon hasn't been able to raise the necessary."

KEITH WATERHOUSE

When the Baloo Goes Up

The Boy Scouts have announced that they are to experiment with spiritualism, and that members will shortly be holding seances in an attempt to make contact with the Other Side.

Mail on Sunday

You know, the day may come when we fellows of the 1st Elysian Fields Troop receive a message from some of our chums on the Other Side.

And you know, that message may not necessarily be in Morse or Semaphore or in the form of smoke signals. As a very famous author named Sir Arthur Conan Doyle noticed, there is a far, far more effective way of getting in touch with us chaps here beyond the Veil.

Some of you may have read Sir Arthur's splendid series of yarns about a detective named Sherlock Holmes, who was known for his powers of observation. Holmes would have made a fine Scout had he not smoked a beastly pipe and slacked about in his dressing-gown all day.

Now it was not always easy to think up plots for those 'tec stories. One morning, Sir Arthur was absently drumming his knuckles on the breakfast table while trying to think up the solution to a mystery tale about a dog which he had to write up that day. To his amazement, the table began to wobble furiously of its own volition, upsetting the coffee pot.

Sir Arthur was a man of the world who had knocked about a bit. So instead of ringing for more coffee he was shrewd enough to listen to what that table had to say. To his delight he found that his abstracted "table-rapping" had accidently called up an old chum of his, a fellow named Carstairs who had been run over by an Embankment tram-car owing to his being a noodle who had not learned what every keen Scout knows when crossing tram-lines – that is, to look both ways. Using a code quickly devised by the fertile brain of Sherlock Holmes' inventor, the two old friends were able to have quite a chin-wag.

Every Scout ought to learn that Table-tapping Code. These are the signals you must memorise to earn your Table-rappers' Badge:

NO .... KNOCK
YES .... KNOCK KNOCK
DECIDEDLY..............KNOCK KNOCK KNOCK KNOCK KNOCK KNOCK KNOCK KNOCK KNOCK, followed by politely upsetting a vase of flowers or turning over a chair, taking care not to damage the polish.
DIB DIB DIB ....KNOCK KNOCK KNOCK
DOB DOB DOB.......KNOCK-KNOCK KNOCK-KNOCK KNOCK-KNOCK

There are also signals for the different letters of the alphabet – Z, for example, is 26 knocks – but I have no space for them here. You will find the full Code in the Angel Scout's Handbook.

But for mortal Scouts who have yet to win their wings, it is not always easy, when in the jungle and such places, to find a suitable table on which to relay a message. Of course, a Scout who was worth his salt would want to make himself a table by splicing bamboo saplings together with reeds or grass. But in the desert or on an iceberg, that may not be possible. And so another way had to be found to signal us fellows here beyond the grave.

Now those of you who have been lucky enough to go to weekend camp in the Happy Hunting Grounds will have met a good chum of the Scouting Movement up here, Princess Pocahontos. The Princess is a thoroughly good sort who will always find the time to teach a tenderwing how to do a war dance or skin a bison. It was a sorry day for the 24th Paradise Cherubim Cub Scouts when Her Highness reluctantly resigned as their Bagheera, owing to her heavy commitments as President of the Seraphims' Institute and Treasurer of the Celestial Choral Society.

One day the Princess was squatting in her tepee eating a dish of ambrosia she had prepared for herself on her cooking fire of glowing, red-hot embers, having first carefully removed all dry leaves and bracken from around the spot to prevent the fire from spreading and damaging the alabaster columns to be found

DEAR
DIARY......

HEATH

in the area, when she heard a disembodied voice not unlike that of a very famous actress named Margaret Rutherford.

The voice asked in quavering tones: "Is there anyone there? Is there anyone there, I say?"

Despite not having finished her breakfast, Princess Pocahontos felt duty-bound to admit there was indeed someone there (remember that a Scout – or an honorary Scout in the Princess's case – will always tell the truth, no matter how inconvenient). No sooner had the answer passed her lips than she experienced a giddy sensation.

Now I know what some of you fellows will be saying to that. You will be saying: "What rot! A good Scout does not swoon", and in the general way I would agree with you. But you know, never forget that the Princess is a girl, and that she had had a nasty shock into the bargain. It also has to be said in her favour that, like the plucky little Red Indian she is, she was very brave in unflinchingly plucking one of her own wing-feathers, singeing it in the cooking fire and holding it under her nostrils to prevent herself from fainting. To no avail. Nor did putting her head between her limbs do the trick. Princess Pocahontos blacked out.

How long these swoons last – for it was to be the first of many – she knows not. What the Princess does know is that, when she came round, it was to find herself inhabiting the corpus of fifteen-stone Brown Owl in Wimbledon, seated on a plastic toadstool in the centre of a ring of crossed-legged Girl Guides, all of them clamouring for hints on haybox manna

cookery, basic harp maintenance, whether Brasso makes the best halo polish and so on and so forth.

Since that experience the Princess has been called upon many times by Akelas, Baloos and Brown Owls up and down the earth, to whom she is always glad to pass on tips and wrinkles from the Happy Hunting Grounds.

So that is another way in which our chums down below may get in touch with us. Any of us, at any hour, may suddenly find ourselves occupying an earthly Scoutmaster or Patrol Leader. And so, just as a mortal Scout always knows what to do should he find a dead body in the woods, every Angel Scout must Be Prepared to take part in a seance, and must remember the best way of bringing an Akela out of a trance (pincering the fingers together, sharply nip the subject in some fleshy part, such as the buttock. See fig XIV of First Aid for Ghost Scouts).

Should you be summoned by a medium by either of the means I have described, remember that as a Ghost Scout you will be an emissary of Paradise, and that mortals will judge the whole Angel Scout Movement by your deeds and demeanour. You will not go far wrong if you remember the Ghost Scout Law:

1. A Ghost Scout haunts cheerfully and without payment.

2. A Ghost Scout is courteous and will always remove his head when encountering a mortal.

3. A Ghost Scout moans and gibbers under all difficulties.

Too Deep For Tears

I wandered lonely as a cloud
That floats on high o'er vales and hills,
When all at once I saw a crowd
Of Texans flashing dollar-bills,
And German nuns, and Japanese
Requesting, "Where is sauna, please?"

Continuous as the stars that shine
Were tourists wearing rubber soles;
They stretched in never-ending line
For skates and squash and indoor bowls.
Ten thousand cars of every make
Lay nose to tail beside the lake.

The guides were working double-shift,
The barmen sweated at their toil:
A poet could not but be miffed
To count the cost of Arab oil.
I gazed – and gazed – and sadly thought
What little wealth to me it brought.

For oft, when on my couch I lie
And think how rich is English earth,
I cannot help but quantify
The paltry sum mere words are worth;
And then my heart with hunger fills –
But not for bloody daffodils.

Roger Woddis

WILLIAM BOYD
Un Bon Homme in un Quandary

I should have been more suspicious, I suppose. Quite suddenly, my editor in Paris – Françoise – started speaking to me in French when hitherto she'd employed her extremely fluent English. Just testing, she said, for the *Table Ronde*. The *table ronde* was an event that had been organised by the British Council in Paris. In return for my air fare and two nights in a hotel I had agreed to participate in an informal discussion about my first novel, *A Good Man in Africa*, which had just been published in France (*Un Anglais sous Les Tropiques*). It seemed a reasonable quid pro quo: a few questions, a few answers, the odd carefully rehearsed anecdote – even my rusty French (product of a year-long sojourn on the Côte d'Azur in 1971) should be able to cope.

I flew to Paris, arriving in the mid afternoon. The *table ronde* had been scheduled for 6pm that day. I had time to check into my hotel, meet at the British Council for a drink with my publishers, and then into the *table ronde*. It had struck me that I wasn't leaving much time for acclimatisation. I had meant to mug up a little on my irregular verbs, check out a few difficult words, but

somehow had never got round to it. Not that it matters much, I told myself as I was driven to the hotel, abstract nouns are the same in French as in English. Keep it simple, throw in the odd *franchement* or *en principe*, a shrug or two, and you're laughing. The lady from the British Council assured me that everyone was very excited about the *table ronde*. Why's that? I enquired. It's so unusual to conduct proceedings in French, she said; most British authors insist on talking English. Oh, I said, do they? Yes, but when we advertise that the *table ronde* will be in French we get a much bigger audience – and we've got a very distinguished panel. My mouth was getting strangely dry. She mentioned their names. No bells ringing. Tell me about them I said. Well, there was Georges Conchon, Goncourt prize-winning novelist, Catherine Rihoit, lecturer at the Sorbonne, famous for her rather raunchy feminist novels, and a celebrated Congolese writer Tchicaya U'

Tam'si. Pronounced tremors had started up in both hands. I tried to translate this nightmare into English terms – it was like being invited to share a panel with Salman Rushdie, Germaine Greer and Wole Soyinka. Imagine some French novelist with semi-efficient English trying to hold his own with these luminaries . . .

In my hotel room I wiped the vomit from my lips and tried to memorise some vocabulary. What was the French for post-structuralist? How did one translate "unreliable narrator". My *Harraps New Shorter* French and English dictionary was a legacy of my sixth form French (grade D at A-level) and was not overburdened with the new literary jargon. I recalled my rule of thumb: all English nouns ending -*tion* are the same in French; all abstract nouns with a Latin root are the same in French – think of the English word, say it with a French accent, no problem. That was my first mistake.

Luckily by the time I ar-

rived at the British Council I was on autopilot. This is a state that descends on me whenever a crisis state reaches panic proportions. Certain segments of my brain – the imagination, those nerve circuits that allow one to think in the future tense, the embarrassment glands, or whatever – are shut down. One enters a sort of solipsistic reverie – the world is a dream, nothing matters. The symptoms are a glazed smile, a dead look in the eyes and conversation pitched at a level of the commonplace and banal.

It was a state that was seldom to leave me during my two days in Paris, but it served me well during the *table ronde* and the dinner with the panel afterwards (nobody told me about the dinner). I remember a huge room, and about a hundred people sitting down facing a dais upon which the panel sat. I was introduced and my decision to speak French was admired and generously applauded. The smile became more glazed. As for the discussion itself, my strategy was to keep my role to an absolute minimum. This turned out to be easily effected because everyone else had huge amounts to say. I remember stuttering to a halt during a lame defence of realism (*le réalisme*, I hoped). Tchicaya U' Tam'si, gamely undertaking the role of spokesman for Black Africa, upbraided me for neglecting to tackle *le racisme* ("*Mais, c'est un roman comique*" was my response) and then got into a 15 minute wrangle with my translator – who was in the audience – over her translation of "French Letter". The term she had used was *capot d'Anglais*. Tchicaya resented this for some reason and, I think, saw it as neo-colonialist. I was as vague as the rest of the audience about the precise nature of his objection, but that didn't stop anyone from talking about it.

Indeed the whole discussion – and this is what I see as typically French – was carried on in the higher altitudes of intellectual debate: the concrete, the empiric, were shunned absolutely – the book disappeared into a fug of abstract nouns. To which,

"I have mixed feelings about you, Prescott. I'm going to recommend you for a promotion, but I'll see that you never get it!"

apparently, I added some new ones. My rule of thumb let me down badly, and after the talk several broadly smiling people admired my way with neologisms. "I do like your new words," one lady said to me. "They sound so much nicer than the old ones."

Problems with words continued the next day. After lunch with a journalist, who mercifully spoke English, I was to be interviewed on French radio. Sadder and wiser I made sure that the publishers had conveyed to the interviewer that I possessed only rudimentary French. It made no difference, and I can only put the interviewer's intransigence and hostility down to rampant Anglophobia. He spoke French with a velocity that in any other circumstances would have been highly impressive. Although we faced each other across a table we might have been separated by thousands of miles of faulty telephone cable. Through the fizz, crackle and interference of his rapid fire I could only make out the occasional word. *"Politique"* was one. *"Plutôt à gauche,"* I

"Okay, okay, my mother doesn't need an operation, but she sure could use a drink."

said. He looked very puzzled. Soon I started asking him to redefine words in an effort to slow him down. We carried on in this way for ten minutes. "How did it go?" I asked the subdued publicity person afterwards. "It was . . .interesting," she said.

That night, the plan was for me to go to a launching party. Not of my book, but of some French author. It seemed that key figures in the French literary world would be present, and it would be greatly advantageous to meet them. Brain death seemed imminent, but I thought I would give it one more try.

My editor, Françoise, drove me out to a small and fashionable bookshop in a fashionable arrondissement. The book being celebrated was a slim monograph on the Paris commune. The small bookshop was very crowded and very smoky. The "look" for French intellectuals and literary folk, for those interested in fashion notes, hasn't changed since the sixties. Key props are a cigarette, a leather jacket, unstructured greasy hair and massive pretension. I was led through the crowd to meet the literary editrix of a major newspaper. She was pale, large, freckled and with a lot of lank ginger hair. "I'm afraid she doesn't like Western literature," Françoise whispered as we approached. But I don't write Westerns," I said, vastly relieved. "No, no," Françoise said. The editrix reserved her admiration for works from beyond the Iron curtain, preferably written by Jewish dissidents. "How do you do?" I said. "I've just been reading Penrose's book on English Surrealism," were her first words to me, in French to boot. We did not find much common ground.

Perhaps as an oblique comment on my small talk, she swiftly introduced me to a translator who wanted to practise his English. Transla-

tors are a curious, generally seriously impoverished breed. Encounters with them can be deeply unsettling. At a party in London I was once introduced to a man who said "Hello, I your Polish translator are." My Swedish translator wrote inviting me to "crash in his pad in Stockholm" if I wanted to "save some bread." Quite apart from provoking anguish over what's happening to your books, you wonder what strange demon drove them to take up the career in the first place. This particular French translator was a suitably tall, dark, starved looking man. I asked him whom he was translating. Flann O'Brien he said. *At Swim Two Birds*. But, I said tactfully after a shocked pause, can it be done? Oh yes, he assured me, he'd been working on it for eight years. Deeply saddened, I was glad to be interrupted by Françoise who said she had to go. She was leaving me in the hands of Francois-Xavier, another editor, who would take me back to my hotel. I liked Francois-Xavier, and not just

because he spoke very good English, and so was not in the least disappointed when he interrupted me trying not to give the French translator my address in London and said we had to go.

Outside, it was clear that Francois-Xavier was in something of a hurry. As we climbed into his Volkwagen he told me why. His mother, who was nearly eighty, was a very celebrated French actress who was currently appearing at the Comédie Française. It was his job to deliver her to the stage door each night. I asked when the play started. Eight o'clock. We had just under an hour, I couldn't see what the problem was. Francois-Xavier explained. His mother, apparently, liked to arrive at the theatre half an hour before her call so she could do her *friction*. Friction? Yes, she rubbed herself all over with a pumice stone. It made her all tingly and hot and was a crucial prerequisite to her nightly performance. If she couldn't do her *friction* all hell

broke loose and tonight we were running a bit late.

Francois-Xavier suggested we pick up his mother before he dropped me off. I agreed, trying to imagine what it must be like to rub yourself all over with a pumice stone. We set off for her flat, we got caught in a traffic jam, we raced up side streets trying to get there more quickly.

As we approached, Francois-Xavier could see his mother pacing up and down on the pavement outside her apartment block.

I jumped into the back of the car as Francois-Xavier tried to mollify the near hysterical old actress. Introductions were scant. The conversation went, approximately, like this:

"You're so late! My *friction*, what about my *friction*!!"

"Darling, you look absolutely ravishing."

"But it's ten to eight!"

"Plenty of time, my little cabbage, plenty of time."

"But my *friction.*"

"You do too much of that *friction*, try just five minutes tonight."

"It's a disaster, a disaster!"

"Nonsense, nonsense. You're so beautiful, so wonderful. Everybody loves you."

Madame, to me: "I have, how you say, pumice? I rub myself. *Friction*. Before the show."

Me: "Ah. Yes."

To Francois-Xavier: "You silly stupid boy. You promised not to be late."

"Oh, darling, don't make such a fuss. We have hours of time. Hours. You will be magnificent."

We stopped at a traffic light. Francois-Xavier kissed his mother's hand. "Keep calm, my lovely, that's the main thing."

I opened the door. "I can walk from here." I faintly said goodbye and thank you. I'm not sure they heard. I watched them drive off. I was on the Boulevard Montparnasse. There had to be a bar around here somewhere. I wandered off. This fiction *friction*, I thought, it can really get to you. I needed a drink very badly indeed: brain death had arrived.

"The last day without Julie Walters in it seems such a long, long time ago."

COTHAM

"Look, lady, all the wishing in the world isn't going to change anything."

"I still say the sentence was too severe!"

"The soup smells terrific today, sir!"

Until Next Term, Then

"...Very good deal, really – ten days in France – Provence, Arles, footsteps of Van Gogh and all that – lectures, tours, practical sessions with local artists...three hundred quid, all in. Then I thought, sod it, and bought a video..."

"You do realise that the last time Wayne looked after the gerbil over the holidays it came back with lice?"

"I'm going away now – but I shall be back very soon."

"Let him lie, Miss Proust – only idiots try to run a detention class on the last day."

"It's over, it's over, it's o-o-o-o-over."

"Get off the corridors! Get off the corridors! The Fifth Form have mistletoe!"

"Makes a change – an incident-free last day."

FREUD ON FOOD

Down Under Nourished

OCKER is a word I had not come across before my visit to Australia; it means "manifestation of all that is most overtly, aggressively Australian". Ocker is beer-gut loosely covered by off-white singlet. Australian voice, expletives undeleted, tone rising at the end of the sentence, in which mention is made of Sheilas and grog, is ocker; "I am going to have a few beers," is ocker shorthand for "When they run out of cans of Foster's lager, we'll try the local wine and finish up with a bottle of brandy, and see whether we can pick a fight with someone who says we can't play cricket." Taking umbrage is ocker.

Barbecued beef sausages are ocker, as are meat pies and tomato sauce and talking about women as if they were a sub-species, and wearing beach shorts at the Opera House. The Opera house is not ocker.

What is the difference between Australia and yoghourt?

One has living culture.

Fussing is not ocker; things like napkin-folding and flower arrangement and gastro-prissiness are looked upon with deep suspicion by the indigenous Oz, therefore much practised by those who wish to show that they have social ambition. I was asked by a New South Wales middle-class family to "Come over, sit by the pool and have something to eat and a few beers"; what in England would be a nicely orchestrated *al fresco* buffet, something they call a *soirée* with a binge on top in Oklahoma. In Australia it means just what it says, and it seems quite in order to push people into the pool, though rather overdoing it – ockery, in fact – to throw up in public.

I went to a fish barbecue in Perth. The people who hosted the occasion were going into avocado farming in a big, sophisticated, computerised way, and said, "Come on over and have a look," and we inspected 2,000 newly planted trees that could be irrigated and fertilised and have their growth monitored from a control shed half-a-mile away.

We then fought our way through the flies to the barbecue area. There was a pit filled with charcoal, and over the pit lay a solid iron wheel, segmented into triangles by metal bars, like a compartmentalised frying pan such as they sell at Ideal Home Exhibitions and you say, "What a good idea," and buy one and give it to the Women's Institute annual sale three years later, unused. It is noticeable that the heat is very much greater at the apex than it is around the circumference, which is useful as dual heat always is.

Our host began with a gallon or two of mussels, poured them into a large segment so that all got direct contact with the red-hot base, and in God's good time they opened to the accompanying smell of charred shells. It was, I think, the least agreeable way of cooking mussels that I have encountered. But there was more.

The good man had bought a 10lb fillet of a huge fish which had the texture of halibut, the delicate taste of monkfish and is called Deep Sea Groper, like some sub-marinal sex-offender. It is absolutely one of the best fish I have eaten. Our host sliced the fillet into pieces the size of a thin baby's hand, sprayed them with cornflour, passed them through a light batter of beaten egg, flour and milk (two, 4ozs, 1 pint) and fried them in a segment of the wheel, into which he had poured a good glug of olive oil and roasted therein a dozen quartered cloves of garlic until they began to brown. The Groper was cooked in this garlicky oil and all fish later barbecued took on much goodness from having had contact with that section of the equipment.

We also had smoked salmon, which in Oz is not the subtle delicacy it is in Scotland; however, served on slices of bread fried in the residual fishy, oily, garlicky juices of the barbecue, it became a most appetising canapé.

And there was calamary, Antipodean baby octopus which comes in smooth, palm-shaped leaves, is cut into strips and sizzled with more garlic and tomato and flared in brandy (which might have been an accident) and was most delectable. One hundred per cent protein and fat, not a carbohydrate in sight, exactly what the doctor did not order.

They do not have barbecue sauce, so with a palette knife I gathered the oil, garlic and scraps of fish that clung to the metal, liquidised them with the juice of a lemon, added three egg yolks and two breakfast cups of olive oil and some salt, and we had an amazing *aioli*. Had I found some cooked rice and gelatin, this would have produced ramekins of considerable interest.

European sociologists who know what a man is by what he eats would be deeply perplexed by Australia. In Perth, a local MP who took me to dinner ordered pea soup and well-done steak, while his driver had oysters and crayfish in lemon butter; they then agreed on cream cake with pink icing as dessert, and as we were in Western Australia a thin patina of fly-spray hung over everything. The driver drank light beer which contains 0.9% alcohol. The ads say you can drink twelve bottles and drive a car; I tried it. One sip was enough – but then I am not very ocker. When I came home last Sunday my daughter said I hadn't even picked up a noticeable Australian accent. ℰ

"Come out, Dougherty – we know you're in there!"

Jonathan SALE
Ace of Clubs

THERE was sword-fighting in the car park. Out there, in the world rumoured to lie beyond the borders of Cambridge, there is massive unemployment, not least for Cantab graduates. At the last count 18% of the class of '83 sociologists were not in receipt of a wage; it might be more. Only 37% of them got round to replying to the Careers Service survey, as opposed to the 100% response from the conscientious geologists.

But here, through the open door of the hall in which the Societies Fair was held last week, broad-sword crashed down on broad-sword, inexpert swipe followed incompetent parry. This was not a fight to the death by a couple of undergraduates terrified of facing a world in which 16% of last year's zoology students are swelling dole queues.

No, it was a rehearsal by members of the Cambridge University Treasure Trap Society, which exists as a recruiting office for folk who want to go on a pilgrimage to "a castle in Cheshire with real dungeons and mouldering towers, which the players explore, carrying padded weapons – you really fight the monsters." Members borrow the communal swords and share petrol money.

The Societies Fair consisted of Treasure Trappers and several hundred other societies trying to catch the eye of fresh, and freshers', faces who will act as new blood (literally new blood, in the case of CUTTS, which admitted to "the odd skinned knuckle"). They are all – animal activists, God Squaddies, Jewish appreciation societies, the Cambridge Options Group (who believe in keeping them open) and the Officers Training Corps (why no Privates Training Section?) – they are all twelve years old.

Or so it seemed to the man from *Punch*, who last attended this particular function 22 years ago according to the almanac, although emotions tell him it cannot have been more than

---

> ## "Membership is open to all sentient life-forms except lizard-men of Antares."

---

three or four autumns past. Either way, the Fair has changed. It is more serious, what with the Alternative Homosexual group on Stall B5, and CARP, the Collegiate Association for Research into Principles, on E11, and the poetry workshop known, but not much, as Virtue Without Terror, not terrorising folk on N19.

It is more frivolous, what with GAS (the Gong Appreciation Society whose lad on G15 boasted, "We don't do much but it's free") and the Dampers Club, restricted to those who have fallen into the Cam, a wine-glass full of whose the waters graced the stand near the entrance.

You may be expecting a gritty Jeremiad against the young swordsmen and co, along such Old Fogey lines as: "At least the *Brideshead Revisited* layabouts had style, or, failing that, cars with long bonnets." You could have had the Jeremiad.

I am, after all, 40. I was 41 yesterday, in fact, a date celebrated by a talk at the C. U. Medical Society, whose stall was decorated with a genuine human femur, on "Sexually Transmitted Diseases". Is this, I could have demanded, the best the university can do – clobber itself with plastic swords while last year's philosophy graduates are stuck in jobs in Hotel Management or, worse, not in jobs in Hotel Management?

That might easily have been the theme, had I not also paid a call last week on Bill Kirkman, a one-time *Times* staffer who now heads the Career Service. My last visit here was also before the Sixties really started Swinging, and it was a quiet building on the outskirts. They told me then that they'd heard of something going in the RAC Press Office, where "it is sometimes necessary to work under pressure." (I followed their advice about the RAC, but only when the car breaks down.)

Now advice on careers is handed out in humming premises just a stone's throw from the rooms of the Hon. Sec. of the Computer Society and Processor Group. The meetings of ▶

"Mama, I don't care how much gold he's got – I don't love him!"

the nearby C. U. Motor Cycle Club would be audible, were it not for the sound of keen fingers riffling through copies of *Opportunities for Archaeologists* (a slim volume, as I am fully aware – my brother is a member of the B.A. trowel brigade).

"Very few graduates are unemployable," explained Mr Kirkman benevolently. "But in Arts subjects, it is very difficult to find work directly related to your subject, except for teaching." The class of '83 bears that out.

By Christmas, only 1% of physicists were not salaried; 11% of English graduates were on the dole, and the ones actually in legal employment sought refuge in "Accountancy", "Management/Administration", "Miscellaneous" and "Other Miscellaneous". Unemployment may be even higher; 31% didn't get round to returning the survey form, which probably says something about English graduates and their lack of salary cheques.

This does not, Mr Kirkman always insists, mean that rounded Fine Arts graduates should have crammed themselves instead into the square pegs of engineering (3% unemployment, and that only temporary, while the fledgling Brunels weigh up the size of the pensions and car engine sizes offered by the competing would-be employers). No, the world does not need second-rate engineers.

What employers want is "skills in numeracy, the ability to communicate effectively, to work co-operatively in groups and to cope with rapid change, and familiarity with computers." Little of this, he did not go on to say, is derived from attending lectures on Shelley (or, in my own case, not attending lectures on Shelley). Much of this, he also did not state, was to be found at the Societies Fair. Numeracy, certainly.

"600 people," stated the membership counter of the Cambridge University Very Nice Society. "We're hoping for a thousand. It costs 40p and you get a free bar of chocolate."

"Are you for real?"

"Yes," he communicated effectively. "Edward Heath is coming down on November 2nd, to talk about his hobbies," which proves the reality of the Very Nice people to the most sceptical of unbelievers.

"Membership," they told me at the other end of the row, "is open to all sentient life-forms except Lizard-men of Antares." The sentient life-forms in question were members of the Science Fiction Society, which used to consist largely of scientists reading comics but has now broadened its appeal to anyone wishing to borrow one of the 3000 books and 2000 magazines in the Tower of Babel library.

It meets in terrestrial public houses for talks on "The Dragonhikers' Guide to Battlefield Covenant Dunes' Edge Odyssey II", its magazine is entitled *The Torment Begins Again* (for this issue only, it keeps transmuting) and the Vice-President is "The Crimson Bat" to his, or its, friends. This creature has, incidentally, no connection with the Bat Group, which meets at the back of Trinity Hall where the flying mammals are thickest on the ground or in the air; the Batmen and Women can recognise them by listening first to the squeaks on *The Bat Tape* produced by the Northants Bat Group.

The Cambridge Students Union's answer to the Crimson Batperson is Martin Tod, Vice-President of the representative association to which all students belong (a form of closed shop decried by a terrifying and not necessarily virtuous band called, among other things, the University Right, which remarked, "We campaign quite aggressively – whoops, someone's vandalised our stand again.")

"Some people come up knowing exactly what they want to be. Someone I know has wanted to be a chartered accountant since he was 12. Either way, the first year is definitely fun, the second mostly fun, but by the third year you have definite attacks of reality."

These attacks can, however, be warded off by signing up with the Cambridge University Dungeons and Dragons Society, which exists as a sort of dating bureau for mortals who want to meet similar for indulgence in this fantastical board game.

But what about the world outside the circulation area of *Stop Press*, the student paper? "Most local war gaming societies have a Dungeons and Dragons society." Graduation, therefore, need have no fears.

Finding fellow enthusiasts in the Great Outside may be more tricky for members of the Gamelan Society, which specialises in Javanese music. Whatever a gamelan is, there are only four of them in Britain and if you miss "the highlight of a full-length programme of classical Javanese music in the Concert Hall, West Road", then you haven't lived and are unlikely to get another chance outside the confines of the university.

The sword-fighters had retired for a word with their sponsors by the time I left the hall. In my hand were leaflets from perfectly worthy groups firmly plugged into reality such as Amnesty, the Life Saving Club, the Malaysia and Singapore Association and the Industrial Society (complete with picture of coal mine labelled "Coal Mine"). But still in my mind was the first conversation I overheard when I went in. A tall young man in a suit, accosted by a girl manning one of the stalls, was saying, "I do like punting to Granchester and I do like eating."

"Here," she said, "take one of our leaflets." ⟳

"It's not the fighting I hate, it's the washing-up!"

ROY HATTERSLEY

Triumph Herald

I T WAS was a great day. Ernest Bevin was guest of honour at a "luncheon in connection with the opening of the exhibition: Historical British Wallpapers." At the School of Slavonic Studies, Miss Bertha Malnick gave a lecture on the History of Russia, 1756 – 1914, and Alan Phillips read his poetry in Kingsway Hall at 1.15 pm. I suspect that all of them hurried home to hear the Prime Minister's broadcast at 3 o'clock. For it was VE-Day and even the afternoon discussion on maternity services (held at the Royal Society of Health, Medicine and Hygiene, and, like the lunch, the lecture and the poetry reading, listed in the *Times* diary of "Today's Engagements") was, no doubt, interrupted to hear Winston Churchill proclaim victory in Europe.

The Times that day must have made immensely reassuring reading to the Officers and Gentlemen in the Halberdiers' Mess. For they knew (see William Deedes in *The Spectator*) that behind the sound of victory bells was the clank of the door slamming closed on old Europe. Yet the notices of the Establishment were printed in good order and discipline. And even the parts of *The Times* which were devoted to the end of the war, rejoiced in a fashion which must have been wholly acceptable in Pall Mall and St James's.

On the leader page was published a poem by the Poet Laureate which, whilst clearly concerned with the end of hostilities in Europe, contained such otherwise incomprehensible lines as "Not terrible with terror and dismay." The leader itself ran to three whole columns and ended with *Non Nobis Domine* and a few explanatory lines of verse in English. Amongst the letters was a note from Robert Birley – yet to be promoted from boss of Charterhouse to head of Eton – explaining the necessity of re-educating the Germans to "respect the Slavs". And the "paper of record" recorded, with careful clarity, the milestones which pointed to victory.

There was a full page "register of events" which chronicled the great occasions of the war months from 1939 to 1945. It was illustrated with portraits of allied commanders – Wavell, who had lost the desert command, no less than Montgomery who had won the desert war, Zhukov and Rokossovsky as well as Omar Bradley and Mark Clark. A second full page charted the same course in continuous prose, whilst the news pages were packed with single-paragraph items which would, on any other day, have commanded front page splash treatment – "Goebbels' Suicide by Poison" and "Eighth Army Enters Austria."

The *Mirror*, it must be said, was less restrained. Its banner headline – "VE-DAY!" – surmounted a photographic cliché, but a photographic cliché which on that day and for that paper must have been irresistible. The caption beneath the picture read "High old time in Trafalgar Square last night. . . Wrens and Allied Soldiers celebrated by climbing the lions." The *Daily Mirror* has, by some extraordinary process, managed to maintain its earthy exuberance over sixty years and the (metaphorically) dead bodies of several proprietors. "This is it," reported an anonymous *Mirror*

▶

"I don't believe he was ever in military intelligence."

Roy HATTERSLEY

man in Piccadilly, "and we are all going nuts."

The *Daily Sketch* recorded the view from Piccadilly itself. Its picture (apart from revealing that one man sat on the bonnet of the bus) revealed no lunacy. The *Daily Herald* on the following day produced a photogrpah of the same street. Again, the crowds were massive, clearly jubilant, but consciously well behaved. In the *Sunday Express* photograph of the adoring masses surrounding Winston Churchill, the mounted policeman looked more like the attendant spear-carriers in a Roman tribute than "necessary protection" in a London Street. Perhaps victory was a sobering as well as elating experience. Or perhaps – except when urged on to mild rumbustiousness by *Mirror* cameramen – we were all better behaved in 1945 than we are today.

The *Morning Star* (né *Daily Worker*, as it was in May 1945) proved that some things have not changed. On VE-Day plus one, it

managed to be both sour and silly. "Both Britain and America," its editorial said, "contain influential men who were ready enough to see the Red Army shed its blood but who are resolved now after victory to thwart and damage the Soviet people in every possible way." Its lead story describes the "Allied forces driving into western Czechoslovakia" and quoted Marshal Stalin's Orders of the Day, which described "our troops fighting valiantly even during the last hours of the war."

I assume that they did and that the British people regarded them with affection, gratitude and admiration – notwithstanding such editorial comments as, "We recall the frank declaration last year by Marshal Stalin that the complete crushing of the Hitler regime was beyond the power of the USSR alone." Fortunately, Spike Milligan and Mother Russia were on the same side.

The now defunct *Star* (neither *Morning* nor *Daily*, but then the best of London's evening papers) used its VE-Day edition to publish Winston Churchill's radio broadcast virtually verbatim. It was a strangely formal statement. "Yesterday at 2.41 am at General Eisenhower's Headquarters. . ."

The next two paragraphs were almost completely taken up with the names of Allied and Axis generals, admirals and field-marshals, and details of the places where they were going to initial, sign and ratify the document of surrender. Today, the story seems inappropriately clinical and quite unsuitable for a front page lead. But then it must have given force as well as flavour to the reality that at last the war was over.

"The German war is therefore at an end," the Prime Minister announced. No wonder "the grass opposite the Houses of Parliament looked like a seaside bench at holiday time." And no wonder the compositors printed an "n" when they should have printed an "a".

Fortunately, the next day even the printers and journalists of the *Star* had time to celebrate or be sad – the two conflicting emotions which characterised the VE-Day papers. The intention had been that no newspapers would be produced on VE-Day plus one. But no agreement was possible. Even in victory, the Fleet Street proprietors remained divided. ☞

Preview 2025

Forty years on, when because of a blunder
Silent are those who are singing today,
One lean and lonely survivor may wonder
How they survived that mad Wednesday in May.

Then there was joy in the booze and the
                                    bunting,
Then there were banquets and food for the soul;
Now he is hungry and does his own hunting,
Stalking a toad for a toad-in-the-hole.

Then there were bells, and the holiday beaches
Rang to the voices of children and dogs,
Then there were leaders and victory speeches;
Now all he hears is the croaking of frogs.

So long ago, but the memory lingers,
Marking the end of the Second World War;
Forty years fêted and Churchill's two fingers:
"That was the last – there won't be any more."

Then there was peace, but it wasn't long after
Suddenly everyone started to run;
Now in his crater and legless with laughter,
Thinks the survivor, "Thank heaven we won."

Roger Woddis

THE WARRIOR'S RETURN

" By Jove, old boy, it's grand to see you back from Africa and Europe and—

Asia and Australasia : come along and I'll show you—

the crater in Brigg's field—

and then the road block in Hyacinth Lane—

and then the F.A.P. at the cross-roads—

and then the bridge over the Dibble the Home Guard made—

and then the battle-course on the Common—

and then what the bomb did to Johnson's barn—

and then what the tank did to Honeysuckle Cottage—

and then what the evacuees did to the Manor House—

and then, finally, one day very soon you simply MUST—

tell me all about Africa and Europe and Asia and . . ."

*". . . And some say that one of the
houses on this estate is made of steel."*

"P.S. I have grown a beard."

*". . . So I wrote to my MP and finally I got
back the job I was doing before the war."*

"Happy new ration book, madam!"

"The Spam is very good today, sir."

"'Ere! 'Oo's supposed to be tellin' their experiences?"

"I shall celebrate Victory-Day by switching over to asparagus."

"He's the chap in the Post-War Planning Section who keeps rushing in and out borrowing my rubber."

ART
EXHIBITION
←

"Let's see – VE-Day plus how many is it now?"

"Only about one in a thousand shows the slightest sign of any individuality."

". . . And Fen End A.A. site kindly offered to help our celebrations with a little flood-lighting."

"I'm afraid the list for flats is now closed, but if you like you can start queuing up for the cinema."

"In fairness, I must warn you that there's a ghost – it keeps on shouting 'Put that ruddy light out'."

"The switch-over from war-production was rather sudden."

"I don't know who he is – the children brought him back from their evacuation village."

"Oh, Mr Gimbel, would you mind just settling an argument?"

"In the book they were Germans."

TERENCE BRADY
Pardon Me, Boy

I don't fly. Particularly in aeroplanes. I'm a fully paid-up and card-bearing member of the If God Had Intended Us To Fly Club. Or rather I was until I took a railway journey across the entire United States of America, because up until that time my notion of Hell was either stacking eternally in a thunderstorm over Epsom or sitting in an overbooked 707 perpetually waiting for take-off. But then I discovered Amtrak . . .

The reason for going to America was because the missus and I had been asked out to Hollywood to work on the Americanisation of a comedy series we'd written called *Pig In The Middle*. For my co-author, née Charlotte Bingham, flying happily holds no fears. All except flying with me. I just flatly refused to go at all, at first. And when finally coerced, I agreed – provided we could go my way. I then planned what I thought a most attractive alternative itinerary which involved railroading it across Siberia to Vladivostock, bussing it down to Ning-Po, sampanning across to Yokohama, then tramp-steamering it over to San Francisco.

However, at the eleventh hour it was pointed out that – since this route would take at least the best part of two months, since our Hollywood deadline was only two weeks, and

since this was the chance of a lifetime – if I didn't get on a plane, Madam would fly out there *toute seule* and write the script with Warren Beatty. I got on the plane.

And if you want a thumbnail description of what sort of flight it was, I believe it's what's known as a knuckler. We flew through the kind of weather you usually only see in disaster movies. The ones where George Kennedy, as irascible but lovable head maintenance engineer, keeps saying: "Of course they'll make it, goddammit! Sure as hell they will!" Even though the hijacked plane's been missing in the freezing fog for the last two reels.

It wasn't just turbulent. It was positively diatrophismic. Mid Atlantic, conditions got so bad that by popular request the cabin steward did an encore of his inflatable life jacket number, only this time to a much more attentive audience, and a rumour spread like wildfire that even the automatic pilot was being airsick.

By the time we'd made a one-point landing two and a half hours late in the full fury of a blinding snow-storm, I thought there was nothing left in the book that could be thrown at us. But I'd reckoned without the courtesy helicopter into New York practically turning turtle in the blizzard and nearly coming down

in the Hudson, and a kamikaze cabbie whose bag was shooting red lights on frozen city streets at ninety miles an hour *en route* to our hotel.

So you can imagine that, by the time it came to make leg two of our broken journey to Los Angeles, I was not really what you'd call match fit. However, the storms had abated and they'd promised a real great flight out West. What they neglected to tell us, though, was that this was also launch day of all the major airlines' Give - Us - 99 - Bucks - And - We'll - Fly - You - Anywhere campaign; as we prepared to embark, all hell let loose. What happened next gave new meaning to the term "overbooking". On this flight, even the crew couldn't get on board. And if you suffered from any of the major phobias (and personally I have them all from Agora to Xeno) this bulging Boeing was no place to be.

As the crowds engulfed us I passed out, was diagnosed as dead – or at the very least dying – and consequently refused further transit. The plane took off without us but with all our luggage, and that was how we came to Amtrak it across America armed only with the contents of Charlotte's handbag and my brief-case.

We had no alternative. Due to the $99 fly-you-anywhere scheme, there wasn't an avail-

"A working miner's wife actually, squire."

able flight for days. Besides, by now I'd had flying. Driving it was out of the question. In deep mid-winter and with a national 50mph limit, it would take a week. So the only option we had left was to Amtrak it. And if you don't know what Amtrak is, it's American for British Rail.

Any notion that American rail travel was going to be like it was on the movies was dispelled the moment we entered Grand Central Station. Central it may certainly be, but Grand – no no no. Not unless, that is, you're heavily into dope, dereliction or self-exposure. We found the only safe bar, where we stopped the show when it was discovered that we were intending to railroad it all the way to San José. And when we got on the train, we could see the reason for the martini quaffers' mass mirth. The rolling stock obviously hadn't been up-dated since it first brought Mr Deeds to Town.

Our "De Luxe Cabin" consisted of a broken armchair, an *en suite* khazi and two steel beds requisitioned from Alcatraz. Half an hour out of the terminus, the lights failed, to be followed shortly afterwards by the entire heating system. Since the temperature without was well on the minus side of sub, this didn't bode too well for the passengers' comfort. The lights recovered and sporadically flickered on and off through the night, but the heating had completely gone to the wall.

One of the consequences of this was that, by midnight, the entire sanitation system had frozen solid and was completely unusable. We pointed this out to our Pullman attendant when he finally answered our bell after a couple of hours, but since he was well over six foot twelve, black, fighting drunk and in the middle of what was later to prove a riotous all-night party in the next door suite, we felt that perhaps we shouldn't press the point.

In fact we had to wait to "freshen up" until we changed trains in Chicago, some fourteen hours later. By that time we had both developed funny walks and Charlotte had contracted flu. The ambulatory disorders were readily cured, but the influenza wasn't. This being America, about the only analgesic available without prescription was something called Toddlerspirin – which is probably fine if you're teething, but not if you're developing double pneumonia. A few shots of bourbon proved much more efficacious, as did a six-hour game of single syllable Scrabble. But, by midnight, delirium had set in. And, as we rolled into Cleveland, Ohio, the patient was convinced it was Basingstoke, Hampshire, and tried to get off in order to visit her late Aunt Mae who used to breed Farfella ponies. Fortunately, the train which was now taking us to LA was the very latest doubledecker Superchief, and had fully operational heating and sanitation, so I could at least keep the patient washed and warm.

Unfortunately, I couldn't keep her in bed, since – due to the budget for uprating the track being cancelled in about 1919 – Amtrak's flagship experienced great difficulty in staying on the rails round corners. So, whenever even the slightest bend was encountered, we were hurled like rag dolls out of our beds or chairs across and around our "De Luxe Observation Suite".

Not, I might add, that there was a great deal to observe from our berth. Sod's Law ordains that if there is any notable scenery on a railway journey you will inevitably pass through it by night, and that by day you will see only the backside of the country. This goes 101% for crossing America east to west, a journey which contains the most boring countryside through which I have ever travelled.

Highlights of the journey were one visible Rockie (we passed by the rest at night, natch), a hundred-mile spread called Charlie's Ranch (which, to the naked eye, seemed to contain only three starving cows and a privy), the original Las Vegas (deserted), Dodge City (deserted), La Paloma (one resident, a Gabby Hayes lookalike), six derailments (rusting), the Colorado Desert (deserted) and the Grand Canyon (night).

The Amtrak cuisine wasn't exactly remarkable either, both trains sharing the same menu. Meatballs, Chicken With All The Trimmins, Turkey With All The Pickins, or Steak au Jus. The chicken and the turkey were inedible, the meatballs were indescribable and the "Steak au Jus" was a huge lump of grey meat served in hot, greasy water – the "Jus". Broiled steak in greasy water is apparently a great Mid-West speciality. So, too, is the great Middle West. So too is Amtraking.

When it was time to leave California and return to England, we came out the way we should have gone out there originally. Pan Am First Class over the Pole. The flight was sensational, the service was impeccable and the scenery – including the Northern Lights – unforgettable. And the first thing I did once we'd hit London was to call in at my club, the IGHIUTFC, remember? And hand in my yellow badge and matching stripe to its lily-livered secretary. ✥

"Richard and I think Mrs Thatcher is perfectly right to over-react."

TELEVISION: JENSEN

DYNASTY JOAN COLLINS *as Alexis*
CORONATION STREET JEAN ALEXANDER *as Hilda Ogden*

THE LEVIN INTERVIEWS ALAN AYCKBOURN

CHAMPIONSHIP SNOOKER STEVE DAVIS ALEX HIGGINS

JOURNEY INTO THE SHADOWS ANNA MASSEY *as Gwen John*

Virgin Soil

AMAZING really. There are actually people in this world who wake up of a morning in their Totteridge mansions, gaze into Moorish-style vanitory units in their avocado bathroom suites, and become fired with a sense of mission: namely, to spend a small fortune flying 4,000 miles across the Atlantic to a tropical Caribbean isle for the sole purpose of regaling a wider audience than Totteridge can provide with the full, epic text of "Adventures with My Ovaries".

And if there aren't, how does one account for Mrs P.? I first came across her off the steaming coastline of Antigua sitting swathed like a mummy under an awning on the poop deck of the *Jolly Roger*. "An Hilarious Pirate Wedding at Sea! Snorkelling over a Picturesque Wreck! A chance to 'Walk the Plank' in True Pirate Style! Barbecue Steak or Lobster Lunch complete with Tempting Side Dishes! Free Bar together with our Wickedly Enjoyable *Jolly Roger* Pirate Rum Punch! And all for only $28 (lobster extra)."

Cutting through the squeals of honeymooning stenographers from New Jersey, through the megaphone bawls of the Pirate Cap'n (*"Hey dis is de Jolly Rah-ger, not a funeral home! We closin' de bar if you don't drink it all up now!"*) through the confidences of Katrina, the fat little meteorologist from Mississippi who's in Antigua hurricane-hunting in a C130 plane *("When Ah tell guys mah job is droppin' thayings into the middle of hurrcaynes, it gets 'em so horny they keep tryin' to get theyah pinkies into mah britches, know what Ah mean?"*) – throughout the

whole six hours of it all there came this steady, blow-fly drone: *"So, finally, the Doctor said, Mrs P., he said, let's have the whole lot out. . . not doing us any good. . . never seen anything so big. . ."*

That night, as I fell asleep in the Half Moon Hotel to the sound of the surf soft-shoe-shuffling up the moonlit beach, I dreamt that a mummified ghost climbed out of a C130 and glided towards me through the whispering palms ". . .Whole lot out. . .theyah pinkies. . . not doing us any good. . .mah britches. . ."

"Contrary to lurid tales, they turn out not to be woad-clad primitives with buttered toothpicks in their hair."

Don't remember much else about my day trip on the *Jolly Roger*. Took a lot of notes of course, but there are strange stains in my notebook, and ah, what valuable aperçus now lie crushed beneath those drunken consonants reeling through the skewed Navajo tepees of my vestigial shorthand? "Brls/ *fgrpt ? spgt frpng §35 gln spq!" Dead, dead, and never called me author. . .

All I can say is that, as far as I know, the sea was made of silk, the beaches were bone-white, and the sky the colour of bleached denim. But then I don't need "brg? stlp/fgs" to tell me that; it's all in the brochures.

Trouble is, "free bar" usually means that

whatever's on offer will contain only as much alcohol as you'd need to pickle an ant: the *Jolly Roger's* free rum-punch, on the other hand, is fierce enough to make a shark cry "Mother!" before its teeth fall out. It's thus one of the cheaper ways of getting drunk in Antigua which, partly thanks to the dollar, is not a cheap island at the moment. Antigua has had a drought now for four years (inland, cattle like hairpins drag feebly at thorn bushes on flayed-leather fields, just like the backdrop to a Jonathan Dimbleby Special), so maybe the "Pirate" company is just saving on water.

Despite the expense, the way some hoteliers tell it Antigua in summer is overrun with a much-loathed tribe known as "British cheapies". Contrary to lurid tales, they turn out to be not woad-clad primitives with buttered toothpicks in their hair, but simply harmless Midlands folk with bright red skin and wobbly thighs, who prefer to cook baked beans for the kiddies in their self-catering "units" rather than chuck away good overtime money on five-course meals, served in expensive hotel restaurants with traditional Antiguan surliness. Sound thinking to my mind.

"Cheapies! I *hate* 'em! They come here because it's got the best beaches in the Caribbean and hardly ever rains, but they don't like spending money!" spat one hotelier as he watched a group of self-catering "cheapies" innocently setting up a parasol on the flawless sands of Dickenson Bay. Approaching the cheapies for a friendly "I'm-on-your-side" chat, I was stopped dead in my tracks: from beneath a nearby sunshade, the blow-fly drone of Totteridge's Ancient Mariner fulfilling her mission ". . . so he said. . . straight out. . . not doing us any good. . .never seen anything . . . whole lot out . . ."

Well at least, I thought, settling into the LIAT flight as it began its leisurely chunter north to the British Virgin Islands, Totteridge's most famous ovaries won't be on offer where I'm going.

Their owner won't have heard of the BVI (as we cognoscenti like to call them). Well, be honest, have *you?* I mean, if I tell you I've just come back from the British Virgin Islands, you're not likely to yawn and say, "Ah, the dear old BVI! How are they these days?" You'd make me embark on an elaborate geography lesson – didn't know we British still had any virgins, ha! ha! Where are they? Do they speak English? And are there missionairies still for tea . . . ? That sort of thing.

Okay, see that map in the back of your diary? Look for Miami, then move down into the Caribbean and a little to the right until you see Puerto Rico and then just off there you'll see a tiny freckle of dots. That's them. Fifty of them, with names like Mosquito, Prickly Pear, Dog, Beef, Fallen Jerusalem, all of them consisting of humpy emerald-coloured hills surrounded by blue-green opaline seas, all of them fringed by secret, untrodden beaches, and only a handful of them inhabited. Fifty little chips of pure, unadulterated paradise. So *now* are you jealous?

Well, OK, I'll try again. Take Peter Island for example. Of course it's not so pure and unadulterated as to be full of bugs and swamps and naturalists with baggy shorts. The Crusoes who wash up here come complete with designer teeth, pants and nose-jobs, and if one aims to split a coconut with them while roughing it in the Peter Island Hotel (which apart from a couple of discreetly-hidden millionaire mansions, is the only building there), one simply has to accept their tribal mores. (Presuming, of course, that the bank robbery was a success and you can thus afford the bill.)

I mean, *if* one's going to indulge in the simple life, darlings, one *simply* can't do without one's own in-room fridge, one's complimentary bottles of chilled white wine, one's individually-wrapped tropical-fruit selection, one's emperor-sized bed, one's in-island boutique and oh, those thousand-and-one little necessities without which life away from Beverly Hills or Fifth Avenue becomes barely supportable. And one really *can't* contemplate putting one's Iced Peach Sundae toenails onto sand which hasn't been swept clean of seaweed by armies of Man Fridays with bulldozers at dawn! And, let's face it, one tends to get *disoriented* on an island paradise if one can't occasionally hear the sound of a million-dollar yacht softly gargling with gold coins as it sets off barracuda-hunting with Crusoes like oneself.

Of course you must give honour where it's due: so here's to the housewives of the Middle American suburbs, without whose daft devotion to buying buckets of wrinkle-cream from door-to-door salesmen Peter Island would not be possible. Here's hoping their hearts are gladdened by the news that, thanks to their efforts, the two gents who founded the Amway Corporation were able to scrape together enough of the crinklies to buy Peter Island, refurbish its hotel, and thus bring such unpretentious joys into the careworn lives of the deserving rich.

And, my dear, the deserving rich who patronise the BVI do have such dreadful problems! At Peter Island one hears them all. See that chap sunbathing on the deck above the stateroom of the *Xanadu*? That's "controversial" millionaire art dealer and racehorse owner Daniel Wildenstein; his little hol with the family at Peter Island is costing him around $100,000 but even here he can't get away from the cares of owning some of the fastest nags in the world. Telexes keep arriving at the hotel from his trainers telling him which million-dollar lump of horseflesh has developed wonky ankles, and what's more the island is now abuzz with the sad news that *Xanadu*'s owner won't be able to hang his spare masterpieces on the walls of the stately pleasure-dome he's building on nearby Virgin Gorda, because the salt-laden trade winds will rot the lot.

Well, short of buying a few Poussins from old Dan to ease the pain, there's not really a lot you and I can do to help him out. But one must, in all charity, grit one's teeth and buy as many Boy George records as one's humble purse can stretch to – otherwise poor young

Richard Branson of Virgin Records might not be able to finish the vast conical mansion he's building atop his very own Necker Island, and that *would* be sad.

But even the paradise of Peter Island isn't totally without drawbacks. It communicates with the outside world via radio telephone and so, as the brochure placed in the lush expanses of one's rattan-and-chintz bedroom warns, in capital letters, "CONVERSATIONS ARE NOT CONFIDENTIAL". (Must remember that next time I plan to zap the copper futures market.)

From Peter Island to the Bitter End. The Bitter End Yacht Club, on the tip of the North Sound of ravishing Virgin Gorda, "aims, Ann, to be livelier and more informal than Peter Island". Oh well, so will I. Forget my lack of designer teeth, I'll just sashay into the bar of an evening dangling a diving-tank over my shoulder, and try out lines like "Cozumel? Oh yeah! Great walls!" or "but doesn't the manifest back in Seville *list* the bastard silver in the cargo of 1740?". Just like I was one of *them*, the people round here who know every inch of the Caribbean islands – *but only under water*.

The stuff above sea-level they tend to be a bit foggy about; unless an object's at least 80ft down and covered in fish, it simply doesn't rate. When they do surface, they tend to congregate at the Bitter End, along with the visiting yachtsmen, the people with Interesting Pasts, and the odd shipwrecked drug runner. Bitter End's assets, apart from being the diver's "local", include a dazzling site, airy Somerset Maugham wooden cottages nestling on a hillside ablaze with bougainvillaea, hibiscus and humming birds – and Janis. She's the

manageress, a jolly, buxom Texan who looks like Sue Ellen's aunt. "Ah'm allergic to the sun, Ann, so Ah'm never tempted to go out in it – that way Ah can spend all mah tahm socialahsin' and carin' for mah guests!"

Some guests have been involuntary. ". . .Well of course, they'd emptied the evidence overboard before we came to rescue them, but there were these bags hangin' from under the hull. . . they must have got lost, Ah mean the Anegada Reef's way off the usual course from Colombia for the cocaine smugglers. . . no ship's papers either. . . well of course Ah made them sit in the far corner of the dining-room, away from mah other guests. . . Then these three gennl'men from Miami flew down, wearin' dark glasses and *suits*, so then we knew. . ." (Lissen, Salvatore, how was we to know it was da *suits* – dey was Tony da Tailor's best – but they didn't have no rubber flippers atta da end, *dat* was da mistake!)

Back at Antigua airport awaiting the BA flight home to reality, the lounge is knee-deep in duty-free rum bottles and singing cheapies wearing "ethnic" banana-sack shirts and palm-frond hats topped off with bouncing birds on prongs and . . .my God, there she is again! ". . .so he said. . . not doing us any good . . .what, dear? Oh, yes, it was a lovely holiday. . . whole lot out. . ."

She spots the "British Virgins are Best" sticker on my luggage. "What's that, dear?" I'm not bloody telling you, Mrs P. Are not Antigua's mead-halls vast enough for the great word-hoard of Totteridge's ovarian Bard? Must British Virgins suffer too? ℮

"This is going to be tricky – I cannot, ethically, defend a man I know to be guilty. On the other hand, unless you tell me where you buried the loot, I don't know whether you can afford me."

ALEXANDER FRATER

Bali Nuisance

> **"He crashed into the wall and got up with his mask over his left ear, reeling and barking like a seal."**

EARLY this year I spent an afternoon on Bali, travelling there from the neighbouring island of Lombok aboard a small airliner piloted by a man whose wife, as he struggled to maintain his heading and altitude in very wild weather, shouted abuse at him through the locked flight-deck door. The plane bucked and banged through the turbulence like a twig in a tide rip. Lightning periodically seared the dark sky, and I reckoned I could hear the thunderclaps even above the shriek of the turboprops and the babbled prayers of the elderly couple across the aisle. Meanwhile, this slim, rather good-looking woman, with her head wrapped in a towel, stood wedged between the front seats, effortlessly riding the storm as she yelled at poor Captain Kowalereng in Bahsa Indonesian, a language richly endowed with offensive and intimidatory epithets. When she began breaking the door down I remembered it was also the language that gave us the word "amok".

The man in the next seat, an animal husbandry expert from Lombok ("I am really best husband for goats") explained that our pilot, over the years, had acquired a reputation throughout the Indonesian archipelago for unusually promiscuous behaviour. Mrs Kowalereng, a jealous woman, was travelling to see her aunt in Bali and, unfortunately, had happened to book herself on the very service that he was commanding. Well, yes, I followed that, of course, but why was she attempting to dismantle the plane while it was still 5000 feet above the Flores Sea?

"I think maybe he has someones in there now."

I stared at him, too shocked to speak, imagining Captain Kowalereng engaging in congress only inches from the throttles, perhaps striking the reverse thrust toggle with a random knee or, worse, shoving a foot through the windscreen. But then the NO SMOKING sign came on to indicate that we were on finals and all was well. Mrs Kowalereng fell silent and returned to her seat. The landing was a tempestuous affair, the aircraft suddenly attempting a whip stall and double snap roll before Captain Kowalereng overruled it and brought it to earth with a comforting thump. We taxied in to the terminal through streaming rain, passing a Garuda 747 all lit up and heading out towards the runway threshold with its wheels making waves in the flood. The plane parked and cut its engines. Nothing hap-

pened. The passengers fell into a doze, lulled by the drumming of the downpour on the roof. I picked up a copy of the *Jawa Pos* - the *Java Post* - and glanced at the Flash Gordon strip. A youth with horns on his head was addressing Flash and the Witch Queen, Azura, with some urgency. "Tele...tele...wah, kau tahu, bukan, Flash!" the youth exclaimed. Then someone opened the door and we all sprinted to the terminal where, while getting my breath back, I stood looking at a crudely painted sign showing two rows of young European visitors. The tourists in the front row were filthy, unkempt and slouching, those in the second neatly attired and smiling, with very good posture. The legend said, "It Is A Must To Dress Correctly When Visiting Government Offices." At that moment a couple came past who illustrated perfectly the idealised types the artist had attempted to capture, a handsome, personable pair walking hand in hand and gazing at each other with affection. It was Captain and Mrs Kowalereng.

"It's black Shaun's treasure!"

I had four hours before my onward flight to Jakarta, and decided to take a room at a neighbouring hotel. I needed a swim and a sleep and, if the rain eased, I would also do a little sight-seeing. After all, I had come to the most beautiful island on earth, named "The Morning of the World" by Tagore and renowned for its devout, industrious and shyly-welcoming people; it would be silly not to observe it at first hand.

In the taxi the driver asked, "You want women?"

"No, thanks," I said.

"Boys?"

"Absolutely not."

"Smack?"

"I just want a swim," I told him.

He sighed. "Jeeze," he murmured, and I remembered that Bali, in the course of the past decade, had suffered an Australian invasion. Tens of thousands of them now swarmed up annually across the Timor Sea, turning the place into a kind of Antipodean Majorca, and I wondered uneasily to what extent their presence had influenced its gentle inhabitants. But I had come at the trough of the low season and there were none at the hotel. Instead, the place was full of Japanese honeymoon couples who, when the rain ceased, joined me at the poolside. The women wore very elegant haute couture sporting outfits and everyone lay around in pairs, watching each other as guardedly as prison warders. Their charter, clearly, had just got in.

The smiling Balinese barman brought me a beer. "Get this down you," he said. There was a sudden stirring among the Japanese. One of their number was plodding across the grass in full scuba-diving gear — black wetsuit, mask, oxygen tanks, flippers and a depth gauge; strapped to his thigh I noted the kind of sheath knife used for butchering giant squid. He was followed by his child bride, beaming with pride and looking fetching in pedal-pushers, a Lacoste T-shirt, Gucci loafers, a printed silk headscarf and plenty of chunky rhinestone jewellery. There was a low interested hum from their fellow guests which turned into hisses of concern when the diver tripped on his flippers and crashed to the ground.

His bride looked mortified as he slowly picked himself up and staggered on towards the pool, a series of tinny, disembodied oaths echoing from behind his mask. When he arrived at the shallow end he jumped in. He adjusted his equipment, raised a hand to us then plunged beneath the surface. The pool was three feet deep here and, for several minutes, he lay motionless on the bottom. I went and stood beside his wife who was gazing at him with a frowning, troubled face. Could he have fallen asleep? Everyone was watching intently.

"Perhaps he's got the bends," I said.

She gave me a scornful, dismissive glance and turned away. I was considering the wisdom of reaching down and prodding him when, all at once, he kicked violently with his flippers, shooting forward like a torpedo being fired from its tube. He crashed into the wall and got up with his mask over his left ear, reeling and barking like a seal. He was standing there, going "Kaark! Kaark! Kaark!" when, without any prior warning, the heavens opened up again. Everyone dashed for cover. A little green snake crawled to the end of a branch overhanging the pool and dropped in, swimming gravely past me as though doing lengths. I went to settle up with the barman. "Have you got poisonous snakes in Bali?" I asked.

"Too bloody right we have," he said, washing glasses. "They're small green jokers that can kill in seconds."

"There's one in your pool," I said and went indoors. The rain was drumming down with such force that it vaporised on impact and formed itself into a low-lying cloud, like marsh gas. I had wanted to go to Ubud, the artistic centre, to soak myself in the cultural life of the island, to see for myself its phenomenal outpouring of painting, sculpture and dancing, but I turned on the telly instead.

I got Flash Gordon again, this time in English. Flash was being menaced by a demon with blazing yellow eyes and smart purple tights. It was growling.

"Sounds like he hasn't had breakfast," Flash observed. Then grew serious. "After the carbonite ray, the only thing left to throw at that creature is the kitchen sink. It's the most powerful thing on Mongo."

An aide advised him that the demon was made of vegetable matter with a silicone base; that was why it had not responded to the carbonite ray.

Next we saw them in their space craft, the Sky Train, making for a new galaxy; unknown to them, however, the demon had crept in the cargo hold and, putting a tentacle out the window and reaching up to the front, it smashed the windscreen and seized Flash by the throat. Flash advised everyone that he was losing his power. He was also turning green.

This reminded me that I too had a flight to catch and, gathering my belongings together, I set off through the monsoon to the airport. We took off in the early evening, the little Fokker jet clambering up through swirling cloud until, suddenly as a blind being drawn, Bali vanished and all I could see was a stormy orange moon, low on the horizon where Bali had been.

"We've succeeded in persuading a very distinguished scholar to write an introduction. He thinks your book stinks, and says so, but people will have bought it before they find out."

MORE TROUBLE OVER AT GENETIC ENGINEERING

And another thing... The food stinks

Albert's New Year dissolutions

"Gaz has decided to give up biting his fingernails."

"I always do quite well until the January sales."

"So much for the twenty press-ups a day."

"Looks like they're serious this year."

" . . . Beluga caviar. How about you?"

"We haven't even finished Auld Lang Syne yet and you've already mugged your Grandad!"

JOHN WAIN

Poet Laureates

Dryden   Masefield

Betjeman

MY impression is that most people regard having a Poet Laureate as one of those endearingly goofy English institutions like Black Rod or the Chiltern Hundreds; yet most of these things tend to have their own kind of logic when one looks into them.

People of radical views who dislike the Establishment have no use for the notion of an official poet who will tend to reflect its attitudes, and that's fair enough. But there is another source of the uneasiness with which the Laureateship is regarded, and that is the view that the poet ought to express his or her individuality in its pure form, relying totally on mood and inspiration, so that the notion of writing a poem to order, on a set theme, is a contradiction in terms.

This idea is of course one of those that were born of the Romantic movement, the last large-scale injection of new ideas into the European mind. It was the Romantics who saw the poet as the solitary seer, working in an isolation that was at worst no hindrance to him and at best a positive strength, since it freed him from the inevitable corruptions and delusions of society. To those who hold this view in its most uncompromising form, the poet not only may but *ought to* remain deaf to any prompting from the society at large, except at the deep and almost mystical level of the *Zeitgeist*.

This attitude became current round about the point where the eighteenth century moved into the nineteenth. Before that, people's idea of

the poet seems to have been a person with a supreme gift of expression, who could be trusted to put anything into attractive and memorable language; a somewhat more exalted version, in fact, of the way the writer is regarded in a modern film studio: give him a story-line and he'll provide it with a good shape and convincing dialogue. The tribal societies of the very early Middle Ages retained poets whose function was to memorialize great events and celebrate heroes; the poet of *Beowulf* was one such, and so were the bards who flourished at the courts of the Welsh Princes. All these did the job that we should nowadays think of as appertaining to the Poet Laureate.

With the coming of the more splendid courts of the Renaissance, not only poets but painters and musicians, indeed artists and entertainers of every kind, found their niche at court. A brilliant architect and stage designer like Inigo Jones, who worked for James I, was a typical court artist; for that matter, the company that Shakespeare belonged to was known for a time as "the King's Men," and Shakespeare's slightly younger friend and contemporary, Ben Jonson was effectively Poet Laureate – he received a regular salary as a functionary of the Royal Household – though evidently he was not known by that title.

When Charles II made John Dryden his Poet Laureate in 1670, the notion was not at all new, though the actual title

seems to have been first used then. Dryden was appointed Historiographer-Royal at the same time, and the linkage is significant. He was supposed to give the official version of events.

Dryden was a poet with a natural taste for writing on public themes, dealing with issues that involved the entire society first and the individual only as a consequence; his style was trumpet-like, clear, sonorous and flashing; and he wholeheartedly adopted the political and social attitudes of the restored Stuarts. He was never in any doubt that what he drew his money for (£300 a year for the two posts, later with a butt of canary wine thrown in) was not simply for writing good poems, which he did, but for backing the Royal party in the various controversies of the day. In the early 1680s Charles was having trouble with a faction headed by the Earl of Shaftes-

bury. Dryden weighed in with a poem called *The Medal*, in which there is a magnificently energetic denunciation of Shaftesbury; according to Joseph Spence, whose painstaking collection of scraps and fragments about literary men appeared in the next century, the King personally gave Dryden the nudge to start writing on this subject:

It was King Charles II who gave Mr Dryden the hint for writing his poem called *The Medal*. One day as the King was walking in the Mall and talking with Dryden, he said: "If I were a poet (and I think I'm poor enough to be one) I would write a poem on such a subject in the following Manner –", and then gave him the plan for it. Dryden took the hint, carried the poem as soon as it was written to the King, and had a present of a hundred broadpieces for it.

Dryden was deprived of the Laureateship in 1689, one year after James II had been booted out and the Stuarts replaced by a new dynasty: a fair indication of how closely his position was seen to be knitted in with that of Charles and then James. I know of no other case when a Laureate lost his job except by death, or, as we call it nowadays, "natural wastage".

IT seems reasonable, then, to see the office of Poet Laureate not as a simple compliment to the most distinguished living poet but as a job for someone who likes, and is able, to write poems of a public nature. The essentially private and individual nature of Romantic inspiration, which still gives us our dominant idea of the poet, is flatly against this. So, who's going to give way?

I personally would not mind much if the Poet Laureateship disappeared, but before abolishing it a few things ought to be borne in mind. First, the notion that the poet's sole concern is with his own individual perceptions, that he shares nothing (except by chance) with the rest of the people who make up his society, has never really won the agreement of the bulk of humanity. Most people who have strong opinions in any direction – who are pacifist, or patriotic, or religious, or anti-religious, or feminist, or whatever – are rather pleased than otherwise when they find their particular opinions given a voice in poetry. During the Vietnam years, for example, when the youth of America (and by magnetic attraction of the Western world generally) achieved a great degree of unanimity, a shared attitude to that war and beyond it a shared rebellion against authority generally – during those years they liked nothing better than to crowd into cellars where, with or without intervals of folk-song, they heard poems read out which gave them back their own opinions and attitudes.

Most of these poems seemed to me then, and seem to me now, to be loose oratory rather than poetry. The language had to be so open in texture, the positions adopted so simple, that there was not much chance for the poets to load them with the rich *nuances* of poetry even if the writers had been capable of it. The fact remains that the young felt a need for verse of a kind that would make a public statement; just as long as the statement was what they wanted to hear.

It follows, then, that the con-

"He was hoping to change his will and leave the lot to the cat."

vention forbidding the poet to speak for a society, or for a substantial segment of that society, has never really prevailed. And if it hasn't, why not have a Poet Laureate? It's true that such a Laureate would naturally express views in his verse that (broadly) went along with those of the established power. But if we feel that to be immoral, we are making a judgment on politics, not on poetry. If we think that the monarchy, and Parliamentary government, and the mixed economy, are wicked and tyrannous, then of course our idea of a Laureate will be someone who attacks these things and sure enough a Communist poet like Hugh McDiarmid was treated, by his admirers, very much as a Laureate.

An example from the opposite extreme might be Kipling, who during the years of expansionist Imperialism accepted those values and enshrined them in verse. Kipling was never Laureate; yet during that entire period it was he who actually fulfilled the duties of the position, in so far as these involve supporting the official views of the leadership and boosting the morale of the military and administrative power.

We are likely at any given time, then, to have a typical Laureate (expressing Establishment attitudes) and a typical Counter-Laureate (expressing subversive or revolutionary views). Perhaps they should both be institutionalized. For instance, the subject of the birth of a new Royal Prince or Princess would be commemorated in terms of satisfaction by the Laureate, and of savage mockery by the Counter-Laureate. Which was the better poem would then become an interesting, and real, question.

One thing is certain, though: most people, from the most sophisticated to the simplest, would prefer the poem that expressed their own opinions.

They would say, of course, that it was the better poem.

John Wain is Emeritus Professor of Poetry at Oxford University

"Well, that's enough about world domination, now I'd like to talk to you about double glazing. . ."

LOVE'S

"Are you sure you're not seeing someone else?"

"I sent myself a Valentine's card this year and it didn't turn up."

LABOURS LOST

MICHAEL HEATH massacres St Valentine's Day

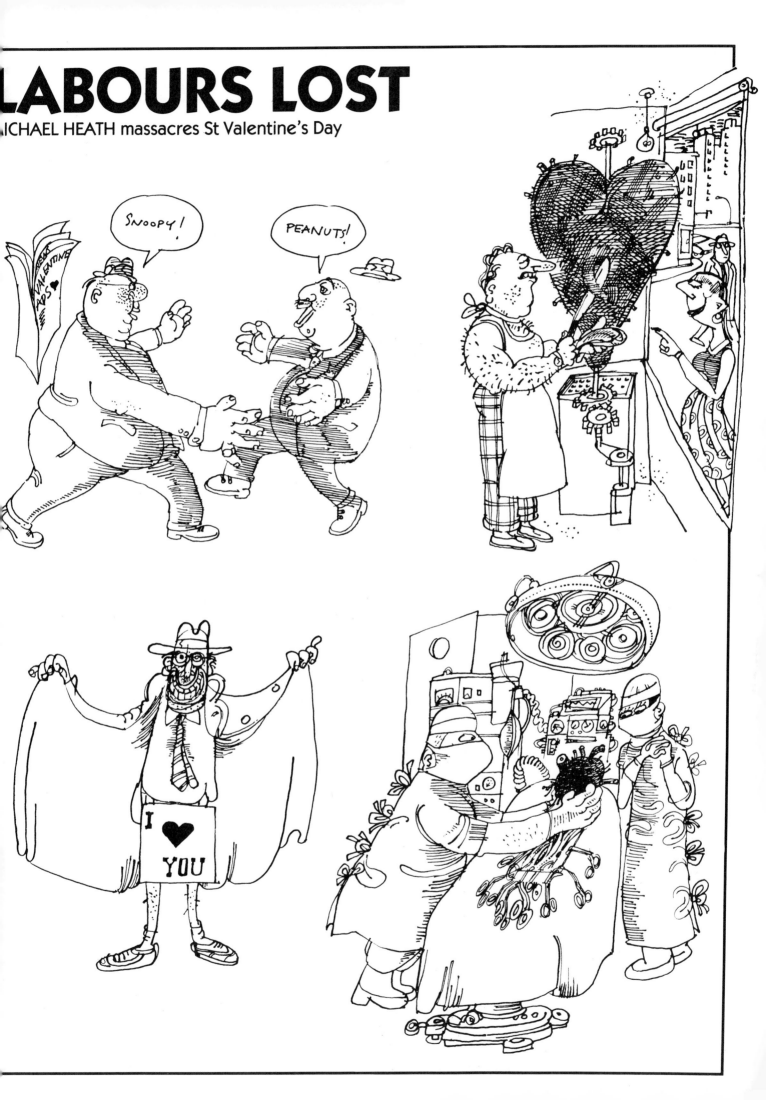

· J E R E M Y · L E W I S ·

DESPITE THE best endeavours of stuffies and fogeys of all ages, a good many much-loved ingredients of English life have been removed from the communal store cupboard over the past thirty years or so, from half-a-crowns and bowler hats to bottle-nosed ex-majors eking out a living as prep-school masters, hobbling across games pitches on their gammy legs and lashing out clips to left and right.

Foremost among our Endangered Species – on a par, perhaps, with Distressed Gentlefolk in South Kensington, crouching over gas fires in Drayton Gardens in well-worn tweeds and sipping sherry out of tooth mugs – is that finest example of womanhood, the English maiden aunt. In the days of my youth the country positively pulsated with maiden aunts – running WIs, waving walking sticks, transfixing small boys with looks of thunder, rescuing underprivileged Spanish donkeys, arguing with greengrocers, knocking up sponge cakes, keeping nephews and nieces supplied with 10/- postal orders, showing visitors round the local church ("The stained glass windows are at least a hundred years old," explained a scholarly aunt, referring to Fairford's famous fourteenth-century glass, "and they were taken down and hidden during the Civil War"), agreeing with every word in the *Daily Express*, and displaying symptoms of alarm at the goings on of that foaming revolutionary, Clement Attlee. Even more plentiful were great-aunts, of the kind that terrorised Bertie Wooster: their numbers were accounted for, we were told, by the slaughter on the Western Front, which had left these ladies with no one to marry and energy to spare.

Like many children of my generation, I grew up hemmed in by maiden aunts, mostly of the "great" variety. My favourite great-aunt was Auntie Annie. A wizened, bent figure, with an enormous curved nose like a Brazil nut and big, round eyes like prunes (the family claimed – or at least my mother claimed on their behalf – a sizeable dash of gypsy blood), she lived alone in a tiny flat up in Onslow Gardens. Annie had spent most of her life as a nurse in the East End: winter or summer, she wore an

aged fox fur slung round her neck and a green felt hat, held firmly in place by one of those enormous, pearl-headed hat pins that featured so largely in mystery stories between the wars. She had legs like broomsticks in stockings, on the bottom of which could be found a highly polished pair of brown "sensible" shoes.

A keen amateur carpenter and electrician, she frequently fused the lights in the entire block of flats, and liked nothing better than to engage my father in technical debate about lathes and chisels. Though hospitable to a degree, she lived off diminutive chops or the occasional kipper cooked over an ancient Baby Belling (the culinary equivalent of the Austin Seven, perhaps): the walls of her midget-sized bathroom were covered with useful and cautionary notices designed to assist the unwary visitor ("Pull chain down STRAIGHT" by the lavatory chain). Despite her proper demeanour, she was game for anything, tossing down the sherry at the least provocation and more than once – when far too old for such antics – joining my parents in various wild sprees, her fox fur and green felt hat remaining firmly in place as she scaled a six-foot wall or was lowered down a drainpipe into the garden of some unsuspecting party-giver. She must have been well over eighty when she eventually deserted Onslow Gardens and moved down to Eastbourne to join two of her sisters. Away from her beloved London, from the peeling stucco and the sulphurous winter smogs, she seemed a shadow of her sparrow-like self, and within a year she was dead.

Though tirelessly good and generous, her Eastbourne sisters were altogether less magical to a child. Auntie Mary, the forceful one, was a short, stout woman, with bristly grey hair and pendulous jowels of the kind unflatteringly referred to as dewlaps. She was, I suspect, a kind old thing, but her gruff voice, ferocious gaze and more than a touch of the regimental sergeant-major made her a force to be reckoned with. Before moving to Eastbourne, she and her sister Ada had lived in Blatchington, a genteel part of Seaford with a golf course to hand, a large number of hydrangea bushes concealing spacious Edwardian

houses, and an engagingly upper-middle-class population of retired tea planters, prep-school masters, solicitors in lovat green tweeds and rival teams of maiden aunts.

Seaford in those days was much favoured by stern-looking ladies in demob suits, trilby hats and string ties who moved about the town with enormous strides and (I liked to think) smoked huge cigars in the privacy of their suburban gardens: Auntie Mary looked, at first sight, as though she might have been a member of this curious sorority, though in fact she cherished a melancholy, unrequited and lifelong passion for a major over the road. As a motorist she was a public menace – which was hardly surprising, since once she had lowered her enormous frame into the bucket seat of her Vauxhall, little could be seen above the windscreen but the top of her head and her hands, firmly gripping the wheel in the approved "ten-to-two" position. On the day of her funeral, as we were walking away from the church, my Auntie Annie turned to her surviving sister, tapped her watch and said in sepulchral tones, "Ada, I think she must be nearly there by now." If Mary's motoring was anything to go by, she must have spent a great deal of time mounting the kerb and mowing down innocent pedestrians *en route* for the Pearly Gates: but like most of my family, she was a stickler for punctuality, so Annie's prognosis may not have been so far out after all.

Auntie Ada, who outlived them all, was the only remotely rich relation we had, and far and away the saddest. Even as a young and – judging by the photographs – very fine-looking girl in the early 1920s, she had a wistful, haunted look about her. She had spent a good deal of time in China, and her houses were crammed with pop-eyed turquoise porcelain pekes, lacquered gold and black wardrobes with impenetrable oriental locks, jade Buddhas on circular black stands, and glass cabinets in which tiny, colourful figures enacted forever the elaborate rituals of an Imperial Chinese procession; and over them all there hung a curious musty smell that remains for me – quite wrongly, no doubt – the quintessential whiff of the Orient. While out in the East the sad-

seeming Ada met and married an amiable, well-heeled Yorkshire businessman, a good many years older than her; within only a few months of their wedding he was dead.

Ada returned home to England, where she moved into a large, red-brick, tile-hung, mullion-windowed Edwardian house, along with her sister Mary. With its rhododendron bushes, tennis court, clipped hedges, tradesmen's entrance, vegetable gardens, crunching gravel drive and bell-push discreetly positioned under the dining-room table within reach of the proprietorial toe, it was exactly the kind of house Richmal Crompton's William Brown must have lived in: unlike William, Ginger and Henry, those great-nephews and great-nieces who occasionally paid a visit were very much on their best behaviour, politely picking at neatly trimmed cucumber sandwiches and speaking only when spoken to, and exhaling sighs of relief as polite farewells were said, and the benign but somewhat daunting elderly aunts disappeared from view in the back window of the car. For all her kindness and the protective affection she inspired, poor Ada remained an unhappy, nervous, dissatisfied figure: the only one of those particular aunts to have married and yet, perhaps, the one that most embodied all those wearisome, condescending clichés about the sadness and the frustration of the maiden aunt.

Maiden aunts are a dying breed, and are likely to become ever scarcer as the years roll by. Smaller families, the notion that women – whether married or not – have the "right" to a child, sexual permissiveness, the oppressive and patronising stigma attached to those who, often for perfectly good reasons of their own, choose to remain single or even (shame upon them!) chaste: faced with such pressures as these, the classic English maiden aunt – eccentric, forceful, devoted to good causes and curious branches of knowledge, source of solace, anecdote, family lore and endless jars of pickle and home-made jam – seems doomed to follow cane-swishing schoolmasters in mortar-boards and gowns and scholarly, absent-minded vicars into the Elysium reserved for those whose time is past. ⟲

MARK HACKETT

"It was held firmly in place by one of those enormous, pearl-headed hat pins that featured in mystery stories."

MALCOLM BRADBURY
Blotting the Landscape

1. INT. STUDY. DAY.

Since Christmas last, I have done little else but write television drama, or more specifically write adaptations of novels, two by Tom Sharpe and one by myself, for television serial performance. Now, as the autumn begins, I feel the need to explain to myself and others this peculiar yet compulsive temptation. I am by birth and custom a novelist, and, when I write, writing novels is what I usually do. As is well-known, novelists are of all the forms of writer the most virgin and virtuous. Playwrights are regularly invited to stay at the palazzi of Italian film-directors, and there they engage in unspeakable orgies on international co-funding. Poets write very short things and get out a lot, drinking in public houses and putting their hands up the skirts of the wives of their friends.

But we, the novelists, live shuttered up, mostly in small country rectories, where we work extraordinarily long and unsocial hours. Our voices are few: drinking before dinner, and fantasizing about unusual couplings – but that is how one gets to be a novelist in the first place. It is a very decent, peculiarly private activity. Yet there is little doubt that, if it is practiced continuously for too long, it can, as Homer discovered, make you blind. Writing television is a communal activity. Admittedly, writing six one-hour episodes means long solitary hours in the study at the typewriter, but one starts from someone's existing work, in order to create instructions for someone else's future work. It is not like writing novels.

This winter the work in question has been Tom Sharpe's *Blott on the Landscape*, a very funny novel about a hideous country house owned by a well-established brewing family which is threatened by a motorway. To me, this is a happy and buoyant combination of authors. I find Sharpe one of the great contemporary farce writers and deeply enjoy the collaboration between his farcical, outrageous comedy and my

own rather severer kind. He has been not only tolerant but very encouraging. We met in a London restaurant, where he arrived breathless, having, he said, just returned from Snowden. I looked for snow on his boots; in fact he had just had his photograph taken. Photography (as we shall see in later episodes) proved to be a Sharpe obsession.

"Throw the book out of the window," he told me, and though I have not done that I have had to change it. It has six enormous, outrageous set-pieces, but these must be rearranged to the end of each episode. The characters plot against each other, in an elaborate seesaw. I must keep the seesaw rocking, and give to each role character-progression and continuous dialogue.

Sharpe goes for extraordinary situations; these must be given motive and probability, to the point of supplementing the narrative. Delighting in his ever-extending, outrageous situations, I add more comedy to his. As a result I write in condition of comic delight, even though at times some lines prove strangely painful to type, like, for example, THEY OVERTURN THE ROLLS ROYCE. Why not something cheaper? Isn't this going to cost a lot of money? And will Tom Sharpe like it?

2. INT. PRODUCER'S OFFICE. DAY. OVER SEVERAL DAYS.

Out of the house and into society; television is essentially a communal activity. So communal, indeed, that one does

not write for it at all, one re-writes for it. The rule of the business is that anyone whose hands a draft-script passes – producer, executive producer, assistant producer, director, set-designer, members of the cast, and the spouse and mother of any or all of these – is entitled to propose the most radical changes. Let's put it in a different decade, a different century, another country. Can't it be done in one episode? In twenty? Can't it be funnier? Less funny? More relevant? More fantastic? Can't we have a scene in the Houses of Parliament? Much profitable thought and discussion is contributed to the script, until it is time to leave society and go back to

3. INT. STUDY. DAY.

Anguish, doubts. What is the nature of this activity? Can a book honorably and decently be transformed into another medium? But you believe the answer is Yes. All writing, you are convinced, is a form of re-writing, all literature a commentary on other literature, and on literature as an institution. You do, that is what you believe. Sharpe has created you, a reader, and that reader has turned writer and is re-creating. You have kept to his spirit, you are adding your spirit. But now the readers have multiplied and are adding their versions. They are professional and convincing and it will be their work as well as yours. Sit down, write again, re-write again. Is it better? Possibly, probably. But it has to be done, the deadline is near, and soon we are due at . . .

4. INT. REHEARSAL ROOMS, ACTON. DAY.

Television is an essentially communal activity. This means getting up very early, risking British Rail from Norwich to London, where the diesel engines frequently explode and the fire brigade is permanently posted all down the line, and then taking the Central Line from Liverpool Street to North Acton, a day's work in itself. If one were a social realist dramatist, they would not only rehearse in Acton, they would film there as well. Never be a social realist dramatist. The series has been marvellously cast: George Cole, David Suchet, Simon Cadell, Geraldine James. How will Cole feel about being eaten by a lion? Geraldine James about romping naked through Handyman Hall after a stark Cadell, shouting "Tallyho"? How to explain the essential creative principles that make these scenes absolutely and irrevocably necessary? And why is it that, at rehearsals, nobody ever seems to eat? Perhaps because there is only a week of rehearsal and then everything moves on location to . . .

5. EXT. MARKETPLACE, LUDLOW. DAY.

Coming into Ludlow has been a peculiar sight. The roads have been blocked with large containers filled with savage animals. Lions. Gorillas. Zebra. Rhinos. I wrote an abstemious script, letting words do the work. Only small parts of animals were employed; I thought they would probably use Muppets. How will they feel in Ludlow, a place where little has happened since Milton wrote *Comus*?. The town centre has been cordoned off for the riot. Market stalls have been set up, and a number of cars strategically placed among them, one of them the Rolls Royce. The police are out in very great force. It turns out they are actors, and that I wrote them. Or rather Tom Sharpe wrote them, and I re-wrote them.

The one person there whom I did not write, though I did rewrite, is Tom Sharpe himself, busily taking photographs; naturally enough, since he was once a professional photographer, and photographs play a substantial part in this as in other of his stories. He discloses the most remarkable thing about the entire situation: the location is the one he himself had in mind in his own INT. STUDY fantasy when he wrote the scene. The book by no means makes this clear, though, knowing Ludlow, I had suspected, and so, independently, had the location-finder. As a result,

"Good morning, sir. The Bureau of Statistics is conducting an inter-regional survey into how many men actually use the little slot in their Y-fronts, and wonder if you'd like to help."

the door from which Geraldine James and her savage band of rioters now emerge is exactly that of the Sharpean imagination. In Sharpean spirit, they flood the square, throwing vegetables, setting fire to the stalls, and burning the cars. THEY OVERTURN THE ROLLS ROYCE turns into the overturning of the Rolls Royce. Did I write this? Why are they doing it? Yet more remarkable, why is it that the square, returned to an hour later, is clean, without damage, and with all the apparently broken windows restored? But it is time to move on to . . .

6. EXT & INT. "HANDYMAN HALL". DAY.

In the book and the script, 'Handyman Hall' is a hideous late Victorian building with Gothic features. This does not quite explain why the chosen location is a beautiful Georgian house set in a fine valley in the Welsh Marches. But compensation is being applied.

A hideous green latex covering is being stuck to its entire facade.

A vile Gothic tower is being added to its roofline by a crane. Fencing is being erected to keep in the screaming wild animals who will shortly eat George Cole.

Tom Sharpe, who has come to take photographs, is also somewhat mystified as he surveys the product of such extraordinary and brilliant ingenuity from the superb set-designer – who is also building a forty-foot, four-storey gatehouse in a gorge near Bristol and the entire centre of an Oxfordshire village, both, like so much else in the production, to be destroyed. Tom looks at the house and asks me a potent question. "It didn't really have to be Gothic, did it?" he said. "Why didn't you just rewrite the line?"

7. INT. STUDY. DAY, AFTER DAY, AFTER DAY.

Two and a half million pounds have been spent on the products of the typewriter that sits there, in all its modesty, under its dustcover. Mayhem of a serious kind has occurred in Shropshire, Oxfordshire, Gloucestershire, and St. John's Wood. People have been eaten by lions and killed by the ball of a swinging crane. I have always made it clear the truly essential quality of fiction is its fictionality. Unlike politics, religion, sociology or science, it is the one form of expression that insists in its very name and its best practice that it is not true; and this is its most profound truth. Yet, out of fiction there has come a curious order of fictional factiticity, an extraordinary combination of people and talents, a community so real that it seems like a funeral when it all breaks up. I put down my tired briefcase. I shut the shutters. I remove the typewriter dustsheet, roll in some paper, and type

RATES OF EXCHANGE
EPISODE ONE
1. INT. STUDY. DAY.

"Brightest horse I ever had – broke a leg and shot himself."

A COLD FOR CHRISTMAS

RUSSELL DAVIES

The New Kamelot

Moscow, Thursday

THEY'RE really painting the town Red tonight! In the Moscow skies it's Marx and sparks as fireworks shower over the city's onion domes. Down in the streets, there's vodka à gogo as Muscovites go gay in a new and exciting way.

All along the Leninsky Prospekt, exuberant charladies in fur-lined boots are doing a peasant stomp to the best of electric balalaikas. On Red Square, youths are openly sniffing British sherbet through tubes of licorice. In the outermost suburbs, senior citizens are hot-wiring tractors and heading downtown. And it's all because of one individual – champagne-swilling Mikhail Gorbachev, the man they're already calling the Ron Atkinson of the Steppes.

It's only a matter of days since fun-loving Mikhail ("Call me Mickey, like your famous Mouse") took over the reins of the ship of state. Yet life here is already transformed. It used to be impossible to get your burnt-out toaster mended, yet suddenly there seems to be a blacksmith on every street corner. The windows of the giant department store GUM are ablaze with fantastic geometrical displays of clothes pegs painted in luminous colours – a thing never seen in Moscow before. Old men gather in knots to gawp and wonder, oblivious to the giggling children who, given half a

chance, will tie an inflated black condom to your leg and run away with a joyous cry. It's not like the old days here.

Moscow folk are not slow to credit a number of the changes to Gorbachev's stunning wife, Raisa "Bubbles" Gorbachev, a former can-can dancer from the Folies Berlin. It is she, they say, who inspired the plan to issue a pliable 45 rpm disc by Johnny Ray as a giveaway insert with *Pravda*. She, too, is said to have given the go-ahead to the Taganka Theatre for their sell-out satirical smash *Sick As An Apparatchik*, in which Stalin is depicted as an unpleasant old party who caused literally dozens of decent Russians to be put to death. And who was it who persuaded Gorbachev to appear on the new video by Moscow's top new-wave band, The Philbys? Why, "Bubbles" of course. She determines hubby's style from the crown of his polished head (pomade by Trumper's of Mayfair) to the tips of his Gucci shoes. Catch him banging those on the negotiating tables of the United Nations!

Politically speaking, Gorbachev does not dye his hair but has believable eyebrows which he is capable of raising or lowering independently. Already these pantomimic skills have magnetised the Iron Lady. But there is more. It is also rumoured that Mr Gorbachev can execute a lively tap-dance while playing *Bei Mir*

Bist Du Schoen on the kazoo; that he has a collection of English real-ale beermats unrivalled in all the Soviet republics; and that, in any forthcoming documentary dramatisations of international affairs, he would like to be played by Rod Steiger in a blue, double-breasted suit with white buttons.

The first sign of change came in Moscow when, at the funeral of President Chernenko in Red Square, the salute was taken by a row of spindly, hatless figures unfamiliar to the crowd below. These turned out to be geraniums. Mr Gorbachev is known to have a fondness for flowers. At his dacha near Borodino he keenly cultivates poppies, sunflowers, and all manner of flamboyant shrubs. Unusually for a Russian leader, he will sometimes hold private parties in his greenhouse.

Among Gorbachev's close friends are several who look likely to be drawn into his immediate decision-making circle. None is a member of the Supreme Soviet, though many are experienced in organising jazz bands, notably the avant-garde banjoist Yuri Foxtrotsky, and trombonist "Snakehips" Chesnokov, with whom the new President has shared frequent yachting holidays on the Black Sea. At next week's invitational pro-celebrity golf tournament, the KGB Klassic, Gorbachev will be partnered by Anatoly Tarbuk, the Kiev comedian, who by all normal standards should have been purged decades ago.

Over a large Dry Molotov at the newly-opened Playcomrade Klub, Kremlin Press Secretary Igor "The Buzz" Borienko outlined to me the differences in his working day. "Basically, I no longer have to look over my shoulder," he explained. "They have given me a mirror for this. Also the whole look of the office has changed. Where before we were allowed only to hang up portraits of Lenin and the current leader, we now have your much-loved Queen Mother and a whole wall devoted to *Izvestia* Page Three girl Galina Fuchs. In front of this wall we have a waste-basket where many, many pencils are sharpened in the course of a week! I use this expression literally, of course."

As we spoke, a pretty Playcomrade sashayed by, her bear-ears wiggling in the stroboscopic light. "A man!" Borienko assured me. "Yes, we allow this. How could we not? Everybody knows Mike Gorbachev himself swings both ways. At the time of the Moscow Olympics, he was trying to get into the boiler-suit of the shot-putter Yelena Bulova, who, let's face it, is also a man. Sure I feel good telling you all this. We in the Soviet Union have had it with sublimating these things into rockets and stuff. We have an old saying which the Americans picked up on, "Let it all dangle, comrade." That's our philosophy now. What else do you want to know? Most of the members of the Politburo shave their legs – there's one for you! Cheers!"

By the time I set off for my apartment, dawn was breaking, but already the urchin gangs were at work. I watched one small girl climb an immense ladder to whitewash out the moustache on a portrait of Lenin. On the corner of Gorky Street I was almost upended by a phalanx of wheelbarrows propelled by panting soldiers. I asked them where they were headed. "We are delivering this consignment of whoopee-cushions to the Palace of Congresses!" they yelled. "Join us!" And with many a quip and a hiccup or two, they were away, rattling across the ancient cobbles, their jackboots glinting merrily in the amber light.

Now it is night again, and the Gorbachevs – he in a Baku silkette peignoir, she in a dazzling mustard brocade trouser-suit – will be gearing up for another of their legendary, all-night parties out at Kremlin Mansion West. Only a couple of nights ago, at the height of the latest of these inaugural thrashes, the hitherto austere Foreign Minister, Andrei Gromyko, is said to have somersaulted fully-clothed into a Jacuzzi full of *bortsch*. The phrase "a good party man" suddenly has an entirely new flavour. So do the St Petersburgers they give you at Colonel Spassky's Caucasian Fried Chicken, come to that.

There are those who say that none of this can last – that Moscow in six months' time will be a filthy, depraved and remorseful city. As one conservative dissident put it to me, "Many a Mikhail maks a muckhole." But that remains to be seen. I only know that, when I checked the bugging device behind my wall-light this evening, I found a tiny card engraved with the words: "Now find the other one."

"What I miss most about being of no fixed address is junk mail."

"Good morning, sir! I represent Rupert Murdoch. We bought a controlling interest in you as you slept."

· R I C H A R D · B O S T O N ·

WATCHING television the other night I suddenly realised why old films are so much better than those of the past twenty years or so. Think of any great screen performance and the first thing that will spring to the inward eye, which is the bliss of solitude, is not daffodils but hats. What would Chaplin or Bogart or Spencer Tracy have been without a hat? Even Dixon of Dock Green would have cut a poor figure without his helmet. Remember that cap Brando wore in *The Wild Ones*? Of course you do. Remember Gene Kelly singing in the rain, or Garbo in *Ninotchka*? You see my point. The only exception I can think of is *King Kong*, but who is to say that the film would not have been even better if Kong had worn a hat?

The reason why all Westerns are so good is that they all wear hats all the time. The same is true of the great Hollywood movies of the 1930s and 40s: whether it was a light comedy or a gangster film, the actors all wore hats, *even when they were indoors*. Imagine Edward G. Robinson or George Raft without a hat. The idea is laughable.

In the decade or so after the Second World War there was an advertising slogan which went "If you want to get ahead, get a hat." The wisdom of this advice was seen as soon as it was ignored in, roughly, the early 1960s. The films immediately became unmemorable, and the nation began its steady decline. In the days when commuters swarmed over Waterloo Bridge to and from the City in bowler hats, you could get four dollars to the pound. Nowadays, a bowler hat is not to be seen in the City and the pound has nearly reached parity.

The same thing happened with the British Empire. In the days of solar topees, the sun never set on the Empire. Then they stopped wearing them and, before you could say Bwana, all the red bits on the map had gone. Look at it another way. Mrs Thatcher wears hats and she's Prime Minister. Neil Kinnock doesn't, and isn't. That's strange. You would have thought Mr Kinnock had the greater need.

There are many advantages in being bald. It means you have something in common with Montaigne, Shakespeare, Picasso and Elisha, the last of whom was a bit touchy on the subject. When some children mocked him (*II Kings 2, verse 23*) saying, "Go up, thou bald head," he cursed them, "And there came forth two she-bears out of the wood, and tare forty and two children of them."

Being able to call out she-bears is not the only advantage of having a bald head. As Sterling Moss has remarked, a bald head is very cheap to run. Personally, I haven't been to the barber's for more than twenty years. A few snips in front of the mirror and the job is done. Also you're the first person to know when it's beginning to rain and therefore have a head start (so to speak) in the rush indoors to occupy the most comfortable armchair.

I read once that something like 80 per cent of body heat loss is from the head, and for bald people it's presumably more. This is not the disadvantage it might seem, since skilful use of hats gives you very fine temperature control. You can put a hat on when you're cold, take it off when you're hot, or in summer shelter under a Panama which keeps cool air circulating over the dome while poor hairy Esau can only grunt and sweat and curse the non-detachable covering to his head.

I've no idea how many hats I've had over the years. The first was my schoolboy cap at the age of six. During the dark years of arrogant adolescence I went bare-headed, but in my early twenties, like all male members of my family, I began to thin out on top and people made jokes about my tall forehead and the width of my parting. Consequently, in the bitterly cold winter of 1963 I invested in a balaclava helmet. It kept me warm not only through that winter but also the next's, which was spent in Sweden where it's really cold. I was in France the year after and acquired a number of berets of various shapes and sizes. They all made good companions.

This companionship is a source of both pleasure and pain. As with pets, you can get too fond of hats. This means you get very upset when their lives end. Sometimes this is through sheer wear and tear, in which case they are not thrown into the outer darkness of a dustbin, but given a decent resting-place in a rarely-visited recess of the clothes cupboard.

Others simply get lost. They just disappear in the night. Like cats, with which they have much in common, they have a way of going out and not coming back. Not that I am at all blameless. I hate to think how many I have left behind on the luggage-racks of trains. I once bought from my favourite shop, Bates the Hatter in Jermyn Street, a shapeless green tweed hat which protected me for some four years before I lost it while changing trains in Rugby. If anybody found it, I would like it back. The same goes for the brown one which, for all I know, is still shuttling between London and Manchester.

I haven't taken a census recently, but I suppose I have at present about a dozen hats, hats for all seasons, daytime hats and knitted wool-

Rosemary Harrison

ly ones with bobbles on top for bedtime. Until recently my number one all-purpose hat was another shapeless tweed job, but is doesn't fit any more. Either it shrank after being soaked in a downpour, or else my head has got bigger.

Whatever the reason, it had to be demoted and has been replaced by a cap bought, again, from Master Bates of Jermyn Street. It's a biscuit-coloured job, made of Irish tweed, constructed of eight radiating segments crowned with a coin-sized button. In front there's a peak with a popper device, so you can vary the angle according to mood. Unbuttoned, it looks a bit like the kind of motorist's cap that Mr Toad wore. Buttoned up, the cap is flatter and more in the Irish navvy style, as sported in a famous photograph of the early James Joyce. Other variations are achieved by the tilt and direction in which it is pointed. It's so versatile that it goes just as well with a bow-tie as with a spotted handkerchief tied round the neck.

But the greatest thing about this hat — and if I ever leave this one on a train I shall certainly burst into tears — is the bit you can't see from the outside. The inside. For there, carefully stitched in, is its maker's label in which, under a picture of an Irish landscape, are written the following words: "Donegal Handwoven. This tweed was woven from pure new wool in my small cottage in County Donegal, Ireland. Like my forefathers, I have put something of my own character into this cloth, ruggedness to wear well, softness for comfort, colours from our countryside. Joy and health to you who wear this. (Signed) D. Melly. Weaver."

That's not just a hat, it's a poem. Anyone who would rather go about with a full head of hair would have to be as mad as a. . . well, you get my point.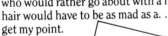

HANDELSMAN

POOR BERNARD'S ALMANACK

A Year's Worth of Misguided Morality

JANUARY

With the old Almanack and the old Year, Leave thy old Vices, tho' ever so dear.

It is never too late to acquire New and Worse Ones.

FEBRUARY

You may put a Man in Office, but you cannot give him Brains.

Then again, he is doing nicely without them.

Alas! Would that we were, as well.

MARCH

It is an ill Windbag that blows no one's Mind.

Well, I hate to blow my own Trumpet, but...

Try blowing your own Stack.

APRIL

Avoid dishonest Gain, & speak the Truth.

To put it bluntly, Madam, this is a Stickup.

INLAND REVENUE

O Sir, I am grateful for your Candour.

A great Talker may be no Fool, but he needs at least one.

O to be in April, now that England's here!

You said that beautifully.

MAY

A spoonful of Honey will attract more Flies than a gallon of Vinegar; but a smidgin of Horse Manure is best of all.

What divine Flies!

Thank you.

Little Strokes fell great Oaks. Or perhaps Pines.

Make up your Mind before I break my Beak.

JUNE

Marry in Haste, repent in good Taste.

I do — and now I should like to take the Best Man as my Lover.

Certainly! Let me just find the appropriate Service.

JULY

Fish stink after 3 Days, but many Visitors can do it in 3 Minutes.

AUGUST

Who desires Privacy, must go to Paris in August.

Be always ashamed to catch thyself idle.

SEPTEMBER

Who has deceiv'd thee as often as thy own self?

He that lieth down with Dogs, shall rise up with Fleas.

OCTOBER

The best Physician knows the Worthlessness of his Medicines.

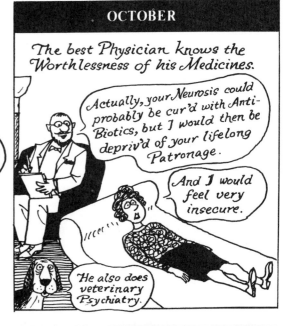

NOVEMBER

A Wolf eats Sheep but now & then; Ten thousands are devour'd by Men.*

DECEMBER

Giving & Receiving are equally pleasant unless thou be a Baboon.

He that drinks fast, pays slow.

MELVYN BRAGG

Volume Sales

ONE of the more enjoyable fringe benefits of being a writer is the company you bump into. Not only other writers – who are, on the whole, as mixed a bunch as any other – but book-lovers of various denominations: fanatical collectors, obsessional readers, devoted connoisseurs or just the generalists whose lives have been enriched, as mine has, by those odd, dumpy little artefacts full of printed words and haunted by the spirits of felled trees. In Shakespeare's day and play, "bookman" meant "scholar". Nowadays we elasticate the word and, though usually in formal circumstances (and rather self-consciously at that), pin it to the lapel of those whose lives have been engrossed in literature – a rare decoration. Alan Hancox is one such.

Living in Cheltenham, he is a bookseller, collector and friend to dozens of contemporary writers whose work he collected (and read) long before Modern First Editions were born; a man whose entire adult life has pivoted upon the desire and pursuit of the book, an object which he has sought out most often for the love of it, sacrificing financial profit by keeping and giving away prize items rather than selling them.

I went down to spend a day with him to talk about the Cheltenham Literary Festival, of which he is a director. In the autumn it will rise up for the 35th time in that pasture-locked West Country spa like an old-time rebellion. It will bring poets and novelists, pamphleteers, biographers, actors, printers and publishers to a town still thought of as the last resting place of our military Raj. For a week, men of words will outrank men of weapons. The theme is to be "The Spirit of Place", a subject very close to Alan Hancox's heart. "I not only like books which have a place inside and outside them, but can remember the very place in which I read a book. When they seem to coincide – *Le Grand Meaulnes*, for instance, which I read in central France – it's quite marvellous."

Alan has the pleasing luck of looking the part: or rather, because he looks as he does, it is his appearance which is the template for others: thick, wavy grey hair; a pair of sturdy, tweed-hugged, English shoulders; a glass of wine; an impatient independence of manner and speech – he's forever jumping up to check on a reference or pull down an example. The room in which we sat, too, is my ideal for a room – panelled floor-to-ceiling with books of such ravishing content, title, binding, rarity (all selected and known by one man; no bought-in-a-lot mercenary dumping ground, this) that you seem to sit in a glow of authors every bit as flickeringly mesmeric as the log fire, every ounce as eager for exercise as Solomon the Setter, who yearns for a gypsy-dog life in the middle of Cheltenham.

There are people you would claim you know well without ever having gone through "the basics". Indeed, after a while, a certain amount of fundamental mutual information is taken for granted; embarrassment leaks through only occasionally when the gaps and holes bring you to the realisation that what you know is almost dangerously incomplete. On a recent snowbound afternoon in Cheltenham – after a lunch cooked by Alan himself and with Solomon back from what is becoming a worrying habit of roving the streets – I talked to him about his bookish life. Alan's wife, a painter, was off to an art class with her youngest son, books lay about us and beech burned quietly in the grate, in a setting fit for the opening of a Victorian novel. "I was just a general reader," Alan began. "Ill-educated would be a good description. Then I happened to go to a WEA class where a Mrs McNeil – a formidable old bird – was talking about Tolstoy, Conrad and Virginia Woolf. The deep end. This was in Coventry, just before the Blitz. I was about 19, working in the motor industry. You might even have called me an engineer. That was the start of it."

He was a conscientious objector: "No religious reason, just an antipathy to killing. And I loathed uniforms and hated taking orders. I was a keen naturalist, more interested in saving life than taking it. To tell the truth, I'm hard put to explain it, really." After an Appellate Tribunal and farm work, he went to the Cotswolds. "Farm work wasn't too pleasant: the farmers hated us – 'conchies'. The land girls hated us too. I saw an advert in *Peace News* – 'Gardener wanted. Peaceful village. Cotswolds'. At Sheepscombe he found his niche. "The man ran a vegetarian guest house. He was an idealist, a Tolstoyan, long-bearded, a socialist and a nudist, farted freely and thought it right, peed on his mustard and cress every day and made them twice as big as anybody else's, the laziest man I ever met. But I remember the first book I read there – David Cecil's *Life of Thomas Hardy*."

He moved on to become a warden of Clevehill Youth Hostel, which he turned into the most thriving in the country, and it was while he was there that the book fever gathered strength. He would walk across to Wynchecombe, to the shop of Mr G. Wincel Tovey. "A marvellous bookseller! There were books I'd never seen before lying on his shelves. I would buy as much as I could afford. They were lovely editions: Old Phoenix Library, Travellers Library, Cobden Sanderson printing. I'd fill my rucksack and walk back over the hills, have a glass of beer, some bread and cheese." Another piece of luck was that in Cheltenham at the time there was a second-hand bookseller who loathed books. He couldn't wait to sell them off – *Prufrock* 2/6, that kind of thing. Thence to an auction where he bought "a Pantechnicon" of books for £50. Almost all of them were despoiled in some way – "If it was a Surtees, no colour plates, if a set of, say, Dickens, two or three missing – but enough to set me off." In a front room. Then a little shop.

"I don't know, sometimes I just feel like walking away from the caravanette and going where my fancy takes me."

I can easily imagine his prolific collecting, his easy generosity. A. L. Rowse, Peter Pears and John Betjeman began to drop in. Betjeman took all his copies (*not* first editions) and wrote, "I, John Betjeman, make this a first edition for Alan Hancox." It was quite late in the day when Alan grew interested in first editions. If he came across one he would put it aside. When he had a thousand, he published his first catalogue, "Feb, 1951. List No. 1. Interesting & Scholarly Books". It included John Clare's *Poems*, chiefly from the MSS first edition, 10/6; Auden's *For the Time Being*, 7/6; Sassoon's *Satirical Poems*, 5/–; Yeats's *The Winding Stair*, 1933, 7/6. If I were a serious collector, I would weep.

Since then, working alone, he has issued 150 catalogues – a breathtaking number. And he always went for writers he loved: "Wyndham Lewis, the Woolfs, D. H. Lawrence of course, Hardy, Blunden, Henry Williamson, the Powyses, Yeats, Jeffries and Edward Thomas in particular. He is my favourite, as much for the man as the writer." Up he shot, over to the particular bookshelf like an owl pouncing on a mouse. And out came the Edward Thomas passage he felt spoke most deeply for him. "My trouble as a bookseller," he says quite happily, "was that, if I liked an author, I preferred to keep the book. Or, if I saw the opportunity of putting together a second collection, I would sell off the first to a university" – for a modest price, although it is not he who told me that.

Nor would he. He is far too absorbed in writers and what they say, in publishers and printers and how they work, in private presses and his huge Cotswolds collection, in his present pursuit of contemporary poets and novelists and the building up of his collections of Greene, Waugh, Rebecca West, Doris Lessing and Orwell. "Orwell is the hardest: but I'll get there," he remarks.

When I asked him about "trends" over the last 35 years, he replied, but his mind was not on it. "Now there are ten part-time booksellers to every one professional, and so all the old stomping grounds – old bookshops, jumble sales, book fairs – are all milked. It's more commercial now, but then everything is. You know that." Other trends? "The Sitwells have fallen right away; T. S. Eliot is not collected anywhere near as much; G. B. Shaw is still down and so is Kipling, save for a few rare early things. There's a move on for some of the poets – Hughes, Heaney, Fenton, Raine – but you know that. And sometimes, if you have a good book, you can ask whatever you want for it."

But his mind was not on it. Trends, prices, dealing. Of course it was part of his life, and a part of which he has made a strikingly visible success, but he wanted to tell me about this extraordinary, odd book collector he had known, called Arnold Yates. "Arnold Yates's collection was based around the art of the book. He became a customer of mine when I was a new bookseller here. . ." The logs barely crackled; Solomon slept; further snow threatened; behind Alan's white mane, the leather spines and gold lettering glittered in the firelight. It was the nearest thing to my Aladdin's Cave, a story and a storyteller inside a magical cavern of stories and storytellers. "He was a fanatical collector. . ."

" . . . and finally, a word from Lloyd on security."

"Tragic really – he died convinced he'd never make it as a trompe l'oeil painter."

DAVID TAYLOR TALKS TO

"He wrote the TV station a letter. He was, so he wrote a tap-dancing knife-thrower from Lightning Ridge, a former sheep shearer and trapeze artist Hogey painted a bit of a picture, as a matter of fac knowing that at the TV station they'd think 'struth, what a dickhead, we'll have to have him on

PAUL HOGAN

STONE him, but Hogey's big. Don't get him wrong. He's not that physically huge. Though as a matter of fact he keeps pretty fit. Used to box a bit, a while back. He does go quite a while back, 44 if you're nosey. No, what he has in mind is big as in Big Time. Down Under, anyways, it's indubitably that. Thet. The way that Hogey assesses it, sort of, he's the first child of Australian TV. Maybe the only one. He used to be a rigger on the Sydney Harbour Bridge. Straight up. Television came along, or as a matter of fact he went along to television. Now he's rich and pretty famous. Doesn't mind that. Helps to keep the dingo from the door.

Sort of a Cinderella story, really, David. Dyvid. All happened overnight as a matter of fact. See, they used to have this talent quest, on Aussie TV, of a Sunday night. Christ, it was grim. On would come a couple of kids with a soft shoe shuffle, or to juggle a bit, sing, whatever, and these truly obnoxious, so-called professional entertainers – the ones in dinner jackets – would be the judges, see? They'd loaf about and really stitch these poor bastards up, gong 'em on the show. The whole idea, as a matter of fact, was to crucify these young hopefuls, either by saying they were no bloody good to their faces, or by saying they were truly great performers, when anyone could see they were nellies. You get a lot of quality programmes going out on Aussie TV.

So anyways, up on the bridge next day, the boys'd all be saying Christ Almighty, did you see that? They meant someone ought to go and get stuck into those bastards, teach them a lesson, know what they meant? And Hogey, as a matter of fact, had sort of a lifetime's habit of being that someone. Someone ought to do this. Someone ought to do that. It was always Hogey volunteered. Or got volunteered. Good on yer, Hogey, mite. Off you go and piss on 'em, Hogey, while we sit at home and egg yer on.

Don't get him wrong. It wasn't as if he was the good fun wag round the camp-fire, goodeye-goodeye-goodeye, the life and soul of the Sydney Harbour Bridge. Whatever. Matter of fact he had a bit of a temper on him, then. Threw a lawnmower at a bloke, once. Never mind that. Thet. So what happened, Hogey got picked to have a go. Think of something, Hogey. He wrote the TV station a letter. He was, so he wrote, a tap-dancing knife-thrower from Lightning Ridge, a former sheep shearer and trapeze artist. Hogey painted a bit of a picture, as a matter of fact, knowing that at the TV station they'd think 'struth, what a

dickhead, we'll have to have him on. They did an 'all – in record time. Whereas one would-be singing mate had waited months.

Only took a week as a matter of fact. He got there, fistful of knives, look on his face said Don't Mess This One About, Sport. He remembers a little kid was coming off in tears just as he was going on. That wound him up good and proper, no mistake. Hogey was not about to come off in tears. Hogey was not about to come off at all, you know? Christ Almighty, Hogey says to himself, old Hogey won't come off this thing till Hogey's good and ready. Any dickhead tries to shove him off, Hogey's still holding the fistful of knives.

Which he can't, incidentally, throw. Any more than he can tap-dance. It was, the way he assesses it, sort of a going on your wits situation, talk a bit, lark about, tell the obnoxious drongoes where they all got off.

They, most of Australia, all went nuts as a matter of fact. Straight up. Switchboard jammed, started to get out of hand. Hogey was back the next week and the week after that. He'd be rigging the bridge all day, then drop by for a jar and a few minutes to camera on his way home to a wife and four kids.

Next thing he knows, the current affairs show, on after the news, wants a bloke to come on and do a bit of a commentating turn, say a few words on the price of beer or the state of the nation, same thing really. Sort of a pub philosopher, they wanted, been looking everywhere, then clocked Hogey on the flamin' talent quest. That started it all. Next thing Hogey knew, he was advertising fags. He'd go on with, say, the Sydney Symphony Orchestra. He'd light the conductor's fag, say *OK, Boris, let 'er rip* and away they'd go with Beethoven's Fifth. Worked a treat for Winfield fags. Then they got banned on Aussie TV, couldn't show fags, or not the kind you set fire to. But they could and did show Hogey, in his own, home-written, one-hour-long show. The show that's now shown in thirty countries, as a matter of fact.

Sometimes seems to Hogey, looking back, that fate's been holding the steering wheel all along. It feels like that. It really does. Wasn't as if the entertainment industry was always in Hogey's blood. Only the rigging industry, really. Same as he reiterates, he'd boxed about a bit, was promising – always promising to beat the other bastard next time – but for thirty years, near enough, it was building, usually twenty-five floors up, minimum, where you got more dollars to the day, you know? Till fate

took a hand at the wheel.

People come up to him. They say Hogey – they all call him Hogey, sort of a nickname as a matter of fact – they say OK, Hogey mate, mite, you're Australia's Number One comic, ahead of Barry Humphries on the TV set at any rate, made a dollar or two, how d'ya feel about Buster Keaton, Charlie Chaplin, whoever? And Hogey's never worked with either. Never seen the films. You don't, as a matter of fact, up on Sydney Harbour Bridge.

Over here, which he is for a few days, it's his own repeats on Channel 4, but mostly it's the ozzy ads for Foster's got him known. In America, by the way, David, Dyvid, he's the face of Come To Sunny Australia. S'like an Aussie craze out there, straight up. They ran the campaign for a few weeks, Hogey strolling about with a jar and a word or two, reckoned maybe a few thousand tourists might be persuaded to give Down Under a try over the next year. They got 200,000 in about a fortnight. They were in all kinds of trouble: nowhere to put them up. Pushed for space in Australia. Jeez.

But it's all more dollars for Hogey, dollars he now plans to put into his first Australian movie: *the* Australian movie, the moving tale of an archetype, a mythical Aussie: *Crocodile Dundee*. The story of a crocodile poacher from up the Northern Territories, sort of a white abbo you could say, but maybe shouldn't, a happy-go-lucky type who halfway through the picture gets dragged across to New York City and into the twentieth century: comedy, romance and adventure, more or less in that order. And all of it Hogey's own work.

The way that Hogey sees it, luck opens a few doors. Then you've got to go at it, stick in there, know what he means? It's sort of a pleasurable feeling to have gone from being stuck for a dollar straight to having a pile of it, without going through the moderately well-off stage. He found he'd bought a bigger place out in Sydney, spot more privacy, spot more room in the yard, then he'd run out of ideas, really, not being possessions orientated, Dyvid, until the movie came along: which he supposes is a bit like doing a book, suddenly, when all you've done till now has been a column or two. Be interesting to see.

He never was a joke-teller, Hogey sums up, and as a matter of fact still isn't. More of a sarcastic sort of a bloke, you know? Seems to make a few people laugh, he's found, so might as well make it a living, sort of style. Fact is it pays better than Sydney Harbour Bridge. ◣

KEITH WATERHOUSE
French Leave

HELLO, dear, sorry to disturb you at this unearthly hour, did I wake you at all? No, only I thought that now this blasted phone's working again at long last, I'd better just call to let you know I'll probably be late.

Do I know what bloody time it is, did you say? Why, is your watch on the blink? Actually, I've left my own watch in the bathroom, it so happens, but I can just hear the church clock across the street striking three. Not that it *is* three, of course, or anywhere near it, because that clock is notoriously seven minutes fast. So it's only seven minutes to three, if that.

By probably late, I mean even more probably late than I am already.

I'm at the office. With Spinks. We have to get this draft tender, er, drafted, and placed in front of Wilkinson before he departs for New York on flight BA175 at 1100 hours, so, as you can imagine, we're working flat out. Definitely the old midnight oil touch.

You can't speak to Spinks, no. Or rather, you can if you wish, but Spinks can't speak to you. Laryngitis. What comes of dictating tender specifications into a tape-recorder for seven hours non-stop.

By bathroom, I meant stockroom. Bathroom is the office joke-name for the stockroom, on account of the condensation running down the walls and forming large puddles. I left my watch there while getting new batteries for Spinks's tape-recorder. The reason I took off my watch was look, this is a very bad line, can I ring you back?

Hello? That's better. Sorry for the delay, only I keep getting a crossed line with the Samaritans of all people, would you believe?

So where were we? Oh, yes – how I came to leave my watch in the stockroom, where I was getting new tape-recorder batteries as a favour for Spinks who didn't want to go in the stockroom himself in case the condensation running down the walls affected his weak throat which as you know is congenitally prone to laryngitis. The reason I took my watch off was because I always automatically do so before taking my shirt off, as you above all people ought to know. And then I simply forgot about it, having weightier matters on my mind.

Yes, I'm coming to why I took my shirt off, if you'll let me get a word in. Why I took my shirt off was to wring out the sleeve. Somebody, Miss Nevinson I shouldn't wonder, had carelessly left a bottle of scent on one of the stockroom shelves, and in reaching up for the tape-recorder batteries I accidentally knocked it over with the consequence that my shirt now reeks of eau de pong. I thought I'd better mention that before I arrive home smelling like a Latin-American knocking-shop at about – let me see, Spinks is mouthing that bar last-minute hitches we should be through at around six, so I should be back in good time for breakfast all being well.

The tinny sound you can hear in the background is the church clock striking the quarter hour, or only eight minutes past as it more accurately is.

By church clock I mean the clock on the church across the – Hello? Hello? You've grown very faint. No, it's no good, dear, I can't hear a word you're saying. I'm going to hang up and come straight back to you.

Hello? Yes, that's a one hundred per cent improvement. I can hear you as closely as if you were here in the office where Spinks is sitting.

Yes, you're quite right, dear, under ordinary circumstances there is in fact no church across the street from the office. This is an inflatable church – an enormous plastic bubble they've erected on that derelict site. A pity we never watch TV-am, because apparently they had some very interesting film of the bubble being blown up, which apparently they do in a matter of seconds. The only part of the operation that takes any time at all is putting up the portable clock tower – apparently it's a very delicate business synchronising the chiming mechanism to within an accuracy of seven minutes.

No, it's one of these American sects apparently. The First Temporary Church of the Universal God. They travel from one place to another spreading the word, which according to them is that we're all descended from the Lost Tribes of Israel and we won't find lasting peace and happiness until we take to the road like gypsies. It's quite interesting – I wouldn't have minded dropping in on one of their prayer meetings, but unfortunately they're moving on to Birmingham at first light.

So there we are. Sorry not to have been able to ring earlier to let you know I couldn't be home for dinner, but as I say the switchboard caught fire and all the lines have been out of action until the British Telecom all-night emergency service finally deigned to roll up less than half an hour ago. I would have gone across and phoned from the pub when Spinks and I were landed with this rush job just as we were about to leave for the evening, but then it turned out that thanks to the switchboard fire

"What's your name? I need it for the menu."

setting off the sprinklers which in turn caused a hiccup in the electric circuit somewhere along the line, the lifts were malfunctioning. I wouldn't have minded walking down nine floors but I didn't fancy slogging back up again, not with the weight I'm carrying. Any messages during this enforced absence, by the way?

Who's been calling me all evening, did you say? Spinks has. Blast – I've run out of tenpenny pieces and the pips are about to go. Pip! Pip! Pip! Don't go away – I'll get some more coins out of the petty cash and ring you back.

Hello? Right – I've put fifty pee in, so no danger of being cut off again.

Spinks, you say. That'll be Derek Spinks – the chap I share an office with. Yes, it won't have been important – I promised to let him know if I could make up a foursome at golf on Saturday. Must ring him back, though of course not at this God-forsaken hour.

I don't think you've ever met Spinks's namesake, have you? Terence Spinks? The chap who's with me here now. The chap who's got laryngitis. He's nodding how d'you do. No, no relation to Derek Spinks – he's from the Brighton branch, just up here on holiday relief. Pitched in at the deep end, eh, Spinks? He's nodding yes.

Ringing from? What do you mean, where the hell am I ringing from? I've told you – the office.

Oh, I see. Look, dear – I'm going to have to ring off for the moment because there's been quite a queue forming while I've been monopolising the phone box. For queue, of course, read Spinks. I'll call you back – OK?

Hello? Sorry about that but Q had to ring his mother very urgently to let her know he's missed the last train. Q for Quentin. Quentin Spinks. Yes, he is called Terence Spinks but his middle name is Quentin. Known to all and sundry as Q.

Yes, I am ringing from the office and I am ringing from a call box. What's so strange about that? I am ringing from the office call box – the one in the canteen. It's the only one British Telecom could get into working order after the switchboard caught fire. No, it wasn't affected by the switchboard fire but it was affected by an earlier, chip-pan fire in the canteen.

Why do you think that? Why should I tell you I'm in the office if I'm at a girl's flat in Streatham?

Had me followed by whom? Look, dear, I just want to recover my watch from the stockroom before it gets corroded by the condensation. Can I possibly call you back? ↩

"Well, there go the mad dogs but there's still no sign of the Englishmen."

BUD GRACE
Cover Story

PAIR OF DICE, LOST

A TRAMP. A BROAD

OLIVE OR TWIST

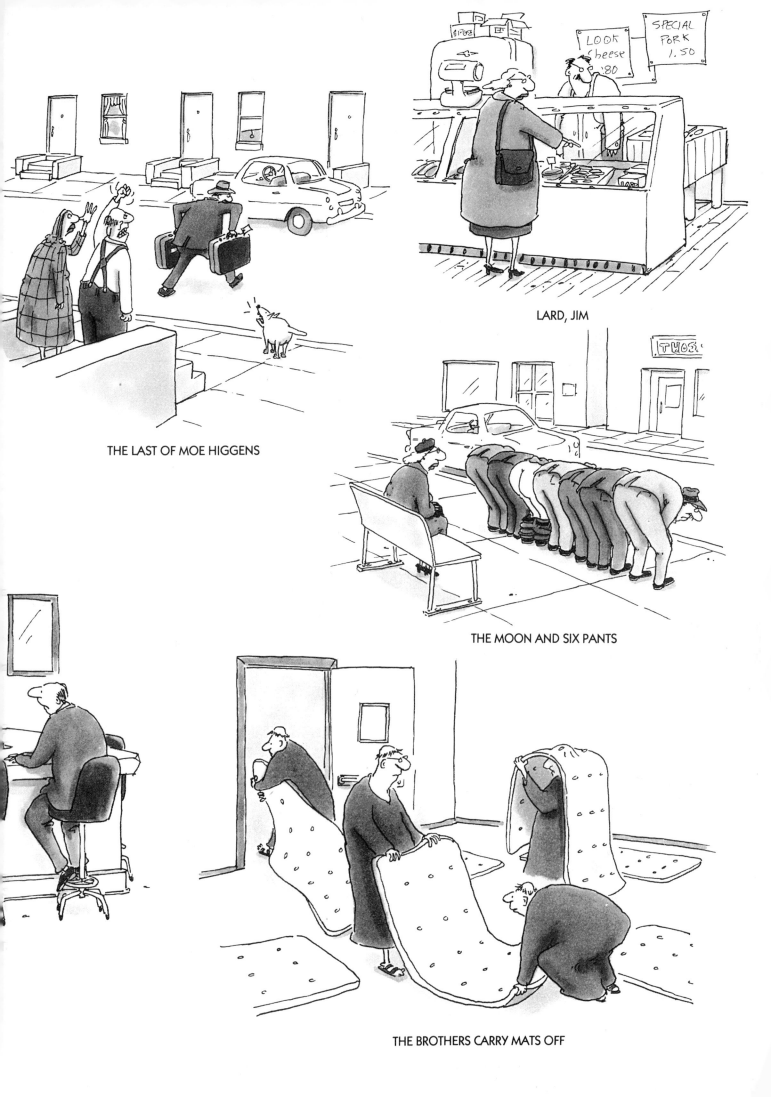

THE LAST OF MOE HIGGENS

LARD, JIM

THE MOON AND SIX PANTS

THE BROTHERS CARRY MATS OFF

ROBERT MORLEY
Off with their Studio Heads

I SUPPOSE forty-eight years is too long a gap. Returning to the M.G.M. studios in Culver City, the fortress seems, if possible, even less attractive, the security guards even more numerous. I remember, all those years ago, my initial shock at discovering each carried a presumably loaded revolver. What could they be guarding, yet another undiscovered script by Graham Greene? How often in all those years have they shot to kill, and whom? Actors trying to get in or out? Pay-rolls for the front office? The front office has spread to the dressing rooms; nowadays the talent has to be content with a small caravan. Gone are the palatial bungalows of the stars, now usurped by eager C.B.S. executives. Huge, grey studios built on either side of narrow streets from which the sunshine or the smog fitfully appears. Stretch limousines with elderly agents and pretty girls plough the lanes and scatter the pedestrians.

In olden times, there were orchestras on the sound stages. Head waiters appeared at eleven to take orders for luncheon. There was a famed chicken soup, always available for twenty-five cents because legend had it Mr Mayer lived on chicken soup before he bought the studios, which included every one who mattered from Garbo to Gary. There was a huge stable of hacks: Scott Fitzgerald, Dorothy Parker, Hemingway, Elinor Glyn.

The acting nowadays is also not what it was, direction a thing of the past: "We don't want a performance", is the cry, "we want it Thursday."

Curious, therefore, that I hugely enjoyed a stint in the current TV extravaganza *Alice in Wonderland*, playing the King of Hearts. Only the beard tickled. The producer, the director and his assistants were hugely kind and considerate. The cast was a glittering assembly of old-timers; Red Buttons, Martha Raye, Sid Caesar as well as present headliners like Carol Channing and Anthony Newley. A veritable Morecambe and Wise Christmas Special, and the conversation an endless reminiscence of time past. Only the child playing Alice, eight years old, tremendously talented and expert, put us all to shame by never forgetting a line and keeping religiously to her marks even when fleeing the Jabberwocky.

The beautiful Carol Channing attempted to

coach me when post-synching a song in the grand finale while we stood in line serenading Alice. "But you don't know the lyric," she told me, and I have seldom seen such astonishment on the face of the White Queen. Everyone knows the lyric in America. In a hundred years we can never hope to catch them up. If you are not on the job, you quite simply don't expect to keep it. Across from my caravan, I watched what I suppose would have once been called a corner sweeper. All day he collected the dust with a broom and an ash can. He never seemed to stop. Chiding me for a fleeting trip to Las Vegas, Irwin Allen, the producer, who never stopped either, and who used to produce disaster epics like *The Towering Inferno* or films about blazing cruise liners and has the odd fifteen million wrapped up in this one, lectured on the folly of playing the tables.

"Natalie Gregory, your child star," I told him, "is prone to far worse than a ball falling in the wrong spot. Chicken-pox, measles, whooping cough. How come you sleep nights? Don't tell me not to gamble." He went on his way

unperturbed, telling me he had just signed Sammy Davis junior for the caterpillar, and Telly Savalas for the Cheshire Cat.

Casinos are opening all over the States, so Vegas is no longer the crowd-puller. Far less crowded and more comfortable now, and on the floor of the Grand Hotel they stage Samson pulling down the Temple and the Sinking of the Titanic twice nightly. The San Francisco Earthquake, a previous spell-binder, has now moved to Reno and Miss Channing who moves there for a fifteen-week engagement when she has finished *Alice*, is determined to take part, though her contract only calls for a singing spot. "But twice nightly with everything falling about your ears? Will it be safe?" "Of course" she answered, "I like to keep working." They all do. The prophets predict that, one day, the economy will go bust. But until then, what the hell?

On a fine Saturday, fifty thousand citizens make their way to Santa Anita, the prettiest race track in the world, shaded by the foothills of the High Sierras. There, I find Mickey Rooney who for the last five years has been touring the sticks with the smash hit *Sugar Babies*, a nostalgic musical in which he stars. A trifle older than when I first saw him in *Babes In Arms* in which he partnered Judy Garland and went on to the most successful soap-opera of all time, *Andy Hardy*. He is now a lively and devout born-again Christian, converted on television naturally by the most successful evangelist in town who builds enormous temple complexes and whose annual take tops ten million. He never appeals for money, Mickey assures me, it just flows in.

Mr Rooney's other extravagance is horse racing, but he is not a fortunate punter. Twice during the afternoon he explained he couldn't after all give me a lift back to Beverly Hills as he was leaving, outraged by the riding of his favourite jockey. However, he finally stayed on to watch his own horse flout his confidence in the last race. "Have you said a prayer?" I asked. "Never bother God with the unimportant" he told me. "But I've backed it" I assured him. "It's important for me." On the way home he reminisced about Louis B. Mayer. "He never paid us properly. What Judy and I should have done was to follow the example of another of Mr Mayer's stars who once demanded two million dollars free of tax to continue making pictures. Mayer showed him the door but a year later after a boardroom meeting he was back with the cash." Mr Rooney subsequently spent a fortune struggling to recover his residuals. "Not for myself but for all the other suckers." But as usual, the suckers didn't get the even break. Nowadays, he loves everyone except the judges.

Christianity and commercials for alcohol-cures keep the home fires burning, and the television networks. Not that Americans watch the programmes as much as they used to. Tapes are the growth industry here as elsewhere. Even the sober lawyer who finally dropped me in Santa Monica offered the choice of *La Boheme* or dirty jokes on his radio tape-player, then decided it was too early for pornography. But, by then, my hearing aid had packed up.

There was a contretemps during the *Alice* shooting when the sound engineer traced a low whistling and I had to confess that a hairpin was making unseemly contact with my apparatus. It meant of course another take for the star who was overdue in the classroom, but everyone took pains to overcome my temporary embarrassment. Afterwards I wore my wig simply clamped to my head with a heavy crown, and dared it to shift.

The first time I attended the Academy Awards Ceremony it was with the redoubtable Louis B. Mayer himself. He was in a tuxedo, a bowler hat and an exceedingly bad temper when I called for him. He was on the telephone, apparently trying to reverse, at the very last moment, a decision of the Awards Committee.

"Damn it" he expostulated, "it's a disgraceful result. We are the only studio to have given the world a genuine screen artiste, Miss Garbo, unless of course you count that Goddam Mouse!"

This time I watched on television. They don't seem to make them like Mickey and Greta. Departing from custom, the organisers had dispensed with the services of Johnny Carson and consigned the task of compèring the proceedings to Jack Lemmon, not on this occasion the most cheerful of companions. The trouble with growing old in our profession is that one has never heard of any of the winners except Peggy Ashcroft and David Lean. Dame Peggy seldom accepts awards in person; she has after all a life to lead. Sir David was heavily outmatched by Mozart, or *Amadeus* as he is called these days.

The Lord Olivier made a brief appearance. A God descending from Olympus, intoned his near-contemporary Mr Lemmon, who then apologised for his understatement. The great thing about our business is that if you can't be pushing nine years old, it's best to be pushing ninety. The president of the Geriatrics for Entertainment Club, the great George Burns, was shocked the other day by a suggestion that he smoked expensive tobacco.

"If I paid five dollars for a cigar," he told them, "I'd expect to go to bed with it." ꝏ

"I've taken the liberty of calling in two of the nation's leading medical practitioners. The other is a gifted amateur."

Doctors

I am a Doctor, yes, a Ph.D.
My thesis has been read by almost three.
I am a Doctor also, a D.Mus.
I live for fugues. Not everybody does.
I am a DCL, the topmost rung
Of civil law, so keep a civil tongue.
I am a D.Sc. Upon my coffin
I see the label now: "An Unknown Boffin."
I am a first-class Doctor of Divinity,
Unfairly saddled with the Blessed Trinity.
I have a quite respectable D.Litt.
It pulls no women, so to hell with it.

Hi There, Strasbourg!

What fount of wrongs the peevish soul delights?
What causes honest men to sweat at nights?
Alas! It is the Court of Human Rights.

Publisher To Author

Your *Byways In Cheam*
Might give us a *succès d'estime.*
If it's all the same to you,
We'd rather have a *succès fou.*

Vive La Différence!

Thoughts will ever idly bubble.
Pensées take a lot more trouble.

The Start Of It All

A self-styled King of the Jews
Made too much news.
The Romans were greatly pained.
Later a man was detained.

Rebuff

The man who fixed the interest rates
Reported at the Pearly Gates.
St Peter, wholly unimpressed,
Said, "Here you rate no interest."

Military Error

Here lies a Colonel, of good reputation,
Who, overlooking a Queen's Regulation,
One vivid day, while wearing spurs, was seen
To stride into a powder magazine.

As Seen On TV

Pete and Pam screech nose to nose,
    Scolding half an inch apart.
Here we have, as I suppose,
    Nature imitating Art—
Art as seen by faithful flocks
Watching "two-shots" on the Box.

As Heard On TV

The Dane, the Swede, the Portugese
All speak good English on TV,
Unlike the British people – *Yuk!*
Who might be speaking Volapuk.

A Media Pioneer

"I break down all taboos," says Mr S.
"I stretch the frontiers of permissiveness."
You must not ask the fellow, "Who are you
To do such things?" for that is quite taboo.

E. S. TURNER

Lewis Burke Frumkes

What Will You Be In Your Next Life?

Believe it or not, what you will be in your next incarnation is determined almost entirely by the last two digits of your birth year. Thus, if you happened to be born in 1945, you will be reincarnated as a fly. Yes, a fly. I'm sorry, I know you would rather have come back as a jewel or a Rolls Royce, but you're quite unmistakably a fly. I've checked my figures a hundred times over. 1945 is a fly, a common house-fly. Look, it's not as bad as you think – the ability to soar through the air effortlessly, taste a dozen different meals at a single restaurant, buzz. Just watch out for scrolls of sticky paper hanging from the ceilings and swatters and you'll be quite all right, trust me. And get your nose out of that stuff, right now! Yuck!

In any event, quite obviously not all of you will come back as flies. Many of you will come back as princes, and water-lilies, and business moguls with estates on the water in East Hampton, and Palm Beach – it's sort of like the lottery, you don't know until your number comes up. But in the interests of the curious, impatient, or just those who have to learn now so they can prepare for the next life, I have set forth the future incarnations of those born in the following years:

1937 – 37 was a good year. You will all come back as magnums of Lafite Rothschild wine, the best. Of course you will be different vintages, since you won't all expire at the same time. That's only natural. For what it's worth, 1987, 1992, 2004 will be the great years, and 2007 the very greatest. If you can make it to 2007, by all means do, since you will not only make great drinking at special occasions and society dinners, but set auction records as well. Salud!

1938 – Pin curls. What can I say?

1939 – The men of 39 will return as major stakes race horses who will retire in their prime as studs. The ladies will be brood mares. If you've got any sexual hangups such as fear of doing it in front of other horses, or spectators, get rid of them now. And if I were you, I'd eat lots of fresh figs and oysters. Capice?

1941 – Chairs. You will come back as chairs. Arms, Chippendales, Rockers, Queen Annes, Captains. A mixed blessing. Depends on what room you wind up in, and who sits on you. For example, you could be just a bar stool in an Irish pub, God forbid, or the guest chair next to Johnny Carson on the *Tonight Show*. As you can see, it's all in the luck of the draw. And in case any of you creative types were wondering, there is a chair in the dressing-room of the Dallas Cowgirls upholstered in the finest silk moiré.

1944 – You will return as a business tycoon, regardless of whether you are male or female. Deal after deal will turn into success and you will be pictured on the cover of *Time* magazine. So affluent will you become, in fact, that small governments and Adnan Khashoggi will approach you for loans. Women will fall all over you, hypnotised by your power, and strong men will envy you. Unfortunately, you will look like a haemorrhoid. Try to remember the bargain you made with Mephistopheles and improve on it next time.

1949 – People born in 1949 will come back as wands. Magic wands, silver wands, bubble wands, glass wands. If you've ever wanted to be a wand, 1949 was the year in which to be born.

1952 – Tell the truth, whenever you've thought about reincarnation you've imagined that someone could come back as a butterfly, right? Well, congratulations, those of you born in 1952 actually will. You will be coloured like the rainbow, able to ride the wind like a hot-air balloon, and alight as soft as a feather on pollen-sweet flowers. Except for you, John. You will be a lunar moth.

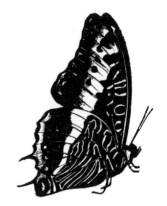

1957 – Wires of all kinds.

1959 – 59s will return as food. Some will be crêpes-suzettes, some will be chicken McNuggets, and still others roast beef Hovis sandwiches with the works. It's hard to know in advance just who will be what, but if you have cauliflower ears, or are called sugar, honey or cookie on a regular basis, chances are you have a rough idea where you're heading.

1960 – Diamonds – great! What can anyone say if you come back as a diamond? Like the erections (substitute steel girders if you prefer) of '53, you will be hard.

BASIL BOOTHROYD

Lot going on we don't know about

Ouagadougou (AFP) – Burkina Faso has called on the Ivory Coast to account for an explosion at a hotel there last week apparently aimed at Captain Thomas Sandara, the visiting Burkina Faso head of state.

The Times

Magnusson: And you have two minutes on your chosen subject, recent events in West Africa as they affect the ordinary man and woman in places like St John's Wood and Nottingham, starting NOW. General Booth founded the Salvation Army, Colonel Bogey is a composition for military bands, Major Speeches are made at weekends by politicians, who is Captain Sandara?

Boothroyd: A head of state.

Magnusson: I'll allow that. Where is Ouagadougou?

Boothroyd: Pass.

Magnusson: Is that how to pronounce it?

Boothroyd: Your guess is as good as mine.

Magnusson: Correct. The initials NACODS mean something to do with colliery shitfiring, shotfiring, sorry, an SPSO is a Senior Principal Scientific Officer, what do the letters AFP stand for?

Boothroyd: Pass.

Magnusson: In an edition of *The Times* newspaper dated Monday February 18 there appeared no fewer than nine short news items essential to the ordinary man and woman's understanding of the extent to which occurrences in parts of the world as far apart as Ajaccio and Bangkok may influence political thinking in Nottingham or St John's Wood.

Boothroyd: Pass.

Magnusson: I haven't finished, so I'll go on.

8m Viewers: Bloody unfair. These questions are miles longer than he gave the deputy head dinner-lady from Chepstow.

Magnusson: Two of those items were headed respectively "Gromyko Trip" and "Reburial Halted". What was the one in between?

Boothroyd: Pass.

Magnusson: How far apart are Ajaccio and Bangkok?

Boothroyd: One hundred and eighty miles.

Magnusson: Eleven thousand, two hundred and three. You're thinking of Nottingham and St John's Wood. Whose reburial was halted?

Boothroyd: Pass.

Magnusson: What did Gromyko trip over?

Boothroyd: Pass.

4m Viewers: What's any of this got to do with his chosen subject, recent events in West Africa as they affect the ordinary man and woman, for God's sake?

4m Ditto: Pass.

Magnusson: At whom, according to the *Times* man in Oubagou . . . in Gougbou . . . in Boogiewoo . . .

Boothroyd: Ouagadougou.

Magnusson: Thank you. At whom, according to the *Times* man there, was an explosion at a hotel, and I quote, "apparently aimed"?

Boothroyd: Michael Heseltine.

Magnusson: Bishop Tutu. I'm sorry. Stop the clock. I have a wrong card here. No, it was Captain Sandara. What is the opposite of West Africa?

Boothroyd: Mogadishu.

Magnusson: Could you be less specific?

Boothroyd: East Africa.

2m Viewers: Good God, even I knew that.

Magnusson: Right. Correct, I should say. Edmund Burke was a well-known statesman and author of something called *Reflections on the Revolution in France*, often referred to, of course, as the French Revolution, published in 1790 and running into twelve editions by the end of the year. *Burke's Peerage* is a genealogical and heraldic history of the peerage, baronetage and knightage of the United Kingdom. A Berk is rhyming slang for Berkeley or Berkshire Hunt. What does this tell you about Burkina Faso?

Boothroyd:

6m Viewers: Pass, you berk.

Boothroyd:

Magnusson: It's on the tip of your tongue.

Boothroyd: Something in the *Times* bit on Tuesday February 19.

Magnusson: I'll accept that. Actually, Monday February 18. Where is the Ivory Coast?

Boothroyd: East Africa.

Magnusson: West Africa. What was it formerly called?

Boothroyd: The Gold Coast.

Magnusson: No, the Ivory Coast. What is its principal export?

Boothroyd: Ivory.

Magnusson: Cotton, coffee and cocoa. It used to be ivory but it ran out of elephants.

Boothroyd: What did?

Magnusson: I can't accept that.

Boothroyd: Suit yourself.

8m Viewers: He's just wasting time, trying to be funny.

Magnusson: Marks and Spencer have discontinued their recent policy of selling books. Why?

Boothroyd: Too many people taking them back and wanting to change them.

Magnusson: No. Too many asking for something about explosions in foreign hotels. Where is Sandara?

Boothroyd: Who knows by this time? Pass.

Magnusson: Who is Burkina Faso?

Boothroyd: You've asked me that. Pass.

3m Viewers: He'll have to be red hot on his General Knowledge round.

Magnusson: The war in Vietnam caused the resignation of London's Jane Bronson – Lyndon Baines Johnson – and the Boston Tea Party caused the American War of Independence. What influence will the *Times* report from Oogledoogloo have on the ordinary man and woman in this country, the falling pound, the future of the coal industry, poor road-gritting and overcrowded prisons, and the circulation of *The Times*?

Bleeper: Bleep, bleep.

Magnusson: And you may answer.

Boothroyd: Pass.

Magnusson: And at the end of that round you have scored four points and *no passes!* Sorry. You passed on eleven. You're going to kick yourself.

10m Viewers: Daft bloody programme. I don't know why we watch it.

SOHO

I CAN'T help feeling about Soho as I might about a woman. Forgive the metaphors and the odious comparisons but there it is. I met and fell in love with her when I was sixteen. We had a mad and passionate affair for a few years until Lord Wolfenden ruined her by putting her on the straight and narrow. The honeymoon has long since been over and we're quietly settled down. When I look at her now – and I see her nearly every day – I don't get the same throb of excitement but I still love her and with great fondness. Her mascara is smudged and she's what Charlie in Berwick Street market would call an "old scrubber" but she's been good to me in spite of having led me astray day in and day out for years.

Twice I've been unfaithful to her, once with a flighty but pretty village in Suffolk and once with a real tart of a village in Berkshire. But Soho has always taken me back. She is very forgiving and her arms are always open. I just wish she could be more discriminating but I suppose one shouldn't expect that of a whore. Take a last look at her before the property developers and pornographers make her unrecognisable with dreadful transplants.

It was by accident that I first went into Soho. My brother was a student at St Martin's School of Art and he one day suggested I meet him there in a café by Foyles where the students went in their coffee breaks. It was instant magic for a repressed schoolboy brought up under the severest discipline. Here was everything that I had been led to believe to be wicked. There were poets, layabouts, bums, thieves, eccentrics, and, above all, girls. Masses of them. I thought I was in some sort of Aladdin's Cave. There was a mad, debarred solicitor called Redvers Gray who had taken to invention and had recently tried to patent a submarine made out of blotting-paper – surfacing was the chief stumbling-block – and there was "Ironfoot" Jack, so called because he made up for a short leg with an iron frame. He wore a cloak and looked like Dr Caligari.

The students who had grants or who lived at home with parents fared well enough but the rest kipped and dossed on other people's floors and sofas and survived on the freemasonry that existed between would-be painters, failed poets, novelists without pens or paper, and Charing Cross Road bookshop thieves. And what thrilled this teenage school-leaver was the fact that all of these people believed in "free love" and some of them even lived "in sin". It was very heady stuff for a boy who told his mother that he spent most days in the Science Museum or National Gallery. Surely such occupations couldn't have accounted for the pallor and the nicotine-stained fingers?

But apart from this chiaroscuro of humanity, the state of mind of Soho, there was the physical Soho. There is now barely a single dirty bookshop, strip club or amusement arcade that wasn't then a bistro, delicatessen, restaurant or café. And money seemed less important, not simply because we were younger but because we could nurse a cup of tea for hours. Being broke was acceptable and expected. None of us had then entered for the rat race. You could spot a rat easily in those days. He was the man who could order chicken or veal escalope, both of which were 3/6d – 1/6d more than you could earn in an hour washing dishes – and I did just that for Victor Sasse when he had a café called the Budapest, years before the Gay Hussar.

All this and that was the first half of the game and affair with Soho. After the interval in National Service we embarked on the second half, which was the transition from café society to pub-going. Now, into the 1950s, Soho blossomed for me with the change of friends and companions that I met in the pubs and clubs and who seemed to accept me as being part of the furniture and fittings. It was like *The Boyhood of Sir Walter Raleigh*: I listened spellbound at the feet of painters like John Minton, Robert Colquhoun, Robert McBryde, Francis Bacon and Lucian Freud. Poets like George Barker, Dylan Thomas, Louis Mac-Neice and Sidney Graham and the composers Alan Rawsthorne and Malcolm Arnold. This is not an exercise in name dropping. I mention such people merely in an attempt to convey the quality of the people who lurched and staggered in and out of the Gargoyle Club, the Mandrake Club, the Club des Caves de France and the Colony Room Club. Six of those people are now dead and their replacements are a pretty disappointing bunch.

I feel a particular nostalgia for mornings in the French pub. At opening time the first arrivals were local shopkeepers and the French girls of the street who were a charming bunch and who did no one any harm in spite of what Lord Wolfenden was later to report. Aperitifs were swapped and Soho village life was discussed. It was all so civilised. There was no such thing as a denim-suited advertising executive. At the other end of our rainbow even the crooks and ne'r-do-wells had a sort of style if not class. They were nearer to Damon

> "Here was everything that I had been led to believe to be wicked. There were poets, layabouts, bums, thieves, eccentrics, and, above all, girls."

Runyon than they were to the *News of the World,* although they frequently featured in the latter. There was Sid the Swimmer, Handbag Johnny, Italian Albert Dimes, French Albert and No Knickers Joyce. You didn't interfere with them and they weren't interested in drawing you into their little web. You had a drink with them and passed the time of day. Frank Norman and I regarded our morning appearance in the French pub as arriving for work. And Soho was Cinderella. Hampstead and Chelsea were and are the ugly sisters.

Well, as I say, Cinderella has lost her looks and a bit of her charm but I am still obsessed with her. Soho still makes me feel safe. Wherever I have had the good luck to travel to in recent times, the return journey is enhanced by the feeling I have that I'm going *home*. It does, after all, still make you feel welcome when you know it. The other day a bunch of us in the Coach and Horses got chatting to a salesman from Glasgow who was paying his first visit to Soho as he passed through London. He obviously enjoyed it. He came in for one drink and stayed until closing time and missed his train. He did the same thing the following day and the day after that. Eventually he did get back to his wife and his home. We got a card from him in which he wrote, "You have ruined my life. Will you all be there next week?" Admittedly he was Glaswegian and so more likely to be led astray, but I doubt whether, say, Notting Hill Gate or Islington could get such a golden seal of approval.

Although the wheels may be at last falling off my village, I can after all these years savour some of its defects. I'd be lost without Norman's rudeness in the Coach and Horses. If he hands me a menu instead of throwing it at me, if he serves me promptly without swearing at me, then I know he has most likely just suffered a deeply tragic and personal loss. In this event we regulars make solicitous enquiries. I myself suffered a sense of loss recently when I spent an entire hour in the Colony Room without spotting a single cockroach. Can this be what they mean by cleaning up Soho?

And now, as both Soho and I are passing peacefully away to our rest, I have taken up the role of teacher. In recent months we have been inundated by young men who all think they are "Jack the Lad" and who desperately want to become what they call "Soho Characters". Not that they will ever have the presence of a Maurice Richardson or be able to conduct a conversation standing on their head as Robert Newton could, but I think they should have the equal opportunity to be able to do so. At any rate I feel it my duty to pass on my obsession with Soho if I can. At least it would keep them off the streets and in the pubs. è